*Japanese Politics*

AN INTRODUCTORY SURVEY

AN INTRODUCTORY SURVEY

Japanese Politics

Nobutaka Ike

STANFORD UNIVERSITY

Alfred A. Knopf   NEW YORK

1957

L.C. catalog card number: 57–5065
© Nobutaka Ike 1957

THIS IS A BORZOI BOOK
PUBLISHED BY ALFRED A. KNOPF, INC.

FIRST EDITION

TO

Tai,

Linda,

&

Brian

✿ *Preface*

The purpose of the present work is to present an overall view of Japanese politics in terms of its setting, the dominant political forces, and basic political processes. I am fully aware that this is indeed a rash undertaking, given our present state of knowledge. Yet those of us who teach and undertake research on Japanese government and politics must seek to relate, explicitly or implicitly, the parts to the whole; and the present work was undertaken on the assumption that it would be useful to set down —even if only in a preliminary way—a general framework for analyzing Japanese politics in its totality.

In preparing this book I was assisted by numerous individuals. I wish to thank in particular Professor C. Easton Rothwell for enabling me to take an extended leave of absence; my colleagues, Professors Mary Wright, Arthur Wright, Thomas Smith, and Dean Carl Spaeth for their encouragement; Professor Kyogoku Jun'ichi, of Tokyo University, for spending many hours giving me the benefit of his insight into Japanese politics, and Professors Saito Makoto and Hayashi Shigeru, also of Tokyo University, and Mr. Okubo Genji, of the Canadian Embassy, for their guidance and advice; and Professor Kurt Steiner for reading the manuscript and offering a number of valuable suggestions. I would also like to extend my thanks to Mr. Ueda Takao for his assistance in checking references, to Miss Akiko Inui for typing portions of the manuscript, and my wife for helping me not only in preparing the manuscript but also in seeing it through press. I am solely responsible for all errors and omissions.

I must also express my appreciation to the Ford Foundation which gave me a fellowship to travel and write this book. That Foundation is not, however, the author, owner, publisher, or proprietor of this publication and is not to be understood as approving by virtue of its grant any of the statements made or views expressed therein. Grateful acknowledgment is also made to Stanford University for a Supplementary Faculty Research grant.

Except for a few items, all source materials used in writing this book were found in the Hoover Library and the Stanford University Library, and thanks are due the staffs of these libraries for their assistance.

NOBUTAKA IKE

Stanford, California
September 1, 1956

❀ *Contents*

�֍ *Tables, Charts, & Maps*

TABLES

CHARTS

MAPS

PART | *The Setting of Japanese Politics*

Chapter 1

The Problem of Government:

A Historical Sketch

Japan's relations with the rest of the world were characterized, until modern times, by relative seclusion. Her geographical position off the eastern coast of the Asian continent away from the main routes of migration and invasion helped her remain isolated from her neighbors whenever she so desired. Until 1945 the Japanese were able to boast that they had never been invaded by a foreign power. Conversely, Japan remained over the centuries relatively aloof from political developments taking place in China and Korea. To be sure, in the early days the Japanese actively intervened in Korean affairs. Late in the 16th century, the famous military leader, Toyotomi Hideyoshi, attempted an invasion of the continent; and it was in this period, too, that Japanese traders and pirates roamed the Far Eastern waters, even establishing settlements in far-off places like Siam. But even when due weight is accorded these facts, one can conclude that in the long view Japan was not involved politically in the affairs of the near-by continent in the way, for instance, that Britain was involved in Europe.[1]

Japan's political seclusion, however, was not accompanied by cultural isolation. The strong impress of Chinese influences on Japanese civilization is apparent even to the casual observer. But, as Sir George Sansom has noted, the Japanese accepted Chinese influences "willingly and under no kind of pressure," with the result that they were in a position to accept or reject as they pleased.[2] Thus, despite extensive borrowing, Japanese civilization managed to retain a special character. "No nation," to quote Sansom again, "has been more ready to consider new teaching, and yet none has been more tenacious of its own tradition."[3]

In Japan's history, periods of active foreign intercourse have alternated with periods of national isolation. One such cycle began in the 16th century. At that time Japan appeared to be on the verge of overseas expansion into parts of Southeast Asia. Then the Tokugawa family, which had succeeded in establishing its hegemony over Japan, decided to pursue a policy of national isolation, fearing that its rivals might, with the help of the Portuguese, then active in the Far East, succeed in overthrowing them. From about 1640 until the middle of the 19th century, Japan remained in relative isolation from the rest of the world.

In the meantime, far reaching changes occurred in Europe. The most notable of these changes was the industrial revolution, which led to the expansion of Europe. The story of how parts of Asia were made into colonial dependencies of European nations is well known and need not be repeated here. In time the wave of expansion reached Japan, and although she was

[1] The effects of isolation are discussed in Edwin O. Reischauer, *The United States and Japan* (Cambridge, 1950), pp. 95–115; George B. Sansom, *The Western World and Japan* (New York, 1950), pp. 167–180.

[2] Sansom, *ibid.*, p. 168.

[3] *Ibid.*, p. 169.

not reduced to a colony she was forced to abandon her policy of isolation and conclude unequal treaties with the major powers.

The historical circumstances under which Japan ended her isolation made difficult her adjustment to her new status as a member of the family of nations. For one thing, she had not joined the world community voluntarily, but had more or less been coerced into it. Even more important, because of her long history of relative isolation, Japan lacked the sense of participation in a large community of nations. In this respect, Japan differed from the nations of Europe, which had historical memories of once having belonged to a universal community. As Sansom says, "the universalist view is exceptional in the history of ideas in Japan," while "the extension of the Roman Empire and the spread of Christianity in Europe, North Africa and Western Asia made the idea of a universal political and spiritual empire familiar and even natural to European minds."[4]

The Internal Crisis

The difficulty of adjustment was further aggravated by certain internal developments. When the Western powers knocked on Japan's door, Japan was in the throes of an internal crisis generated by the breakdown of the political and social system established by the Tokugawa family in the 17th century. At the risk of over-simplification, it may be said that the crisis was characterized by a growing disparity between political power and social prestige, on the one hand, and economic power, on the other. The elite of the country—the feudal nobility and their retainers, the samurai—had become progressively impoverished, while some urban merchants and rural landowner-entrepreneurs had become progressively wealthier until they controlled a good

[4] George B. Sansom, *Japan in World History* (New York, 1951), p. 34; also Maruyama Masao, "Nihon ni okeru nashionarizumu" (Nationalism in Japan), *Chuo koron* (Central review), January, 1951, p. 297.

part of the wealth of the country. The transfer of wealth from one class to another led in turn to increased exactions on the peasant population which provided the bulk of the revenue for the state. But there was a limit to the amount that could be levied on the peasantry, and as this limit was reached the latter rose in revolt.

By the middle of the 19th century, there was a great deal of discontent in the air. The samurai were discontented because of their chronic poverty, the merchants because of their low social status and restrictions on trade, and the peasants because of increased tax levies. Much of this discontent came to be directed against the Shogunate, controlled by the Tokugawa. Eventually a small group of low-ranking samurai from several fiefs in western Japan which had been traditionally hostile to the Tokugawa family formed an alliance with some nobles from the Emperor's court, wealthy merchants from the big cities, and rural landowner-entrepreneurs and overthrew the Shogunate. These samurai then set up the Emperor who had been relegated to obscurity by the Tokugawa rulers in place of the Shogun. This seizure of power known as the Meiji Restoration occurred in 1868, and it opened a new chapter in the history of modern Japan.

Because of the alignment of forces in the Restoration movement, the key positions in the new regime came to be held, for the most part, by men who stemmed from the lower ranks of the old governing class.[5] Most of them had a samurai background, which meant that they had some understanding of military problems. They readily saw that it was futile to try to fight against cannon with samurai swords. If Japan was to become strong, her entire military establishment would have to be revamped. They realized that instead of fighting forces made up

[5] More detailed accounts of this period may be found in E. Herbert Norman, *Japan's Emergence as a Modern State* (New York, 1940); George B. Sansom, *The Western World and Japan;* and Nobutaka Ike, *The Beginnings of Political Democracy in Japan* (Baltimore, 1950).

of samurai exclusively there would have to be a national army composed of conscripts and equipped with modern arms. To make the army and navy an effective fighting force, a modern communications and transportation system would have to be built. Finally, they saw that Japan would need modern large-scale industry because of the close relationship between industrial capacity and military power.

But there were serious obstacles in the way of these goals. Technologically Japan was backward, her capital accumulation was small, and her natural resources were meager. There was the added problem of time. Japan was in a hurry and wished to achieve in a few decades what Western countries had achieved in centuries. Under the circumstances, those in control felt that the state would have to play a leading role in the modernization program. The state would have to provide the capital and direct the industrialization process. Japan could not afford a slow and haphazard industrial development based on individual entrepreneurs starting up important industries with private capital.[6]

But if the state was to play this role successfully, it would need the full support of the population and control over the allocation of the resources of the nation. Much of the funds needed for modernization would have to come from internal taxation and currency inflation, measures that called for sacrifices on the part of the governed.

It must have been evident to the leaders that a program of modernization of this nature could not be executed successfully by a political structure in which power was divided among more or less autonomous units, as was the case under the Shogunate. They believed that what was needed was a unified and highly centralized nation-state governed by an elite. A few who presumably knew best what to do and how to do it would make

---

[6] Thomas C. Smith, *Political Change and Industrial Development in Japan; Government Enterprise, 1868–1880* (Stanford, 1955), p. 103.

the high policy decisions, and the remainder of the population should be willing to abide by these decisions.

"Western Technology and Eastern Morals"

But ironically the very program of making Japan rich and strong contained within it certain features which tended, in the long run, to make difficult the perpetuation of government by a few. The creation of a conscript army, for example, led eventually to the argument that if a citizen had the obligation to bear arms and fight for his country, he ought to have some voice in government. The spread of education and literacy gave rise to mass circulation newspapers and magazines which conveyed to their readers news and opinions regarding political matters. Unlike the days of Tokugawa rule, the behavior and pronouncements of high officials became the concern not of the few but of the multitude. In her program of industrialization, Japan had to depend heavily on the West for machinery and technological skills. But with industrialization there also came scientific knowledge as well as Western political doctrines, such as liberalism and socialism which conflicted basically with the prevailing political myths.

Finally, if Japan was to carry weight in international affairs the sense of nationalism had to be strengthened. Successful diplomatic negotiation depended on convincing your adversaries that the diplomat's voice was not a solo but a national chorus. The bargaining power of Japanese diplomats was strengthened to the extent that they could show that their demands represented the demands of the entire nation and not those of a small elite. But with the rise of nationalism there came increasingly the feeling that politics and international affairs were everybody's business, and public opinion became a factor of increasing importance.

Thus it may be said that underlying the politics of modern Japan there was a central problem: how to modernize the country and become a world power without changing the oligarchic character of the political structure. Japan might become strong militarily by Westernizing; yet Westernization might lead to internal disunity and political weakness. One answer to this dilemma was the formula: "Western technology and Eastern morals." According to this formula Japan was to look to the Western world in matters of technology and science, but with regard to political and social values she was to draw on her own traditions. A clear statement of this point of view may be found in the writings of Fukuzawa Yukichi, educator and a leading student of Western civilization in the 19th century.

> The duty of Japanese at the present time lies solely in protecting our national polity [kokutai]. To protect our national polity is to avoid losing our political independence. In order to avoid losing our political independence, the intellectual capacity of the people must be increased. The most urgent step needed to be taken to increase the intellectual capacity is to sweep away the weaknesses of our old customs and adopt the spirit of Western civilization.[7]

Undoubtedly the formula served a useful purpose in that it allowed the use of traditional values to justify change, enabling Japan to achieve the remarkable feat of modernizing within a generation. But, as Thomas Smith notes, "if old loyalties provided the sanctions for change, they were not in turn strengthened by it."[8] With the passage of time it became increasingly difficult to perpetuate old values in the face of industrialization and urbanization. Experience proved that "Western technology and Eastern morals" could be combined only at a price—"a price in malaise."[9] How the malaise was reflected in the political sphere will be one of the several themes taken up in this book.

[7] Quoted in Maruyama Masao, *"Meiji kokka no shiso"* (The ideology of the Meiji state) in *Nihon shakai no shi-teki kyumei* (A historical study of Japanese society), ed. by Rekishigaku kenkyukai (Tokyo, 1949), p. 195.

[8] "Old Values and New Techniques in the Modernization of Japan," *The Far Eastern Quarterly*, XIV (May, 1955), p. 355.

[9] *Ibid.*, p. 356.

Chapter 2

The Social Setting of Japanese Politics

We see power being exercised all around us. Most of us have had an occasion to remark that a friend or an acquaintance "loves power." The term power is included in everyone's vocabulary, and we all have a notion of what it means. Students of politics, however, find it desirable to be more precise; and so most works on government and politics include a formal definition of the word. For example, Floyd Hunter, who studied the way in which power was exercised in a small community in the American South, defines it in the following way: "Power is a word that will be used to describe the acts of men going about the business of moving other men to act in relation to themselves or in relation to organic or inorganic things." [1] Another definition, this one by V. O. Key, is that power in all degrees of meaning "involves relations among human beings." [2] Finally, Carl Friedrich looks upon power as a "human relationship in which the leader and the led are banded together for the accomplishment of some common objectives, partly by consent, partly by constraint." [3]

There are slight differences in the foregoing approaches to the problem of power, but they share the common view that

[1] *Community Power Structure* (Chapel Hill, 1953), pp. 2–3.

[2] *Politics, Parties and Pressure Groups,* Second edition (New York, 1947), p. 2.

[3] *Constitutional Government and Democracy* (Boston, 1941), p. 19.

power is a human relationship. And if it is true that power involves relations between and among men, it is inevitable that it should be moulded by the way in which men think and behave in the larger society. Political power, to state it more abstractly, is shaped by social institutions and social values.

AN OUTLINE OF JAPANESE SOCIAL STRATIFICATION

It is a common observation that communities everywhere are generally divided. Social distinctions may be based on age or on wealth, or on a variety of other factors, depending upon time and circumstance. Among the major divisions are class distinctions, which divide society into several social strata. "Everywhere," says MacIver, "the social order to which men cling is presented to them as a graduated order. Power and status combine in such a way that it is hardly possible for anyone, except some visionary prophet, to conceive of the social order otherwise than organized by rank and station." [4] Class divisions are usually accompanied by differences in income levels, occupations and the like, and by a sense of status and social distance which prevails among the members of the society.

It is evident to anyone who has taken even a brief look at Japanese society that a strong sense of social status prevails, leading to social stratification. Japanese society, like other societies, may be represented graphically by a pyramid; but it is not easy to draw this pyramid with any feeling of precision, partly because we are dealing with a highly complex and changing society, and partly because our knowledge of it is inadequate. A clue, however, to the way in which people feel about social distinctions is afforded by a recent survey undertaken in six large cities, in which 2,000 men, twenty years of age and over, were asked to rank thirty occupational categories in order of their importance. This survey produced the following results.

[4] R. M. MacIver, *The Web of Government* (New York, 1947), p. 98.

Thirty Occupations in Order of Importance

		AVERAGE RANK
1.	Prefectural governors	3.78
2.	University professors	4.56
3.	Judges	4.69
4.	Directors of large firms	5.51
5.	Doctors	6.97
6.	Section chiefs of gov't bureaus	7.19
7.	Architects	9.51
8.	Owners of factories	10.21
9.	Labor union leaders	10.77
10.	Journalists	11.17
11.	Primary school teachers	11.73
12.	Chief Buddhist priests	12.46
13.	Owners of retail stores	15.30
14.	Officials of ward offices	15.38
15.	Company employees	16.13
16.	Land-owning farmers	16.38
17.	Policemen	16.41
18.	Tailors	17.68
19.	Dep't store clerks	19.76
20.	Insurance agents	20.18
21.	Carpenters	20.22
22.	Barbers	20.46
23.	Bus drivers	20.93
24.	Lathe workers	21.05
25.	Fishermen	22.02
26.	Coal miners	23.07
27.	Coal stokers	24.42
28.	Road repair men	24.80
29.	Owners of street stalls	24.92
30.	Shoe blacks	26.86

Source: Odaka Kunio, *"Nihon shakai no kaikyu-teki kozo"* (The class structure of Japanese society), *Asahi shimbun*, Feb. 10, 1953.

If we look at the foregoing list carefully, we see definite breaks between numbers 6 and 7, 12 and 13, and 18 and 19; and when we subdivide the list of 30 occupations with these breaks in mind, we get a grouping which looks like this:

Upper middle:	Prefectural governors
	Professors
	Judges
	Directors of large corporations
	Doctors
	Section chiefs of government bureaus
Middle middle:	Architects
	Owners of factories in towns
	Labor union leaders
	Journalists
	Primary school teachers
	Priests of Buddhist temples
Lower middle:	Owners of retail establishments
	Officials in ward offices
	White collar employees in firms
	Land-owning farmers
	Policemen
	Tailors
Upper lower:	Department store clerks
	Insurance agents
	Carpenters
	Barbers
	Bus drivers
	Lathe workers
	Fishermen
Lower lower:	Coal miners
	Coal stokers
	Road repair men
	Owners of street stalls
	Shoe blacks

From this list we can get a rough idea of the way in which Japanese society appears to be stratified to urban dwellers. One should note that those who hold important positions in government agencies, who own or control property, and who have specialized skills involving mental, rather than physical, effort are in general esteemed.

It is unfortunate that a survey along similar lines but cov-

ering the rural areas was not carried out, for very likely a somewhat different profile would have emerged. From various
village studies available to us, however, we can make some in-
ferences as to the social strata that enjoy prestige and influence
in the farming areas. Traditionally, ownership of land and long
and continued residence in the community have been the determinants of social prestige and power. Undoubtedly social attitudes are changing even in the countryside as a result of new
influences flowing in from the cities; but available evidence suggests that these two factors continue to be highly regarded.
John Embree reported in his pre-war study of a village that
there was a small group at the top which included no more
than three people in any one *buraku* or hamlet. "There is no
select social function to which they are not invited. They are
given seats of honor at school affairs and as guests in anyone's
house. The village headmen and village schoolmaster are included in this group. All members are old families, natives of
the *mura*. They are all landed farmers except one. He is the son
of a *samurai* and rather poor, but, because of his ancestry, he
belongs in this group without question. A majority of the twelve
village councillors belongs to this class." [5] In a more recent
study of local government by Royama Masamichi, a tenant
farmer is quoted as saying: "It is a commonplace that all official
positions should be circulated among those who, having inherited wealth from their ancestors, are regarded as 'gentlemen'
(*danna*), even though they may be stupid." [6] Thus the evidence
suggests that in the rural areas power, property and status still
form what MacIver has called the traditional trinity.[7]

[5] *Suye Mura* (Chicago, 1939), pp. 158–9.

[6] *Noson jichi no henbo* (Changes in local government in rural areas)
(Tokyo, 1948), p. 16.

[7] "Each so sustained and augmented the other two that they created
a single hierarchy. The pyramid of power coincided with the pyramid of
status and the pyramid of property—until new social forces drove deep
wedges into the previously cohesive union." R. M. MacIver, *The Web of
Government*, p. 82.

Below the top rung of the local social pyramid are found the smaller landowning families. As a result of the land reform program sponsored by the Occupation, this class has been expanded considerably in size and presumably in influence. Local shopkeepers and professional people, notably Buddhist priests and school teachers, now belong roughly in the same class as the smaller landowning families.

The lower levels of the pyramid are composed of craftsmen, such as carpenters, stonemasons, blacksmiths and the like. Poor farmers, tenant farmers, and landless agricultural workers also belong to the lower classes.

When the rural social pyramid is compared with the urban pyramid, two observations may be made. The horizontal divisions seem less sharp and the total height appears to be lower in the case of the rural scene. Hence those at the summit of the rural pyramid would correspond roughly to the "middle middle" classification which we have adopted in the urban situation. Similarly, the smaller landowners, the shopkeepers and the rural professional people would correspond to the "lower middle." Those who belong to these two classes—the "middle middle" and the "lower middle"—make up what Japanese social scientists sometimes call *chukanso* or the "middle strata."

There is reason to believe that the tens of thousands of individuals (and their families) who are included in the "middle strata" play a key role in Japanese politics. An interesting analysis of the role of the middle classes has been made by Maruyama Masao, who has suggested that the Japanese middle classes may be divided roughly into two groups. In the first group he includes the following types of individuals: owners of small factories, foremen in urban factories, building contractors, owners of small retail establishments, carpenters and masons, small landlords and landowning farmers, school teachers (especially primary school teachers), officials in the village government, lower officials in government agencies, and priests. In the second group are found such individuals as urban white collar workers, journalists, and free intellectuals, that is, professors, lawyers, and students. And in Maruyama's view, it is those individuals comprising the first group who provide the focal points of power in Japanese society. [8]

If we look at the kinds of individuals who appear in this group, it might appear a bit incongruous that so important a position should be assigned them. They scarcely fit the conventionalized image of men who hold leadership positions. Nevertheless, Maruyama's observation provides us with a key for unraveling and understanding some of the complexities of Japanese politics.

The reason such relatively obscure persons as foremen, shopkeepers, and landlords can exercise social power will become clearer when we examine in more detail the relation of the individual to social groups.

THE ROLE OF KINSHIP

When a system of ordered relations among men is present, we may say that society exists. Without such a system of ordered relations, chaos would ensue, for there would be no regulation or channeling of human impulses. No individual would know what to expect of other individuals, and hence social action would be well-nigh impossible. [9]

The primary responsibility for inculcating socially accepted ways of behavior lies in the family. It is in the family that the process known as socialization takes place. It is there that a child learns to conform to the ways of the group by discovering that

[8] Maruyama Masao, *Nihon fasshizumu no shiso to undo* (The ideology and structure of Japanese fascism) in *Sonjo shiso to zettaishugi* (The pro-Emperor ideology and absolutism), ed. by Toyama Shigeki (Tokyo, 1948), pp. 149 ff.

[9] MacIver, *op. cit.*, pp. 22–3.

certain kinds of behavior will be rewarded while other kinds will be punished. Thus, as MacIver says, "Wherever the family exists —and it exists everywhere in human society—government already exists." The family, indeed, is the breeding ground of power.[10] It is therefore appropriate to turn our attention first to the Japanese family.

The Japanese Family System

We are accustomed to thinking of the family and family relations as a private matter. Marriage, divorce, and kindred problems, to be sure, are regulated by law; but we feel that behavior of children toward their parents, sentiments of love and loyalty binding family members together, the division of family property and the like belong in the realm of private morality. In Japan, however, for reasons to be given later, the family, or more precisely the "family system," has been traditionally of concern to the state; and statesmen have made it the subject of solemn speeches, parliaments have taken it up in debate, and political prophets have warned that a weakening of the traditional family system would have dire national consequences.

For all the emphasis that has been put on the family system, there is relatively little data on actual behavior. A substantial portion of the literature that exists on the subject is concerned with normative standards as embodied in the rather detailed provisions in the civil code, in the stories and maxims printed in textbooks, particularly those designed to inculcate proper social ethics, and in pronouncements made by national leaders.

It is possible to put together from these sources a composite picture of the officially prescribed normative patterns of family life. According to this picture, the Japanese family is characterized by its cohesiveness. For some purposes the family is regarded

[10] *Ibid.*, p. 26.

as the basic social unit; and the family as a social group is considered to be more important than the individuals who comprise it. Unlike the contemporary American family, which is built around the conjugal unit of husband and wife, the Japanese family puts its emphasis on the continuity of the family line from grandfather to father to son to grandson, and so on. The individual is a mere link in this chain; and hence he is expected to behave accordingly. He must not act in such a way as to besmirch the good name of his ancestors or jeopardize the reputation of his descendants.

According to the Japanese view, the family is more than a mere grouping of close kin. It has a hierarchical structure; and at the pinnacle of this structure, which may be thought of as pyramidal in shape, stands the male head of the family. He gives the family its unity, for it is toward him that devotion and loyalty are directed.

The head of the family enjoys authority and privileges commensurate with his important position, but he also has certain obligations toward his family. He must support his family, educate his children, find suitable spouses for them when they reach marriageable age, and if possible elevate the family's social standing and increase its property holdings so that the next generation may be better endowed. His wife is considered to be inferior. A good wife is obedient and helpful. She is, moreover, chaste, caters to the needs and whims of her husband, looks after her children, and runs the household generally.

The children in return must assume certain obligations. The Japanese term for this obligation is *on*, and the common saying is that a child's *on* to his parents is "deeper than the ocean and higher than the mountains." A child is obligated to his parents for having been born into this world, for having been cared for through childhood and youth, and for having a spouse selected for him. The child thus is heavily indebted to his parents, and the repayment of this debt involved *ko* or filial piety. Specifically this calls for, among other things, obeying one's parents, never thinking of one's self as their equal, using polite language when addressing them, and taking care to keep them in a good frame of mind. Children should behave in such a way that they will be a credit to their parents, their ancestors and descendants, and to the family as a whole. Misbehavior will not only adversely affect one's own standing in the community, but will cause the entire family to lose face. Each child should be willing to subordinate his own interests and welfare to the good of the family as a whole. The following excerpt from a textbook on ethics used in all the schools in the pre-war period sums up this philosophy in a succinct manner:

If everybody in the family does his best on his own assigned task and serves the Emperor's country faithfully, not only will the prosperity of his family be increased but also, in turn, the honorable position of his family and relatives. But on the contrary, if there should be some persons of indolence or of bad behavior in a family, they will bring suffering upon all the family members, and their relatives will have to suffer loss of face in their community. In this manner a person's conduct will immediately reflect upon the happiness of his family and also reflect upon the good name of his ancestors. Therefore, everyone in the family should be of the same mind, to prosper and to honor the family's name, and to be a good descendant of his ancestors and a good ancestor for his own descendants.[11]

Not all children receive equal treatment or are put under equal obligation. The eldest son enjoys the most preferential treatment, because for one thing it is he who carries on the family line. Upon his father's retirement or death he gets the bulk of the family estate. It is he who takes over the family business

[11] Robert King Hall, *Shushin: The Ethics of a Defeated Nation* (New York: Bureau of Publications, Teachers College, Columbia University, 1949), p. 133. Quoted by permission of the publisher.

or the family farm. The eldest son, on the other hand, must provide for his parents in their old age. After his father's death, the eldest son succeeds him as the head of the house; and now he assumes the obligation of looking after his younger brothers and of helping them in case of need.

The training and education given to daughters is different from that given to sons. Girls are expected to become good wives and wise mothers. A keynote in a woman's upbringing is learning to be submissive. An old saying has it that a girl is subject to the will of her father before her marriage, to her husband after her marriage, and to her son when she becomes a widow.

No student of behavior would make the mistake of assuming that these officially prescribed norms are always in agreement with social realities. Yet, an understanding of such normative standards has value, especially if we know something about their historical background. There is reason to believe that the patriarchal, authoritarian, hierarchical family system represented the idealized norms of the samurai class. In the latter part of the nineteenth century, Japanese political leaders, who were mostly of samurai origin, took the norms which were typical of their class and incorporated them into the civil code and into the social ethics courses in the schools. Values held by elites eventually tend to filter down, even in stratified societies, particularly since in this case these values were consciously inculcated among the entire population over a period of decades.

Field studies undertaken recently in rural areas in northern Japan, a section, incidentally, which is least urbanized and where traditional forms of social organization are strongest, show the existence of tightly knit patriarchal families among the upper strata. In wealthy landowning families, the eldest son inherits the family land and other property. The second and third sons either go elsewhere to seek careers or remain at home. In the latter instance, the second son, even after his marriage, lives with his older brother and works for him. After the younger brother and his wife have worked for as many as ten years,

the older brother will give the couple a small section of the an-
cestral holdings as a reward, thus enabling the couple to become independent and establish a cadet family. But often the
amount of land given is not large enough to support a family,
and so the younger brother must rent land from his older
brother, thereby creating in addition to a older brother-younger
brother relationship a landlord-tenant tie. The younger brother
is, of course, subordinated to his older brother, and this subordination is symbolized in certain rituals. During New Year's and
certain other holidays the second son brings rice cakes to his
brother's house and worships at the family shrine. At a more
practical level, the younger brother is expected to help his older
brother at harvest time.[12]

It may be said that in general the wealthy landed families
in the rural areas (especially in northern Japan), and aristocratic families and business families with wealth in the urban
areas appear to come closest to the normative standard. Very
likely economic considerations are partly at work here. Wealthy
families can give their children considerable advantages in the
way of education, social contacts, and property; and in return
the head of the family is in a position to exercise strong authority over the younger generation.

Such is not the case in low income families where the father's earnings are not sufficiently large to maintain the family
and hence other members of the family are forced to go out
and work in order to supplement the family income. In these
families the idea of a child's obligation (*on*) to his parents, a
notion stressed in the textbooks, appears to be very weak or
even nonexistent. A field study undertaken by Kawashima
Takeyoshi to ascertain attitudes toward filial piety produced
some rather startling results. Most of his respondents, who were
either of the middle or lower strata in a village, replied, when

---

[12] Fukutake Tadashi, *Nihon noson no shakai-teki seikaku* (The social
character of Japanese farm villages) (Tokyo, 1949), pp. 69–88.

asked about their idea of *on* to parents, that they felt no obligation and that what they felt was affection.[13]

Recent Changes in the Family System

Kawashima's study suggests that the normative pattern as expressed in law and taught in the schools applies unevenly to the various sectors of the population. Although precise data are lacking on this point, we may surmise that deviations from the normative pattern are somewhat related to class, regional, and age differences. These differences may be summarized as follows: upper class families are closer to the officially prescribed norm than lower class families; and rural families are closer than urban. As already mentioned, families in northern Japan probably approximate the norm more than families elsewhere. Finally the older generation is more attached to the traditional family system than the younger generation, which prefers something more akin to the individualistic nuclear family typical of contemporary America.

Although it is evident that deviations from prescribed standards have occurred, political leaders have consistently resisted efforts to bring about modification in the social norms. Myths are often unassailable; and it was only after the Allied Occupation put its weight behind it that changes were actually made. The 1947 Constitution contains provisions affecting property rights, inheritance, and marriage. Article 24 reads: "Marriage shall be based only on the mutual consent of both sexes and it shall be maintained through mutual cooperation with the equal rights of husband and wife as a basis. Laws shall be enacted considering choice of spouse, property rights, inheritance, choice of domicile, divorce and other matters pertaining to marriage and the family from the standpoint of individual dignity and

[13] Kawashima Takeyoshi, " '*On*' *no ishiki no jittai*" (On the consciousness of *on*), *Chuo koron* (March, 1951), pp. 120–1.

the essential equality of the sexes." As a consequence, a number of amendments were made to the old civil code in order to make it consistent with the new Constitution. The details need not concern us here. What is of greater interest is the fact that conservative political leaders expressed fear that legal changes affecting the family system would have serious political consequences. One representative in the lower house of the Diet argued in the following vein: "After all, I fear that the revision of our Constitution will shake the foundation of the rights of the head of a house and those of parents. What, do you think, will follow a revision like this? I fear that this will greatly affect the filial piety which forms the foundation of all morals. . . . It is a question that requires a careful study that the filial piety, which forms the fundamentals of the peace and order in the country, is also to be destroyed in consequence of the Constitutional revision." [14]

Changes in the Constitution and the civil code have not led to the breakdown of the social order as feared by some people, for as Steiner says, "a system that is as strongly entrenched in the past and has far-reaching ramifications as the Japanese family system cannot be altered by the stroke of the pen of any lawmaker." [15] On the other hand, it does seem reasonable to presume that the adoption of new normative patterns will accelerate change in the direction of a nuclear family in which the individual will enjoy considerable independence.

The Individual and the Family

The day may come when the provisions of the new Constitution and the civil code as amended can be taken as reason-

[14] Quoted in Kurt Steiner, "The Revision of the Civil Code in Japan: Provisions Affecting the Family," *The Far Eastern Quarterly*, IX (February, 1950), p. 173.
[15] *Ibid.*, p. 184.

able descriptions of the relation of the individual to his family in terms of actual behavior. But most observers would agree that such a day has not yet arrived, although the long-term trend probably is in that direction. Meanwhile, it may be said that when compared to the situation in American families, the individual in Japan is still subordinated to his family. The social expectation is that close kin will help one another and form a cohesive social group. Kinship, therefore, still represents a strong social bond. A political manifestation of this may be seen in a remark, attributed to a villager, that "there is nothing so dirty as blood." [16] What the villager had in mind was the fact that rural inhabitants are under strong social and psychological pressures to vote in local elections along kinship lines rather than on the basis of political principles.

So far our discussion has been concerned only with those situations in which the family members were actually related by blood. But kinship ties may also apply to those who are adopted into the family. Because of the value placed on the continuity of the family line, outsiders or distant relatives are often legally adopted and such individuals assume the family name. This may occur in the case of childless couples, and in the case of families without sons. In the latter instance, the adopted son would most likely marry the eldest daughter and in this way carry on the family line.

A variation of this principle sometimes occurs when outsiders are set up as cadet families, much in the same way that second and third sons are given cadet family status. This may be illustrated by taking the example of the Saito family. The Saitos took in a child of a stranger, and as he grew up he became a "resident servant," helping with household chores, working on the farm and so on. Although he was a servant, he lived with the family, and was fed, clothed, and generally taken care of. Eventually when he reached manhood, the Saitos found

[16] See Fukutake, *op. cit.*, p. 103.

him a wife, gave him a house; and he maintained his livelihood by renting some land held by the Saito family. He and his wife and his children came to be considered blood kin, and he assumed the name of Saito. This relationship has been called "ritual kinship" since it is not based on blood, but it entailed the same kind of obligations. He was expected to help the Saito family on such occasions as funerals and weddings, house building and repairing, and worship at the Saito family shrine, thereby affirming his loyalty to the group.[17]

A functional explanation for this practice of incorporating outsiders into the family structure has been given by an American anthropologist. According to John Bennett, it takes a group larger than that formed by true relatives to run large farms. "Yet, in the rural Japanese system of interpersonal relations, unswerving loyalty and devotion to the task are obtained primarily through kinship ties. This is another way of saying that the family is the model for all social relationships, and the family the basic solidaristic unit. Consequently, ficticious kin ties are frequently resorted to in order to achieve the solidarity, cooperation, and loyalty needed to insure economic welfare."[18]

THE FAMILY AS A MODEL FOR SOCIAL ORGANIZATION

We have alluded to the concern Japanese political leaders have expressed about the family system. The reason for this, simply stated, is that the family is looked upon as the model for other social groupings, including the largest and most extensive, namely the nation-state. Thus the smallest and the most intimate group and the largest and most diffuse are thought to be funda-

[17] Michio Nagai, *Dozoku: A Preliminary Study of the Japanese "Extended Family" Group and Its Social and Economic Functions* (The Ohio State University Research Foundation, 1953), chaps. 3–5.
[18] *Ibid.*, p. 2.

mentally alike. It would follow therefore that other social groupings which lie between the family and the nation-state would also tend to model themselves after the family.

The Oyabun-Kobun Relationship

A number of social groups are characterized by the *oyabun-kobun* relationship. The term *oyabun* is made up of two words, *oya* or parent and *bun* meaning part, role or status; while *kobun* comes from *ko* or child plus *bun*. This relationship has been defined by Ishino and Bennett as follows: "The oyabun-kobun system is a particularistic pattern of social relationships based upon simulated patrimonial principles. In social groupings of this type, persons of authority assume obligations and manifest attitudes toward their subordinates much as if they were foster parents, and conversely the subordinates behave dutifully and hold feelings of great personal loyalty toward their superiors." [19]

As is implied in the foregoing quotation, groups of this kind have structural characteristics which are based on principles found in the family. The leader is called *oyabun* and his subordinates are *kobun*. There is also a differentiation among the *kobun*. Those who joined the organization earlier or who are closer to the *oyabun* outrank others, just as the older brother outranks a younger brother. Furthermore, a *kobun* might be in his own right an *oyabun* and have his own followers. In this case the relationship of these followers to the first *oyabun* would be analogous to that of grandsons to grandfather. "The end result is a complex organization composed of linked groups of several hundred or even thousand members, the ties between and within the groups being highly particularistic and personal, rather than contractual and impersonal." [20]

[19] Iwao Ishino and John W. Bennett, *The Japanese Labor Boss System* (The Ohio State University Research Foundation, 1952), p. 1.
[20] *Ibid.*, p. 2.

The fact that relationships in these groups are based on "particularistic" and "personal" ties is important for our purposes. Although *oyabun-kobun* relationships are found in many sectors of the society, they seem to be particularly conspicuous in certain types of economic pursuits such as coal mining and commercial fishing where workers are exposed to considerable physical danger; construction gangs where work is cyclical in nature and hence accompanied by economic insecurity; organized gambling, prostitution, and racketeering which are in the twilight zone of legality and respectability; and in certain trades and professions such as teachers of traditional music and flower-arrangement where there is advantage in perpetuating monopolistic practices. In all of these instances, individuals are subjected to serious insecurity of one kind or another and find that insecurity can be alleviated to a certain extent by attaching themselves to an *oyabun-kobun* organization.

Ishino and Bennett give in their study a detailed description of an *oyabun-kobun* system among construction workers. They reported that the boss or *oyabun* whom they studied found work for his men or *kobun*, coordinated their work and paid their wages. But since the basic wage was so low as to allow little surplus after allowing for the cost of food, it was necessary for *kobun* to borrow or get additional sums from the *oyabun* to meet doctor bills, cost of new clothing, recreational expenses and the like. The workers were thus dependent upon the "benevolence" of the *oyabun*. "By maintaining such dependence, the oyabun is able to demand and achieve greater personal loyalty from and discipline among his workers. It reinforces his symbolic role of the 'father.'" [21]

The father-role of the *oyabun* also involves activities which lie outside of economics. Ishino and Bennett report that the *oyabun* mediated in a quarrel between a *kobun* and his wife, served as a matchmaker for his unmarried *kobun*, gave parties

[21] *Ibid.*, pp. 39–40.

for his men, "and called for a doctor and personally massaged the back of a sick kobun." [22]

Here we see that there is a reciprocal relationship between the *oyabun* and his *kobun:* the former provides jobs and security and the latter works faithfully and is loyal to his boss. But the relationship is somewhat different from a contract which sets forth precisely the obligations and rights of each party. It is different from a situation in which an employee works eight hours a day for a set wage. In an *oyabun-kobun* relationship no sharp line can be drawn between what is "business" and what is "private." The *oyabun*'s authority and influence extend into what we would regard as the private sectors of the *kobun*'s life. The political implications of this are clear enough. For instance, it takes no great imagination to see what would most likely happen if an *oyabun* made a deal with a local political boss during an election.

The "Human Group"

Not everyone is an *oyabun* or a *kobun*. As we have tried to indicate, the *oyabun-kobun* relationship appears to be most pronounced in those economic and occupational groups characterized by a high degree of insecurity. For this reason, this relationship must be regarded as more abnormal than typical.

A more normal kind of social grouping which is on a larger scale than the immediate family may be called the "human group" for lack of a better word. We have taken the term from the title of George Homans' book, where he has this to say about it: "We mean by a group a number of persons who communicate with one another often over a span of time, and who are few enough so that each person is able to communicate with all the others, not at secondhand, through other people,

[22] *Ibid.*, pp. 26–7.

but face-to-face. Sociologists call this the primary group." [23]

In case of the human group in the Japanese social setting, six attributes may be distinguished: [24]

1. *Permanency.* The group is not formed and then disbanded a short time thereafter, but tends to remain in existence over a span of time. The permanency of the group is maintained by such ritualistic actions as the exchange of letters, periodic visits, and the giving and receiving of presents during holiday seasons.

2. *Is all embracing.* The group may be formed for a limited objective, e.g., for the enjoyment and promotion of music or art, for political action, for the solution of common neighborhood problems, etc. But soon the sphere of activity of the group goes beyond its objectives and begins to touch on the private lives of its members, concerning itself with such problems as marriage and job placement of its members.

3. *Weakens individual free will.* The range of activity open to the individual becomes circumscribed. An individual's behavior is influenced less by free choice and self-interest than by the dictates of the norms of the group.

4. *Personal relationship.* The members of the group are held together by personal ties. Face and social prestige are important considerations.

5. *The emotional element.* The emotional element plays an important part in the relationship among members. Individuals react more on the basis of emotions than on calculated reasoning.

6. *Hierarchical structure.* Observers have noted that groups tend to be composed of equals. But in this case, the members of the group are more likely to be unequal in social standing. Individuals or families cluster around a leader or a few leaders.

Groups with these features are found in every sector of the society, and Kawashima calls them the "cellular units" of Japa-

[23] George Homans, *The Human Group* (New York, 1950), p. 1.
[24] This is based on Kawashima Takeyoshi, *"Giri," Shiso* (Thought), no. 327 (September, 1951), pp. 24 ff.

nese society. Neighborhood organizations, youth groups, teachers and their disciples and landlord-tenant groups are some typical examples.

The "Human Group" and Its Norms

Sociologists tell us that all groups have norms which may be defined as "an idea in the minds of the members of a group, an idea that can be put in the form of a statement specifying what the members or other men should do, ought to do, are expected to do, under given circumstances." [25] Nonconformity to norms is punished and conformity is rewarded.

Norms therefore have to do with expectations; and these expectations may be either implicit or explicit. An interesting facet of Japanese social behavior which, incidentally, is pertinent to an understanding of political behavior, is that certain norms are explicitly stated and more or less formalized in social codes. Two of these norms, *on* and *giri* are of special importance.

The late Ruth Benedict was the first American to call attention to *on* and *giri*. Of *on* she wrote:

Both the Chinese and Japanese have many words meaning "obligations." The words are not synonyms and their specific meanings have no literal translation into English because the ideas they express are alien to us. The word for "obligations" which covers a person's indebtedness from the greatest to least is *on*. In Japanese usage it is translated into English by a whole series of words from "obligations" and "loyalty" to "kindness" and "love," but these words distort its meaning. . . . *On* is in all its uses a load, an indebtedness, a burden, which one carries as best one may.

[25] Homans, *op. cit.*, p. 123.

A man receives *on* from a superior and the act of accepting an *on* from any man not definitely one's superior or at least one's equal gives one an uncomfortable sense of inferiority. When they say, "I wear an *on* on him" they are saying, "I carry a load of obligations to him," and they call this creditor, this benefactor, their "*on* man." [26]

The way in which *on* works may be best shown by a hypothetical situation. Let us suppose that Mr. Suzuki's wife is desperately ill and she must undergo a major operation or she will die. But Mr. Suzuki has been barely able to make ends meet and hence has no cash reserves to meet an emergency of this kind. So he turns to an old family friend, Mr. Tanaka, who is a wealthy wine merchant, for a loan of 50,000 yen. Mr. Tanaka generously loans the needed sum and Mrs. Suzuki undergoes her operation and eventually recovers.

Mr. Suzuki has now incurred an *on*. He has, of course, gotten himself into debt to the extent of 50,000 yen; but more is involved. Mr. Suzuki is not only liable for the 50,000 yen but also for any number of favors that Mr. Tanaka might ask.

Suppose that Mr. Tanaka's son is running for the post of village councillor. Let us also suppose that Mr. Suzuki is convinced that Tanaka, Jr., would not make a good councillor because he would be too partial to the wine industry interests. Suzuki personally favors another candidate. But one evening Mr. Tanaka comes to the Suzuki residence and asks Suzuki to take part in his son's campaign. He hints that he could use some extra helpers to put up campaign posters on telephone poles and also suggests that Suzuki line up votes among his friends and acquaintances. At this point, Suzuki would be caught between conflicting loyalties: loyalty to his political principles and convictions, and his obligations or *on* to Tanaka.

[26] Ruth Benedict, *The Chrysanthemum and the Sword* (Boston: Houghton Mifflin Company, 1946), pp. 99–100. Quoted by permission of the publisher.

This brings us to *giri,* which is related to *on,* and is in effect the other side of the coin. Again we turn to Benedict:

> To an Occidental, giri includes a most heterogeneous list of obligations ranging from gratitude for an old kindness to the duty of revenge. It is no wonder that the Japanese have not tried to expound giri to Westerners; their own all-Japanese dictionaries can hardly define it. One of these renders it—I translate:—'righteous way; the road human beings should follow; something one does unwillingly to forestall apology to the world.'[27]

In another passage she says:

> The rules of giri are strictly rules of required payment; they are not a set of moral rules like the Ten Commandments. When a man is forced with giri, it is assumed that he may have to override his sense of justice and they often say, 'I could not do right (gi) because of giri.' Nor do the rules of giri have anything to do with loving your neighbor as yourself; they do not dictate that a man shall act generously out of the spontaneity of his heart. A man must do giri, they say, because, 'if he does not, people will call him "a person who does not know giri" and he will be shamed before the world.' It is what people will say that makes it so necessary to comply.[28]

Benedict has more to say about *giri,* but the foregoing quotations should suffice to convey its general meaning. We may now return to our illustration involving Mr. Suzuki's dilemma. If he is to follow the dictates of *giri* he must put aside his

---

[27] *Ibid.,* pp. 133–4. See comments by Richard K. Beardsley, "The Household in the Status System of Japanese Villages," *Occasional Papers,* University of Michigan, Center for Japanese Studies I (1951), pp. 68–9.

[28] *Ibid.,* pp. 140–1.

political principles and campaign for Tanaka's son; for by refusing he would not only incur the displeasure of his benefactor
and thereby jeopardize the possibility of getting aid in the future, but he would also be subjected to social disapproval and
criticism. One can begin to appreciate why Japanese do not
like to get tangled up in *on*.

It is worthwhile repeating at this point that when we speak
of *on* and *giri*, we have in mind group norms—the ideas men
have of what they are expected to do under given circumstances.
And the group in question here is the "human group" which
we have already discussed. Contrary to the impression which
Benedict gives in her book, *on* and *giri* generally do not apply
when strangers or casual acquaintances interact. One does not
incur *on* generally speaking when a stranger offers him a cigarette
or when a friend treats him to a soda. *On* is involved when an
individual as an act of generosity does a favor for another individual, and this favor enables the recipient to meet a crisis
situation (such as the one given in our illustration above) or is
vital to one's livelihood (such as a landlord renting farm land to
a tenant farmer). In other words, *on* and *giri* are associated with
group situations in which the group is small in size and the personal element is dominant.

The question then arises: what about large groupings like
the nation-state where members cannot possibly come into an
intimate face-to-face relationship. The Japanese were confronted with this problem when they had to shift from a feudal
state to a nation-state after the Meiji Restoration. It was probably in this period that a more general word for obligation,
gimu, was created.[29] Without going into a detailed discussion of

[29] The term *kenri,* "rights," was created in the Meiji era (Sansom,
The Western World and Japan, p. 446), and one suspects that the term
gimu, which is the obverse of *kenri,* was created at the same time. I cannot
cite concrete evidence to confirm this, but the phraseology of Book 2, Chapter 7 of *Taisei kokuho-ron* (On the laws of the Western world) by Tsuda
Masamichi, reprinted in *Meiji bunka zenshu,* VIII, pp. 88 ff. suggests this.

the difference between *giri* and *gimu,* one can say that *gimu* would apply to a generalized obligation, such as the obligation of a citizen to serve in the armed forces, in contrast to a particular obligation to return a favor rendered previously.

Essentially feudalism is a decentralized political system in which individuals owe political allegiance to their immediate feudal superior. Under Tokugawa feudalism, however, the principle of mutual responsibility was widely used as a method of social control. The habit of person-to-person loyalty, therefore, came to be deeply ingrained. In a modern state, however, individuals owe allegiance to an abstract entity, the nation-state. To change from one system of political allegiance to another in a short span of time is a formidable undertaking; and the Japanese managed it in part by incorporating traditional loyalties into the new system of loyalties. The Meiji statesmen and political theorists sought to solve the problem of new political loyalties by resorting to a specious analogy. The nation-state, they said, was a family writ large. A son incurred *on* to his parents; by the same token a subject has incurred *on* to his emperor, the "father" of the nation.

How much success did the statesmen have? One ought not be dogmatic on this point because little work has been done in this area of Japanese politics. From very fragmentary data, one gets the impression that despite long indoctrination of the idea of *on* to the emperor, it never took firm root, at least not among the middle and lower strata of the society. It may be true that among the elite who could personally get close to the emperor this idea was meaningful; but it is doubtful that the peasant who never saw the emperor face-to-face would feel *on* in any significant way. It must be remembered that *on* and *giri* apply to situations in which the personal element is in the foreground; and this personal element is conspicuously missing at the nation-state level. Of course various devices were used to get around this difficulty. For example, in the Japanese army, soldiers were required every morning to bow in the direction of the villages from which they had come and in the direction of the Imperial palace. Obviously this was an attempt to relate the symbol of home and family to the imperial symbol.[30]

On the basis of a survey of attitudes held by Japanese youth, a French sociologist suggests the hypotheses that *giri*, which was a part of the traditional ethics of the aristocracy, was disseminated by means of the theater, literature, and social intercourse first in the towns and later and to a lesser degree in the countryside; that this concept is correctly understood by about one-third of the population, and that another third are acquainted with the term but do not know what it means; that precise knowledge of the concept decreases in direct ratio to the age of the subject interrogated.[31]

Concluding Remarks

Many aspects of Japanese political behavior cannot be understood unless they are placed in their social setting. That individuals everywhere belong to groups and that their behavior is influenced by group norms goes without saying. What distinguishes Japanese social behavior is the degree to which the individual is subordinated to the family and to small face-to-face groups. Compared to the position of the individual in America, the Japanese individual is caught in a web of obligations which tend to limit the area of action left to choice. The dictates of *on, giri,* and social custom weigh heavily on the individual, and demand much in the way of loyalty to the small group.

Strong emphasis is placed on personal relationships, and this has served to impede the development of impersonal, formalized relationships among individuals. Several consequences flow

[30] Iizuka Koji, *Nihon no guntai* (Japan's army) (Tokyo, 1950), p. 27.

[31] Jean Stoetzel, *Without the Chrysanthemum and the Sword* (New York, 1955), pp. 192–8.

from this state of affairs. First, large groups and organizations are often afflicted by the formation of cliques and factionalism. Large organizations are often nothing more than a conglomeration of small groups. Second, factionalism has resulted in a highly fragmented society composed of innumerable "cellular units" in which individuals are clustered around a leader or a few leaders. The leaders and followers are bound together by a sense of mutual obligation. In many instances, leaders of these "cellular units" belong to the "middle strata" and as has been suggested such leaders often provide the focal points of power in Japanese society. As will be indicated in Chapter 4 they seem to play a part in the system of "informal government." They are, moreover, often in a position to control votes during elections; and they serve as vital links in the transmission of political views and public opinion. It seems fairly certain that large-scale political action cannot occur without the acquiescence, if not the active support, of those local leaders belonging to the "middle strata."

Chapter 3

Political Doctrines and Myths

It is a characteristic of political power that it must not appear naked; it must be adorned by political creeds which seek to explain and justify it. "Those in authority within institutions and social structures," write Gerth and Mills, "attempt to justify their rule by linking it, as if it were a necessary consequence, with moral symbols, sacred emblems, or legal formulae which are widely believed and deeply internalized." [1] We may call these justifications of political power "political doctrines."

POLITICAL DOCTRINES

One would normally expect that, except in periods of revolutionary change, the political doctrine of a society would be more or less in accord with the way of life which prevails. Thus a highly individualistic society would very likely have a political doctrine which extolled the virtues of individualism. Conversely, in a society where the individual is subordinated

[1] Hans Gerth and C. Wright Mills, *Character and Social Structure* (New York, 1953), p. 277.

to the group, the political doctrine will, in all probability, stress the subordination of the individual.

It is extremely difficult at this point in history to set forth with clarity the kind of doctrine which prevails in contemporary Japan. In theory, the pre-war doctrines have been discarded and replaced by new ones which are democratic in character. Yet, since the new doctrines were imposed from outside instead of originating primarily in internal social changes, there is ground for believing that the old and the new doctrines exist side by side at present, with little effective integration of the two having occurred as yet. If this line of reasoning is valid, a historical analysis of the pre-war political doctrine would not be entirely out of place in this study.

Kokutai

A convenient starting point of a discussion of the pre-war myth is the notion of *kokutai* which runs through Japanese political writings like a leitmotiv. The term *kokutai* is composed of two ideographs meaning country and body respectively. As conceived by Japanese writers, *kokutai* is divine in origin, unique to Japan, and eternal in character. An anthoritative exposition of *kokutai* appeared in the opening paragraph of *Kokutai no hongi* (The basic principles of *kokutai*), published by the Ministry of Education in 1937. "The great empire of Japan," it read, "shall be governed for all time under the guidance of the divine injunctions of the Imperial ancestors of the Emperor whose line is unbroken for ages eternal. This is our everlasting and immutable *kokutai*." [2]

As is implied in the foregoing quotation, the cornerstone of *kokutai* was the Emperor and his divine ancestors. Indeed, without the Emperor it would have lacked its *raison d'être*.

[2] Tenth printing (Tokyo, 1943), p. 9. There is an English translation of this document by John Owen Gauntlett (Cambridge, 1949).

Until January 1, 1946 when the Emperor renounced his divinity, the official dogma, taught in the schools and disseminated in publications, asserted that the Emperor was the direct descendant of the Sun Goddess, Amaterasu-o-mikami. Justification for this dogma was sought in Japanese mythology as recorded in two works, the *Kojiki* (A.D. 712) and the *Nihongi* (A.D. 720).[3]

As stated in these mythological tales, once treated as historical truth in official circles, in the beginning there was chaos. After heaven and earth were formed, there were produced divine beings and in the seventh generation there were a brother and sister, Izanagi and Izanami, who were married and later gave birth to the islands of Japan and a host of gods and goddesses. After the birth of the fire-god, Izanami died and went to the Land of Darkness. Izanagi followed her, only to find her a mass of decaying flesh. Overcome by the sight, he fled. He then bathed in a stream to purify himself, and from each piece of clothing he threw on the river bank a new deity was born and also from each part of his person. From his left eye, sprang the Sun Goddess. Eventually the grandson of this Sun Goddess, Ninigi-no-mikoto, received the Imperial Command and descended to earth. His great grandson ascended the throne to become Jimmu, the first emperor. This, say the chronicles, occurred on February 11, 660 B.C.

According to the findings of modern scholarship, this myth tale, which has resemblances to Polynesian mythology, was originally used to justify the hegemony of the Imperial clan over the lesser clans.[4] The myth undoubtedly would have been relegated to obscurity if at a later point in history the Imperial clan

---

[3] The *Kojiki* was translated into English by Basil Hall Chamberlain in the *Transactions of the Asiatic Society of Japan,* supplement to Volume X (Tokyo, 1906). W. G. Aston's translation of the *Nihongi* was published in London in 1896.

[4] George B. Sansom, *Japan, a Short Cultural History* (New York, 1943), pp. 22 ff.

had been overthrown; but since it was not, the mythology continued to survive along with the long line of Emperors.

Although the Imperial institution boasted long continuity, the actual power wielded by the Emperor waxed and waned. In fact, during the Tokugawa period (1603–1867) the Emperor was so much eclipsed by the Shogun that among the common people the existence of the Emperor was probably unknown. Historically, the beginnings of the modern Emperor system go back to the revival of learning in the 18th century, when there developed a school of nationalistic scholars who, through their studies of Japanese history, seized upon the idea that the Shogun was a usurper and that the Emperor was the rightful ruler. In time this idea became influential, until it finally achieved political expression in the Meiji Restoration.

The leaders of the new government that was established as a result of the Restoration used the Throne as an instrument for overcoming the strong sense of localism that had prevailed under the feudal regime. The Emperor was consciously moulded into the symbol of a modern centralized state. But because of the historical circumstances surrounding the emergence of Japan as a modern state, the basic components of the state were not free and equal citizens who owed direct allegiance to it. The Meiji Restoration was not a social revolution which detached, as it were, the individual from his previous social moorings and incorporated him into new social institutions. Rather, as was indicated earlier, a deliberate effort was made to preserve the old social groupings as much as possible, making such modifications as were necessary to meet new conditions. Among the most important of the old institutions that were preserved was the family system. The feelings of loyalty and devotion which individuals had toward their families were, in theory, made the basis of a new patriotism. The formula which was used to link intensely personal sentiments like devotion to one's family to impersonal sentiments like loyalty to one's own nation was the concept of the "nation as one big family."

The Nation as One Big Family

Until the end of the war when their use was prohibited by the Occupation authorities, Japanese school children studied the *Shushinsho* or textbook on social ethics. We find in this textbook the following passage:

> The Emperor, whom we the people worship as God, is a descendant of the Great August Sun Goddess Amaterasu and He rules the country in accordance with the will and desires of Goddess Amaterasu. And the manner in which our Emperor graciously and lovingly leads our people is like the parents' love for their children and like the sunshine that shines equally over all living things and His Benevolence toward His people is deep and boundless.
>
> The manner in which we worship the Emperor as God and [the fact of] having the Imperial Household as the main stock of our family origin is something that is peculiar to the body politic of our country, there being no likeness of it throughout all the world.[5]

There are in this quotation three ideas which are central to the *kokutai* concept. First, the assertion is made that the Japanese state is unique. From this the implication could be drawn that even though Japan may become Westernized, she need not adopt democratic ideas and ideals. Second, the Emperor is likened to a father who loves his children. Third, it is claimed that the Imperial family came first and that the descendants of this family ultimately became the subjects of the Emperor.

With the Emperor considered as a patriarch, and the nation one large family, political obligation ultimately rested on filial piety. Inoue Tetsujiro, a well-known philosopher, stated

[5] Quoted in Robert King Hall, *Shushin: The Ethics of a Defeated Nation*, p. 76.

it this way: "The relation of the ruler to his subjects is like that of parents to their children. That is, a state is an extended family. For the ruler of a country to lead and direct his subjects is no different from parents of a family benevolently singing to their children."[6] A similar view is expressed in *Shimmin no michi* (The way of the subjects), an official publication of the Ministry of Education. "Now in our country filial piety (*ko*) exists because of loyalty (*chu*); loyalty is the root. Within our families we are offspring of our parents; both parents and offspring are subjects. Filial piety as found in our families must be transformed into loyalty without alteration. Loyalty and filial piety are not two but one."[7]

Since loyalty and filial piety made constant demands on the individual there was little room, under the Japanese myth system, for individualism. According to the authors of the *Kokutai no hongi* it was not self-sacrifice for an individual to give up his life for the Emperor. Rather it was to relinquish the ego, which was unimportant, and live in the August Virtue of the Emperor, which was important. It is thus evident that the parts were to be strictly subordinated to the whole.[8]

The Japanese used the phrase "isshin dotai" or one mind —one body to give expression to this idea.[9] An important corollary of "isshin dotai," however, was the view that the parts making up the whole were not of equal value. Hierarchy was the dominant pattern of the Japanese family system; and in the same way, the state took the form of a hierarchical structure. Attacking the Western ideas of equality and freedom as "false

[6] Quoted in Ishida Takeshi, *Meiji seiji shiso shi kenkyu* (A study of Meiji political theory) (Tokyo, 1954), p. 42.

[7] (Tokyo, 1941), pp. 47–8. In an annotated edition the footnote explaining the phrase "not two but one" says: "To be loyal to the Emperor is to be filial to one's parents. In short loyalty and filial piety are the same thing." This edition was published by the Asahi Shimbunsha, 1941, and the note appears on page 60.

[8] *Kokutai no hongi*, p. 35.

[9] See Kakehi Katsuhiko, *Kokka no kenkyu* (A study of the state) (Tokyo, 1930), I, pp. 27, ff. for an explanation of this term.

notions," a Japanese writer said: "The equality and freedom which Japan considers, and moreover tries to realize is the true equality and freedom resting on just principles of nature. That is to say, by recognition of man's inequality, each individual is given his appropriate place. Human beings, who to begin with are unequal are thus enabled to avoid the misfortunes arising from this inequality; and each person is permitted to manifest his talents and ability." [10]

It should be evident that the Emperor was central to the idea (1) that the Japanese nation was unique, (2) that it was a large family under a patriarchal father, and (3) that its component parts were unequal. The Imperial institution was indispensable to the myth system, and this fact was explicitly recognized by those in power in the Meiji era. When the draft of the Constitution of 1889 was being considered by the Privy Council, Prince Ito Hirobumi, one of the architects of the Constitution, told his colleagues in the Privy Council that since constitutional government was new to Japan he could not predict whether it would be helpful or harmful, but that the best way for a state to function was through a constitution. But he added that since the Japanese had no previous experience with constitutions, a focal point for the state would have to be established. If the people, he said, were allowed to participate in government without such a focal point, the state could not be ruled and national fortunes would decline. The Western countries, continued Ito, have had long experience with constitutional government, and they also have a religion that serves as a unifying force. Japan has neither; in fact the only thing that can serve as a focal point is the Imperial house. For this reason, he contended, the draft constitution emphasized the power of the Throne. [11]

[10] Nakaoka Hiroo, *Nihon-teki sekaikan josetsu* (An introduction to the Japanese world-view) (Tokyo, 1944), p. 200.

[11] Quoted in Osatake Takeshi, *Nihon kensei shi taiko* (An outline of Japanese constitutional history) (Tokyo, 1939), II, p. 781.

Kokutai in the Post-war Period

Ito made the foregoing statement in 1888. Since then Japan has undergone many changes, including defeat in a major war and the Allied Occupation. The crucial question is to what extent the idea of *kokutai* remains preserved today. Here we must rely on evidence which at best is fragmentary and circumstantial. The evidence available to us suggests that attachment to the Emperor and *kokutai* still survive among the political elite.

First of all, there is reason to believe that Japan's leaders chose to surrender rather than prolong the war because of their desire to preserve *kokutai*. The late Prince Konoye Fumimaro, a former Prime Minister, for example, is said to have made the following remarks in a conference of senior statesmen toward the end of the war:

> During the past few decades there has been present leftist ideology in one section of the Army. At present some have made connections with the armed forces, the bureaucracy, and the people, and are planning a leftist revolution. This is of greater danger than defeat in war. I personally fear a leftist revolution even more than defeat. This is because the Imperial household and the *kokutai* can be preserved even in defeat, but not so in case of a revolution.[12]

Konoye's views were shared by others. In negotiating with the Allied Powers a year later, the Japanese government tried to modify the surrender terms by adding a clause that it would accept the Potsdam Declaration "with the understanding that

[12] These remarks were recorded by Kido Koichi in his diary. Kyokuto kokusai gunji saiban kenkyukai (Society for the study of the International Military Tribunal for the Far East), *Kido nikki* (Kido diary) (Tokyo, 1947), p. 128. See also Robert J. C. Butow, *Japan's Decision to Surrender* (Stanford, 1954), *passim*.

the said declaration does not comprise any demand which prejudices the prerogatives of His Majesty as a Sovereign Ruler." The issue, however, was not settled, since Secretary of State Byrne's reply merely stated that the "authority of the Emperor and the Japanese Government to rule the state shall be subject to the Supreme Commander of the Allied Powers."

Within the first year of the Occupation several steps were taken to clarify the relation of the Emperor to the state. In an unprecedented Rescript issued on January 1, 1946, the Emperor disavowed his claim to divine origins. After noting that following defeat the people were liable to grow restless and that "radical tendencies in excess are gradually spreading," he affirmed the following:

> We stand by the people and we wish always to share
> with them in their moments of joys and sorrows. The ties
> between us and our people have always stood upon mutual
> trust and affection. They do not depend upon mere legends
> and myths. They are not predicated on the false concep-
> tion that the Emperor is divine and that the Japanese peo-
> ple are superior to other races and fated to rule the world.[13]

The next major step involved the incorporation of the new concept of the Throne into the basic law of the land. It was apparent to everyone that the Meiji Constitution of 1889 was hardly appropriate for a democratized Japan, but there was no agreement as to the kind of constitution that should be enacted to replace it. Japanese leaders, particularly those of conservative persuasion, took the position that the old Constitution should be retained with certain revisions being made to meet new conditions; and in fact had started to work along this line. The Occupation, however, rejected this approach, and in the end decided that a completely new constitution should be drafted. This was undertaken by General MacArthur's staff in

[13] Quoted in U.S. Department of State, *Occupation of Japan, Policy and Progress* (Washington, n.d.), p. 135.

strict secrecy, and the finished document was presented to the Japanese government.[14] "We, the Japanese people," the draft read, "acting through our duly elected representatives in the National Diet, determined that we shall secure for ourselves and our posterity the fruits of peaceful cooperation with all nations and the blessings of liberty through this land . . . do proclaim the sovereignty of the people's will and do ordain and establish this Constitution. . . ." Article One stated that the "Emperor shall be the symbol of the state and of the unity of the people, deriving his position from the sovereign will of the people."

The Japanese government was taken by surprise, but it was powerless to reject the document. Outwardly both sides maintained the fiction that the draft had been prepared by the Japanese government. In due time it was debated and passed by the National Diet. It is significant that in steering the draft through the legislature, the government stoutly maintained that the new Constitution did not alter the *kokutai*. In the debate in the House of Peers, a supporter of the government's position, Mizuchi Chuzo, offered a tortuous explanation as to why the *kokutai* remained unchanged. "Our national character (kokutai)," he said, "has been hotly discussed as the most important of all the problems dealt with at [t]he plenary sessions and committee meetings." He acknowledged that under the new Constitution, sovereignty resides with the people, while the old Constitution rested on the principle of Imperial sovereignty. "From the viewpoint of political science, therefore, [i]t may be argued that there has been a manifest change in the national character." But he did not agree with this point of view because "the constitution stipulated only the form of government." "In Japan alone," he continued, "exists the concept of national character . . . and the national character exists outside of or be-

---

[14] Supreme Commander for the Allied Powers, *Political Reorientation of Japan* (Washington, 1949), I, pp. 94–109.

hind the sovereignty. Therefore, I subscribe to the Government's view that the constitutional revision may alter the form of government but not our national character. . . ." Moreover, it was his belief that a basic feature of the national character was the fact "that the Emperor, who comes of the Imperial Line Unbroken for ages eternal, forms the center of the unity of the people." He noted that under Article One, the Emperor was the symbol of the state and of the unity of the people. "This stipulation," he concluded, "makes us firmly believe that there is no alteration whatever in our time-honored national character." (Applause).[15]

This speaker was followed by another member who argued that sovereignty rested in the people, and that the Emperor as Emperor was included in the word "people." He disagreed with the government's position, which was that the Emperor was included in the "people" but only as a private individual. "In other words," he said, "the sovereignty in this country subsists in the people as an entity through ages past, present and future and as a unity of the rule[r] and the ruled." [16]

We need not go into the niceties of the argument as to whether *kokutai* remains unaltered. What is important is that people in positions of influence apparently still believe in (or profess to believe in) the Emperor system. In recent interviews, two former Prime Ministers, Wakatsuki Reijiro and Admiral Okada Keisuke affirmed their faith in the Emperor system. Wakatsuki said that he does not believe the Emperor to be divine, but added: "As for one's feeling toward the Emperor, one does not analyze it in Eastern morality. If one were to analyze it, one would probably have some difficulties. We are loyal to our ruler and filial to our parents; and we never study why it should be so." Unlike Wakatsuki, Admiral Okada believes that the Emperor is divine. "He is divine not because

[15] The House of Peers, The 90th Session of the Imperial Diet, *The Official Gazette*, Extra, no. 40, October 7, 1946 (English edition), pp. 2–3.
[16] The House of Peers, *ibid.*, p. 5.

of his sterling character or of his vast knowledge. He is a god whom the people worship without question. The divine Emperor is different from the divine beings of Buddhism whom I worship. . . ." [17]

What about popular attitudes? In the long run the thoughts and feelings which the masses have toward the concept of *kokutai* and the Emperor institution will most likely prove to be decisive. But the problem of ascertaining popular attitudes in this area is complicated by at least two considerations: the subject of the Emperor was taboo for such a long time that people are not accustomed to discussing it freely, and systematic research in this field has not yet been undertaken. To get anything resembling a total picture, one would have to relate attitudes to social status, and this, of course, would require a fairly large-scale survey.

Our remarks, therefore, are based on incomplete and inconclusive evidence. The various public opinion polls that have been undertaken since the end of the war suggest in general that the great majority of the population support the Emperor system. [18] The data suggest, moreover, that the strongest support comes from farmers, fishermen, the less educated portion of the population, and the older generation. The least enthusiastic support, and in some instances opposition, is to be found among intellectuals, industrial workers, and the youth. But even in the case of the younger generation, according to Jean Stoetzel, devotion to the Emperor system remains. "It is clear that, notwithstanding Japan's setbacks and political upheavals, attachment to the imperial house remains strong. This attachment, however, is much more political, or philosophical, than personal; in other words it is directed more towards the

[17] Shiso no kagaku kenkyukai (Institute for the science of thought), *Watakushi no tetsugaku* (My philosophy) (Tokyo, 1950), pp. 107, 116.

[18] Hugh H. Smythe and Masaharu Watanabe, "Japanese Popular Attitudes Toward the Emperor," *Pacific Affairs*, XXVI (December, 1953), pp. 335–44.

imperial regime than towards the person of the present sovereign, His Imperial Majesty the Emperor Hirohito." [19]

An interesting analysis of the various ways in which the Imperial institution is justified by the public has been made by Tsurumi Shunsuke, on the basis of extensive interviews. According to Tsurumi, there are seven methods of justification:

1. *Analogy:* The Emperor is often compared to the main pillar of a house, or to the national flag, or to the father of a family. "When we look at a family, we find it needs a father, and when there is no father the family becomes very gloomy and sad."

2. *Personal sentiment:* Some people merely assert their personal need for the Imperial institution. "I just want the Emperor over us."

3. *National sentiment:* The assertion is made that the nation feels devotion to the Emperor. "I wonder if it isn't a national sentiment."

4. *Origin:* The emphasis here is on tradition. "The Emperor has been the center of our country since ancient times."

5. *Utility:* The Emperor system is justified because it performs useful functions. "Japan won't develop without an Emperor." "If there are evil ministers, he will make them quit and put in good men."

6. *Inherent authority:* According to Tsurumi, not many use this reason to justify the Imperial institution. "My father told me that the Emperor is the greatest person in Japan."

7. *Supernatural power:* The Emperor is divine; if not, at least he is different from the rest of the people. "You may say that the Emperor is not a *kami;* but he lives in a distant palace, so I can't help but believe he is a *kami.*" [20]

[19] Jean Stoetzel, *Without the Chrysanthemum and the Sword,* p. 159.

[20] Tsurumi Shunsuke, *"Nihon shiso no tokushoku to tenno-sei"* (Special characteristics of Japanese thought and the emperor system), *Shiso* (Thought), no. 336 (June, 1952), pp. 49–50; also Smythe and Watanabe, *op. cit.,* pp. 341–2.

In Search of a New Doctrine

Democracy does not have a specific creed; nor does it have a set number of authoritative texts, or a systematic ideology. It rests rather on certain basic assumptions, attitudes and ideals which have to do with the relation of man to society. Broadly speaking, if democracy is to be a living idea, it must become a part of the "way of life" of a people.

One can appreciate the fact that it must be difficult for a people like the Japanese who had become accustomed to a carefully defined political creed to be deprived, as they were under the Occupation, of their traditional ideological guideposts. The Meiji Constitution was replaced by a new Constitution based on a vastly different political philosophy, the *Kokutai no hongi* was banned by the Occupation, and a famous document, The Imperial Rescript on Education, was rescinded in 1948. In the eyes of some Japanese, an intellectual vacuum was thereby created, leading—according to this school of thought—to chaos in the moral order and to social unrest.

It would appear, at least to an outsider, that the effectiveness of these officially prescribed political dicta was vastly overrated. The Imperial Rescript on Education is a case in point. Its promulgation in 1890 was a part of the conservative reaction to the spread of liberal Western ideas. "The excessive Westernization of Japan," recalled Yoshikawa Akimasa, who was Minister of Education at the time, "very naturally aroused strong opposition among conservative people, especially scholars of the Japanese and Chinese classics, who thought it dangerous for the moral standard of this Empire to see this process carried even into the moral teachings of the people." [21] Until the end of the war, the Rescript was read on important school occasions in an atmosphere of solemnity, and there were even instances in

---

[21] Quoted in Hall, *op. cit.*, p. 36.

which school principals were deprived of their jobs for having mispronounced one of its syllables.[22]

But did the Rescript, for all the reverence that was accorded it, actually succeed in inculcating the desired moral and political attitudes? One thinks not. It was, to begin with, written in a flowery difficult language, making it almost incomprehensible to the average person. It dealt, moreover, with abstractions and generalities, so that it was almost useless as a guide to social behavior. The following comment by Yoshiya Nobuko, a well-known woman novelist, would appear to characterize succinctly the intellectual impact of the Rescript: "As I think back on it now, it was too difficult. When I was in primary school, it used to be read aloud on the Emperor's birthday; but I could not understand its meaning. It seems to me that it did not have much spiritual effect; it was a kind of ceremony." [23] The evidence suggests, then, that the officially approved dicta were not always internalized, as the sociologists would say, by the citizen-subjects. But if the Rescript was without practical value in guiding the everyday life of the individual, it did provide individuals with shibboleths about social ideals and behavior. It was useful for individuals to have a prescribed set of precepts to which they might pay lip service. Equally important, it helped create an illusion of political unity and social harmony.

As we have seen, pronouncements like the Rescript on Education were officially disavowed under the Occupation. At the same time, there was a general loosening of social controls which the Occupation either intentionally or unintentionally fostered. The result was that social conflicts which had been present in prewar Japan but which had been either restrained or kept hidden now stood out in full public view. Thus, to cite an example, there was by no means unanimous devotion to the Emperor be-

[22] Willis Lamott, *Nippon: the Crime and Punishment of Japan* (New York, 1944), p. 137.

[23] Shiso no kagaku kenkyukai, *Watakushi no tetsugaku, zoku* (Tokyo, 1950), p. 21.

fore the war, but so long as discussion of the Emperor system was taboo, the existence of differences in points of view remained hidden. Under the Occupation, the taboo was removed and differences of view emerged to the surface, leading to an open debate on the pros and cons of the Emperor system.

The loosening of social controls and the dislocations attendant on war and defeat led to a breakdown of the social order. Crimes of violence increased sharply, prostitution was openly practiced, erotic literature came to be widely sold, new forms of entertainment, such as strip tease, attracted crowds, and gambling of all kinds, including pinball machines, became a craze.

There arose as a result a widespread feeling that moral standards had declined severely. Among those who remembered the pre-war era, there emerged a feeling of nostalgia for the "good old days." This nostalgia for the past was given expression in a popular novel, *All hope is not lost* (*Nozomi naki ni arazu*) by Ishikawa Tatsuzo. Originally published in serial form in one of the leading metropolitan newspapers, the novel, when issued in book form, became a best seller. Later it was made into a stage play as well as a movie, and finally it was dramatized over the radio.

There are two types of characters in the novel—those representing good and those representing evil. The hero, an ex-navy captain, is pictured as the upholder of traditional values. A man of integrity, loyal to the Emperor, he is the only one in the novel who worries about the future of his country. But the hero has been "purged" and thus is excluded from many occupations. In order to make a living, therefore, he gets involved in blackmarket operations, but he still believes that he can preserve the purity of his innermost self even if the world around him is full of impurity and chaos.

The other figures in the novel represent "democracy" in one way or another. There is the hero's wife, who buys foreign-style dresses and goes out dancing with a university student who rents a room in the hero's house. This student is a disillusioned unemployed man who looks back with nostalgia to the wartime period when he had a job in a factory. At present the student spends his time drinking, dancing and carrying on a love affair with a wealthy war widow who lives next door. Living in a kind of a dream world, the widow makes believe that the young student is her deceased husband.

The student invites, without first obtaining his landlord's permission, two roomless friends to come and live with him. These two men are aggressive self-styled "revolutionaries" and when the hero tries to put them out, they refuse to leave on the ground that this is a free world and they have a right to stay. Finally through the carelessness of these men, the hero's house is burned to the ground. So we find the hero suffering many injustices inflicted upon him in the name of "democracy."

The novel gives the general impression that the pre-war period was superior, and that "democracy" is the source of evils —blackmarkets, sexual license, the emphasis on individual rights at the expense of duties and obligations—that plague the country. To be sure, *All hope is not lost* is a caricature and draws an exaggerated picture; nevertheless it apparently struck a responsive chord among its readers.

Many people, confronted by the apparent breakdown of traditional morality, came to attribute it in part to the abolition of officially prescribed precepts like the Rescript on Education. They believed that what was needed to restore moral standards was a new Rescript. It was this feeling which finally moved Amano Teiyu, Minister of Education, to draft a document which he called "An outline of ethical practice for the Japanese people" (*Kokumin jissen yoryo*). It was published in November, 1951, in the conservative newspaper, *Yomiuri*.

The Outline consisted of four parts: the individual; the family; society; and the state.[24] Unlike the pre-war Rescript, the

[24] R. P. Dore, "The Ethics of the New Japan," *Pacific Affairs*, XXV (June, 1952), pp. 150 ff.

Outline recognized the dignity of the individual personality, but at the same time it tried to bolster certain traditional concep- tions, such as self-restraint, and the moral character of the state. With regard to the Emperor, the Outline stated: "We have the Emperor as the symbol of the State, a unique form of national polity. Our special characteristic lies in the fact that we have had an Emperor throughout a long history. The position of the Emperor has the character of being the focus of morality as the symbol of the State."

The document immediately became the center of a heated controversy. There was widespread objection in the press and other quarters, particularly to the section on the Emperor. Even when Amano stated that the views expressed in his Outline were his private views and not those of a Minister of Education, his critics remained unsatisfied. On November 26, 1951, the Commit- tee on Education of the House of Councillors summoned nine witnesses to give their views on the Amano Outline. The wit- nesses, many of whom were educators, all took a negative stand. One witness, Yano Ichiro, president of the Daiichi Life Insur- ance company, told the committee that he could understand why Amano would wish to issue such an Outline, but doubted its effectiveness. He felt that among those over 50 years of age, there would be many who would be sympathetic to what Amano was trying to say, but that this would not be true among those in the 20 to 40 age bracket. "For example," he went on, "when Amano uses a word like state and Emperor, the denotation would be the same for everyone, but the ideas associated with such terms and the feelings aroused by them would differ from person to person. So occasionally these words would have an unfavorable effect upon those who associate them with totali- tarianism." [25] There was so much adverse comment that in the end Amano was forced to retract his Outline.

[25] *Shugiin mombu iinkai kaigiroku* (Proceedings of the Education Committee, House of Representatives), 12th session of the National Diet, no. 4 (November 26, 1951), p. 3.

The furor that the Outline aroused is merely one indication of the divisions which are now apparent within the Japanese body politic. An even more graphic illustration is provided by a celebrated case of patricide argued before the Japanese Supreme Court.

The case rose out of an incident which occurred in the fall of 1949 in the city of Iizuka in northern Kyushu.[26] Yamato Shigeki, age 53, his wife and children were sitting around the dinner table one evening when the father turned to one of his sons, Toyomi, and accused him of having stolen his younger brother's overcoat. When Toyomi denied the accusation, the short-tempered father got angry and told his son that he ought to confess. Then he threw at his son some iron pots which were nearby. Toyomi threw these pots back, and one of them hit his father on the head. Later the father died from an injury received on this occasion.

Toyomi was charged with patricide and tried in a district court. Article 205 of the criminal code prescribed that "Every person who has wounded or otherwise bodily injured another person and thereby caused the latter's death shall be punished with limited penal servitude for not less than two years. In case the crime is against a lineal ascendant of the offender or of his (her) spouse, punishment shall be penal servitude for life or not less than three years." But the district court refused to apply the provision in Article 205 governing the death of a lineal ascendant because in its view it was unconstitutional, and gave Toyomi a three-year suspended sentence. The court held that the provision for more stringent penalties for crimes against lineal ascendants was "feudalistic," "anti-democratic," and opposed to human rights. It concluded that the provision was contrary to Article 14 of the Constitution which declares that "All of the people are equal under the law and there shall be no discrim-

---

[26] Nakagawa Zennosuke, *"Oyagoroshi"* (Patricide), *Tembo* (Outlook), no. 68 (August, 1951), pp. 38–44, gives the background of this case.

ination in political, economic or social relations, because of race, creed, sex, social status or family origin." The government appealed the case, and it was finally argued before the Supreme Court, which handed down its decision in October, 1950.

The Supreme Court reversed the decision of the Fukuoka District court and held that the provision was constitutional.[27] The court held, through its majority opinion, that Article 14 of the Constitution stated the general principle that human beings were of equal worth, and that it did not prevent the application of concrete rules within the general framework of equality. The court's view was that it was permissible for concrete rules to take into account such things as age differences, natural conditions, occupation, and special relationships between people. It held that the provisions in the criminal code were based on the moral obligation of the child to his parents. The Supreme Court rejected the district court's argument that such provisions were found only in familial societies which uphold the idea of the "oneness of loyalty and filial piety" and of "ancestor worship." According to the Supreme Court, the morality which governs husband and wife, parent and child, older brother and younger brother is the basis of human ethics, is a universal moral principle recognized in the past as well as in the present, in the West as well as in the East. In other words, said the Supreme Court, it pertains to "natural law."

Two justices, Mano Tsuyoshi and Hozumi Shigeto, wrote dissenting opinions. Justice Mano contended that the basic principle of democracy was the equality of human beings. This is stated, he said, in the U.N. Declaration on Human Rights and is engraved on the United States' Supreme Court building where we find the words, "equal justice under the law." Justice Mano went on to say that the basis of equality lies in the spirit of independence and self-respect whereby an individual acts, not as

[27] "*Sonzoku shogai chishi hikoku jiken*" (Case of fatal injury of an ascendant), *Saiko saibansho hanreishu* (Supreme Court reports), IV (December, 1950), pp. 2038 ff.

a result of pressure from the outside, but from guidance coming from within. The imposition of heavier penalties for patricide is clearly discriminatory and contrary to the principle of equality before the law. The devotion of a child to his parents is the concern of individuals and ought not be regulated by law. In a rational democratic state, law and morality should be kept strictly separated.

Justice Hozumi disagreed with the contention that Article 14 of the Constitution merely stated a general principle. He argued that if exceptions are made in application, the principle would become meaningless. Justice Hozumi stated that he was not opposed to filial piety, but was opposed to making it a concern of law.

In a sharply worded concurring opinion, Justice Saito Yusuke took issue with the dissenting opinions. Justice Saito maintained that filial piety was the basis of ethics and that it was universal. He said that for law to recognize superior status in order to emphasize filial piety is a very rational step in maintaining order within the state. Justice Saito dismissed the lower court's opinion that Article 205 was feudalistic, anti-democratic, and anti-human rights by saying that this was "infantile diseased democracy."

Thus the Supreme Court showed by its action a disinclination to tamper with the ideology of the Japanese family system, a cornerstone of Japanese conservatism. This is not altogether surprising. What is noteworthy is the open split within the court and the caustic tone of the opinions. There has been a tendency in Japanese politics to value outward unanimity, and one would presume that the justices were under strong pressure to present a united front on so important an issue as the family system. But apparently this was not possible and so the Supreme Court became openly divided.

Both the controversy that followed the Amano statement and the split within the Supreme Court are indicative of the divisions that exist within the body politic. Of course, the existence of divisions is to be expected in a complex modern state. We know that there was in fact disunity in pre-war Japan just as there is now. The chief difference is that before the war disunity was more or less camouflaged, whereas now it is not. But to a people long accustomed to surface unity, the sight of open cleavages can be rather disturbing, giving rise to a feeling of insecurity. Such a feeling, if it became sufficiently widespread and strong, could very well pave the way for the emergence of a totalitarian state which, by suppressing dissident opinion, would restore the façade of national unity. Japan's problem is not to cover up the cleavages, but rather to find appropriate means of achieving accommodation and compromise among competing groups and ideologies. But steps toward a solution cannot be taken until there is full recognition of the problem.

POLITICAL MYTHS

Political doctrines are usually embodied in formal declarations such as constitutions and charters, and in reflections on government by political philosophers. There are, in addition, basic assumptions made by large sectors of the population with reference to political affairs. We shall call these assumptions political myths. Because they are seldom treated systematically, it is not always easy to describe the political myths which underlie a political system. In the Japanese case, we may distinguish at least three basic notions: the ideal of social harmony, subservience to authority, and fatalism.

The Ideal of Social Harmony

A striking feature of political thinking in the Western world is the central place held by the idea of justice. The problem of how to attain justice has been the concern of Western political philosophers ever since the time of the Greeks. In the Japanese political tradition, however, justice does not occupy so exalted a place. Instead of justice, the Japanese have emphasized the idea of social harmony (*wago*). A well-known legal philosopher has described social harmony in the following manner:

> Social harmony is a principle of Japanese civic life. It rejects quarrelling among ourselves. The idea is rooted in our traditional customs which are a part of our racial heritage; but philosophically it has been modified greatly by Buddhism. The spirit which guides Buddhist monastic orders is that all members become united like water and milk which have been mixed together, and avoid conflict. Such was the life of Buddhist priests in temples. In our country Buddhism has been accepted by a large proportion of the population; and this idea has contributed greatly to nurturing the cooperative spirit of our people. It has especially penetrated rural life in modern times. . . . It is alien to our traditional spirit to urge individuals to fight for their rights and to stress the class struggle for materialistic gain. . . .[28]

Students of Western political theory will perceive that social harmony as described by Maki differs from the idea of civic harmony which characterized political thinking in the Greek city-states. In the latter case, civic harmony was coupled with freedom and respect for law; [29] whereas in the Japanese instance the emphasis is on the avoidance of conflict through restraints on the individual.

In Japan, as in traditional China, morality is given precedence over law. Indeed, in the Tokugawa period, texts of laws were supposed to be kept secret from the public on the theory

[28] Maki Kenji, *Nihon kokutai no riron* (The theory of Japan's *kokutai*), revised edition (Tokyo, 1940), p. 538.
[29] George H. Sabine, *A History of Political Theory* (New York, 1937), p. 17.

that if the people found out about laws they would promptly seek ways to evade them. There was (and still is) a distaste for litigation; and compromise and conciliation were preferred in the settlement of disputes. The relatively underdeveloped state of law and legal institutions in Japan may be regarded as a corollary of the value placed on social harmony.

A sidelight on the idea of social harmony is afforded by a list of traits which are said to be in disfavor in Japanese villages. According to a survey, individuals with the following traits were generally unpopular: Those who were greedy, stingy in money matters, headstrong, stubborn, argumentative, selfish, independent and egotistical, perverse, sullen and aloof. These are, of course, traits which are usually associated with non-conformists. The same survey also revealed that individuals who refused to participate in village undertakings were criticized by their fellow villagers. Thus those who were late to village projects, who neglected to take part in road repair work, who refused to attend village meetings, who would not participate in village festivals, and who would not call on neighbors and friends on such occasions as births, marriages, and deaths, were subject to censure. We see therefore that the willingness to cooperate and to get along with one's friends and neighbors commands a premium; it is rewarded by social approval.[30]

Cooperation and harmony, no doubt, are valued because they are consistent with, or contribute to, the attainment of group ends. It is plausible to assume, in this connection, that the idea of social harmony is related to the practice of intensive rice agriculture. As Smith has pointed out, rice must grow in standing water and this calls for a "vast and complex system of ditches, dams, dikes, ponds, tunnels, and water gates that can be constructed and maintained only by community effort." Every cultivator, therefore, must subordinate himself to the community.

---

[30] Suzuki Eitaro, *Nihon noson shakai gaku yoron* (The essentials of Japanese rural sociology) (Tokyo, 1949), p. 168.

"A man may wish, for example, to turn an unirrigated field into paddy, but he will not be allowed to do so if this would impair the water supply of others; and he will refrain from insisting on his wish because he has been taught he must, and village opinion will be ranged solidly against him if he does not." [31]

Subservience to Authority

Modern Japan still retains vestiges of her authoritarian past. When a people suffer under oppressive rule, they tend to develop—one suspects as a form of protest—folk sayings about government. One such saying which came into being in the middle ages was "*nagai mono ni wa makarero*" which translated literally means "to be bound by something long," in other words, "one is forced to submit to authority." Several years ago, the National Public Opinion Research Institute sought to determine what the prevailing attitude was toward authority. The Institute undertook a public opinion poll in which it asked:

"People say '*Nagai mono ni wa makarero*'; have you heard the phrase?" Of those who were asked, 32 per cent said they had never heard of the phrase. A more detailed analysis of those in this category shows that the percentage declines as age and education level goes up, and that more rural people than urban dwellers were unaware of the phrase.

The National Public Opinion Research Institute then asked: "Do you think such an attitude is bad; or do you think it cannot be helped?"

Forty-one per cent of those questioned disapproved of the dictum while 27 per cent said that it could not be helped. The following table gives the breakdown of the latter category by age:

[31] Thomas C. Smith, "Old Values and New Techniques in the Modernization of Japan," *The Far Eastern Quarterly*, XIV (May, 1955), p. 362.

Percentage of those who think "it can't be helped"

(by age)

AGE	MEN	WOMEN
16–19	17	14
20–24	30	22
25–29	27	28
30–39	38	35
40–49	35	38
50–58	40	43

Source: Sori-fu, Kokuritsu seron chosajo, *Shakai kyoiku ni tsuite no seron chosa* (Public opinion survey on social education), Report No. 51 (March, 1953), p. 23.

It would appear from the foregoing data that the younger generation is more independent than those in the older age brackets. Yet Stoetzel, on the basis of other surveys as well as projective tests, comes to the conclusion that "Japanese youth appears disposed to show more independence in the face of civil authority, but a study of the available data from investigations leads us to conclude that this attitude is still not very firm and is more the exception than the rule." [32]

For further evidence of subservience to authority we may turn to a recently published book on "How to deal with people." The author, instructing his readers on how to approach officials, lays down eight principles: (1) quietly apologize; (2) do not make excuses; (3) have a sense of gratitude toward officials; (4) be sympathetic; (5) make them feel goodwill toward you; (6) do not treat them as friends; (7) never treat them as public servants; (8) get acquainted with officials. [33] Here one can almost see the humble subject prostrating himself before the proud official. But it might be pointed out at this juncture that there usually lies an ulterior motive behind this servility. The author whom we have just quoted suggests that officials should be in-

[32] *Without the Chrysanthemum and the Sword,* p. 150.

[33] Quoted in Minami Hiroshi, *Nihonjin no shinri* (The psychology of the Japanese people) (Tokyo, 1953), p. 6.

vited to banquets. "The objectives of an organization, irregardless of what kind it may be, can be more easily achieved if officials are invited to its banquets and treated cordially. Even if it is just a social club, the official will feel goodwill toward it with reference to all kinds of matters in the future."[34]

Fatalism

The idea that man is not a complete master of his destiny is deeply rooted. What happens to an individual in his lifetime, it is believed, is affected by factors that are to a considerable extent out of his control. Man may be likened to a drop of water in a moving river. In the same sense, history is believed to be propelled by some outside force. Sometimes this outside force may be expressed through heroes, who, by their actions, affect the course of history. The average individual, however, merely goes along with the currents of history.

Man, then, is subject to the influence of outside forces, call it what you will—luck, fortune, chance, fate.[35] Almost every Japanese speaks of *un* or *unmei* (fate, destiny). Man is subject to *un;* and those who are favored by *un* will achieve their aims in life, such as economic well-being and security, while those whose *un* are unfavorable, will not get far, no matter how hard they try. A recent work on the subject puts it this way: "Every person, when he gets to be forty or over, begins to feel that in his lifetime, he comes across *un*, which lies beyond effort. When

[34] *Ibid.*, p. 5.

[35] For this section, I have drawn heavily on a number of recent studies published by those associated with the Shiso no kagaku kenkyukai (Institute for the science of thought). I should like to mention in particular the following works: Tsurumi Shunsuke, *"Nichijo no ronri"* (Everyday logic), *Shiso*, no. 325 (July, 1951); Shiso no kagaku kenkyukai, *"Nomin no uso to makoto"* (Falsehood and truth among peasants), *Chuo koron* (August, 1951); Shiso no kagaku kenkyukai (ed.), *Yume to omokage* (Dreams and phantoms) (Tokyo, 1950).

one is in his twenties and thirties, he refuses to admit the existence of *un*. We feel that it is a sign of defeatism to speak about it and think about it. When we are young we believe that nothing can stand in the way of effort, that there can't be anything like *un*. I, too, was one of those who felt this way. As I look back I feel a sense of nostalgia for my youth. Everything was in a dream." [36]

In some societies when there is a discrepancy between individual merit and social reward, people attribute it to mystical forces.[37] The idea of *un* probably provides a kind of safety valve for those who have been unable to achieve their ambitions. In this sense, it serves to ameliorate social tension. Politically, it may contribute, as a Japanese social psychologist argues, to a perpetuation of subservience to authority. "There are probably few civilized peoples like the Japanese who try, even today, to explain what happens to men and society in terms of fate (*unmei*) and destiny (*shukumei*). Since the olden days, various views on human affairs and heaven's decree (*tenmei*) have been published; and those in power have used them, directly and indirectly, as ideological weapons to perpetuate their rule and control the masses." [38]

[36] Ifukube Takahiko, *Un, don, kon* (Fate, dullness, perseverance) (Tokyo, 1952), p. 13.

[37] Robert K. Merton, *Social Theory and Social Structure* (Glencoe, Illinois, 1949), p. 138.

[38] Minami, *op. cit.*, p. 115.

Chapter 4

The Political Structure

The formal structure of any government is seldom fully congruent with the structure of political power. Nevertheless, the formal structure can often provide clues to the state of political affairs that prevails. In the Japanese instance, the problem of the relation of the present legal structure to political practice is complicated by the fact that the legal structure is not the outgrowth of normal historical evolution, but is rather the product of Occupation-sponsored reforms. Accordingly, the allocation of formal authority among the branches of government, the rules of policy-making and execution, the definition of what constitutes the legitimate acts of government, and the ends implicit in the constitutional structure may not necessarily be in keeping with prevailing social attitudes. In fact, at this point one might assert somewhat dogmatically that the formal structure more nearly portrays the goals of government than the state of affairs that actually obtains today.

FORMAL GOVERNMENT

From the point of view of the formal structure, the present Japanese government may be described as a constitutional democracy. A brief outline of the skeletal framework of this constitutional democracy will be set forth in the following pages.

The Constitution

The Constitution provides for the first time a single, all-embracing organic law for the country. Unlike the Meiji Constitution, the 1947 Constitution proclaims in the preamble the doctrine of popular sovereignty. "We the Japanese people, acting through our duly elected representatives in the National Diet . . . do proclaim that sovereign power resides with the people and do firmly establish this Constitution."

There follow 12 chapters of varying length. Chapter 1 defines the position of the Emperor who "shall be the symbol of the State and of the unity of the people, deriving his position from the will of the people with whom resides sovereign power." In Chapter 2, war "as a sovereign right of the nation" is renounced forever. Chapter 3, the "Rights and Duties of the People," guarantees a long list of rights for the people and is intended to provide a full measure of civil liberties. Chapters 4 and 5 relate to the structure and power of the National Diet and the Cabinet. Chapter 6 regulates the judiciary, while Chapter 7 deals with finance. Local self-government is taken up in Chapter 8. Chapter 9 provides for amendments which "shall be initiated by the Diet, through a concurring vote of two-thirds or more of all the members of each House and shall thereupon be submitted to the people for ratification, which shall require the affirmative vote of a majority of all votes cast thereon, at a special referendum or at such election as the Diet shall specify." Chapter 10 enunciates the principle that the Constitution shall be the supreme law of the land; and Chapter 11 contains Supplementary Provisions, mostly having to do with transition from the old to the new Constitution.

The Constitution clearly provides the legal framework for a democratic system of government. But the real test, of course, is whether the legal formulae can be translated into political reality. As one source admits, "The new Constitution is as yet no more than a new set of rules, devised in committee and communicated to the players, in which the players have as yet little familiarity or confidence. It will take time and experience before they know the rules well enough to play by them." [1]

The Emperor

According to pre-war constitutional theory, the Emperor was the source of all legal authority and political power. "The Emperor," said Article Four of the Meiji Constitution, "is the head of the Empire, combining in Himself the rights of sovereignty, and exercises them, according to the provisions of the present Constitution." The Emperor exercised legislative power with the consent of the Diet, gave sanction to laws, and issued Imperial Ordinances.

In contrast, under the new Constitution, the Emperor is "the symbol of the State and of the unity of the people, deriving his position from the will of the people with whom resides sovereign power." The Emperor is to perform "only such acts in matters of state as are provided for in this Constitution and he shall not have powers related to government." Like many monarchs, the Emperor promulgates laws and treaties, convokes the Diet, attests the appointment and dismissal of ministers of state and other high officials, receives foreign ambassadors and ministers, and performs ceremonial functions; but he performs these acts with "the advice and approval of the Cabinet," and "on behalf of the people." Under the new Constitution, then, the Emperor quite clearly reigns but does not rule.

[1] *Political Reorientation of Japan*, I, p. 117.

The National Diet

The pre-war Imperial Diet was fundamentally an advisory body which tried to check, but often unsuccessfully, the actions of the executive. One of its primary functions was to act as a kind of sounding board for public opinion.

The framers of the new Constitution elevated the status of the legislature, making it the core of post-war government. "The Diet," according to the Constitution, "shall be the highest organ of state power, and shall be the sole law-making organ of the State."

The National Diet is composed of two houses: the House of Councillors and the House of Representatives. The House of Councillors, which replaced the old House of Peers, is composed of 250 members who serve 6-year terms. One half of the upper chamber stands for election every three years. One hundred and fifty members are elected from the prefectures, while the remaining one hundred are elected from the nation at large. Each voter casts two votes, one for the prefectural candidate and one for the national candidate.

Like the House of Commons, the House of Representatives is the more important of the two branches. At present the lower house consists of 467 members elected from 118 electoral districts. Three to five members are chosen from each district, but each elector may vote for only one candidate. Members of the House of Representatives are elected for four-year terms, but the lower house may be dissolved before the term is completed. In case of the dissolution of the lower house, a new election must be held within 40 days.

The powers which are conferred by law on the legislature are extensive. The Diet elects the Prime Minister; and in general the Cabinet is made responsible to the legislative organ. The Diet now has complete control of the purse strings, in contrast to the pre-war Imperial Diet, where the government was empowered to adopt the previous year's budget in case the budget bill was voted down. If there is disagreement between the two houses over the budget, the decision of the House of Representatives becomes effective in 30 days. Any bill passed by both houses automatically becomes law. If the upper house fails to pass a bill, it will become law if it is repassed by the lower house by a two-thirds majority. In addition to legislation, both houses "may conduct investigations in relation to government, and may demand the presence and testimony of witnesses, and the production of records."

In keeping with the enhanced position of the National Diet, a number of changes have been made in the legislative machinery. Diet members now enjoy "franking" privileges, they are provided with offices and clerical assistants, and a National Diet Library and a reference service have been established. An important innovation, doubtlessly copied from the organization of the American Congress, is the creation of standing committees of the Diet. There are 16 (formerly 21) standing committees, one for each major field of legislation, such as foreign affairs, budget, education, labor, agriculture, commerce, transportation, audit, and a disciplinary committee. Each member of the Diet must be appointed to at least one committee but no more than three. Committee membership is "allocated in proportion to the numerical strength of political parties or groups in the respective houses." Committee chairmen are chosen by the House, rather than by the committees themselves. In addition to standing committees, special committees are created from time to time to deal with problems that cannot be handled effectively by the regular committees. The committees are empowered, moreover, to hold open hearings which make it possible for interested individuals and groups to express their views on questions of public concern. Obviously, the idea of the public hearing was also copied from American legislative practice. Finally, according to law, each standing committee is provided with at least two qualified specialists who are not Diet members. The intent of this provision was to provide the Diet, whose members are often inexperienced, with "technicians, working for and not against the legislative branch, who can match and offset the ministerial bureaucracy." [2]

The Cabinet

The Constitution provides that the "Executive power shall be vested in the Cabinet." The Cabinet is composed of the Prime Minister, who is chosen by the Diet, and other ministers of state; and the Cabinet collectively is responsible to the Diet in discharging its executive functions. The Prime Minister appoints (and removes) his ministers of state, but the majority of ministers must be chosen from among the members of the Diet. In case a no-confidence resolution is passed by the House of Representatives, the Cabinet must resign unless the lower house is dissolved within ten days.

At present there are eleven ministries represented in the Cabinet through their respective cabinet ministers: foreign affairs, justice, finance, education, welfare, agriculture and forestry, commerce and industry, transportation, postal communications, labor, and construction. There are, in addition, several ministers without portfolio and the chief of the cabinet secretariat. A host of agencies, including the Imperial household agency and the national security agency, are currently attached to the Prime Minister's office. [3]

In addition to performing its general administrative functions through the various ministries and government agencies, the Cabinet is held responsible for the conduct of foreign relations, for administering the civil service, for preparing the budget

---

[2] *Political Reorientation of Japan,* I, p. 165.

[3] John M. Maki, "The Prime Minister's Office and Executive Power in Japan," *Far Eastern Survey,* XXIV (May, 1955), pp. 71–5.

for presentation to the Diet, for enacting cabinet orders to carry out the provisions of the Constitution and other laws, and for deciding on amnesty, commutation of punishments, and the like. The Prime Minister, representing the Cabinet, submits bills and reports to the Diet. Finally, all laws and cabinet orders are signed by the competent minister of state and countersigned by the Prime Minister.

The Judiciary

In the pre-war period, the judiciary was under the control of the executive, especially the Ministry of Justice. Under the new Constitution, the judiciary was made independent and its power and prestige were substantially raised. One of the most important provisions in the Constitution relating to the judiciary is Article 81, which states that "The Supreme Court is the court of last resort with power to determine the constitutionality of any law, order, regulation or official act." By granting the Supreme Court the power of judicial review, the framers of the Constitution made the high tribunal a watch dog of the Constitution.

Today the courts form a separate organization headed by the Supreme Court. In keeping with the independent status of the judiciary, the Supreme Court supervises judicial administration. Provision is also made for funds to be independently appropriated in the national budget.

The Supreme Court is composed of the Chief Justice, who is appointed by the Emperor upon designation by the Cabinet, and fourteen associate justices, who are appointed directly by the Cabinet. It is required that at least ten of the justices must have high professional qualifications in the legal field, but the remaining may be outstanding persons in other fields. Supreme Court justices serve until they reach the retirement age of 70;

however, a popular check is provided by a system of recall elections in which the justices must be approved by the electorate every ten years.

In order to prevent the Supreme Court from assuming too heavy a burden, its jurisdiction is limited to appeal cases requiring a review of issues of law. An important innovation in court procedure is the provision for dissenting opinions. According to one view, "This provision introduces into Japanese law the institution of dissenting opinion which has proved invaluable in Anglo-Saxon countries as source material for legal science and for the progress of judicial interpretation." [4]

At present there are below the Supreme Court eight High Courts, whose districts correspond to the eight geographical regions of Japan. The High Courts take up appeal cases which do not fall within the jurisdiction of the Supreme Court. Below the High Courts are District Courts which at present total forty-nine, roughly, one for each prefecture. The District Court has original jurisdiction over serious crimes and civil suits involving larger sums, and appellate jurisdiction over cases originating in the Summary Courts. There are more than 500 Summary Courts, and their jurisdiction is limited to minor criminal matters and civil suits involving less than 5,000 yen. One index to the place of law and courts in the Japanese political scene is furnished by the legal profession in Japan. Out of a population of more than 85 million, there are only about 6,000 practicing lawyers; and only 1,732 judges are provided by law. [5]

Local Government

Before the war, the central government exercised considerable control over local government through the now-defunct Ministry of Home Affairs, which appointed the prefectural gov-

[4] *Political Reorientation of Japan*, I, p. 202.
[5] *Ibid.*, p. 242.

ernors. The new Constitution enunciates the principle of local autonomy and declares that "local public entities shall establish assemblies as their deliberative organs." It further provides that the chief executive officers and other local officials as may be determined by law are to be elected by direct popular vote. To assure local autonomy the power of the National Diet to legislate on local matters is circumscribed by the constitutional provision that "A special law, applicable only to one local public entity, cannot be enacted by the Diet without the consent of the majority of the voters of the local public entity concerned."

The voters have been provided with several devices which will enable them to exercise more control over local government, if they so desire. First, the power of recall has been established by law. Voters have the power to remove from office governors, mayors, and particular members of the local assembly, to cause dissolution of the local assembly, and to remove certain officials, like the assistant governor, who are appointed with the consent of the assembly. Second, citizens are given the power of initiative, and by taking proper legal steps can force the assembly to consider the enactment, revision, and repeal of laws. Third, citizens have the right to bring suit against local public bodies for illegal actions committed by them and to collect damages. Fourth, citizens now enjoy the right to sue local officials personally for wrong doing.

INFORMAL GOVERNMENT

It is perhaps belaboring the obvious to state that government consists of much more than the formal structure. The neat diagrams in textbooks showing the relation of one ministry to another and their relationship to the other branches of the government tell us only a part of the story. One finds everywhere a good deal of activity, essentially political in character, taking place outside of the confines of government proper. The late Charles

Merriam called attention to the existence of what he called "private government."

> A congeries of associations operates to produce the net result in the community. Many of these associations have their own parallel plans for social action of their own special genre—in family, church, industry, agriculture, professions. Methods of initiation, assumptions of responsibilities, opportunities, duties, forms of discipline and reward, ways and means of meeting the crises of life—all these are the commonplace of all associations. Sometimes they are very explicit, and again they may be very vague, existing in understandings which, however, may be extremely powerful in operation. Government is intimately related to all these cross-sections of social living, and its devices must be closely enmeshed into the others.[6]

It is particularly important in the case of Japan to take note of private, or as we prefer to call it, informal government, because formal institutions in the Japanese political context often serve as a façade, giving legal sanction to what has been already decided by informal and covert techniques.[7]

It is not easy to describe private government with any degree of precision because it is by its very nature a rather amorphous phenomenon. Being informal, it has little in the way of organized and visible structure. One suspects, moreover, that the way in which private government operates varies from area to area. The indications are that it is most strongly rooted in the rural areas of Japan where tradition continues to exercise influence over social relations. A useful way of approaching private government is through the *yuryokusha*.

---

[6] Charles E. Merriam, *Systematic Politics*, p. 236. Copyright 1945 by the University of Chicago.

[7] Paul S. Dull, "The Senkyoya System in Rural Japanese Communities," *Occasional Papers*, University of Michigan, Center for Japanese Studies, IV (1953), p. 29.

Yuryokusha

In every community, whether rural or urban, there are a few individuals who are known as *yuryokusha* (man of influence). These individuals may range in type from men of integrity to those on the criminal fringe, but in any case they are looked upon as the leaders of the community. The *yuryokusha* may or may not hold office; quite often their power is independent of office holding. If they happen to be officials, it is because they are influential in their own right. Traditionally in rural Japan, the *yuryokusha* almost always sprang from the larger landholding families, because landownership and power were related. This is to some extent still the case; but it is also true that new sources of influence have appeared in recent decades as a result of economic and social changes.

An interesting portrait of a *yuryokusha* is found in Norbeck's study of a Japanese fiishing village. In this village there is an elective official known as *sodai* who is responsible for managing the affairs of the *buraku* or hamlet. But the local inhabitants spoke of another *sodai*. "The second '*sodai*,'" says Norbeck, "is the richest man in the *buraku*. He has always been prominent in local political matters and since the formation of Kojima City has served as an elected city council member. His influence and prestige are great. . . . So great is the prestige and fear of this man that he virtually runs the *buraku* and in recent years has, with no show of opposition, often conducted many of the *buraku* meetings (usurping the place of the elected *sodai*). Feelings of other residents toward him are ambivalent. He is feared and disliked for his aggressiveness and selfishness, but he is also openly acknowledged as the most intelligent, influential, and capable person in the community." [8]

[8] Edward Norbeck, *Takashima, a Japanese Fishing Community* (Salt Lake City, 1954), pp. 96–7.

The preceding description suggests two factors—wealth and capability—which presumably induce the residents of this fishing village to listen to the *yuryokusha,* accept his proposals, and in general follow his lead, despite the fact that they dislike and fear him. It is useful in this connection to recall that Japanese society is characterized by a web of obligations which tie individuals together. A person with wealth at his disposal is in a position, if he so desires, to bind people to him by manipulating this wealth. In an economy where it is difficult to accumulate a surplus, the ability to get credit to meet business or personal needs can be of vital importance; and in such circumstances, no one is anxious to "get on the wrong side" of people who can provide funds to meet emergencies. Paul Dull describes a political boss, Mano, who secured control of the *Nogyo kyodo kumiai* (Agricultural cooperative association), and used the manipulation of credit as one means of achieving local influence.[9]

The second factor, capability, is partly related to the ability of the *yuryokusha* to establish contact with the outside world. On this point Norbeck notes that without him "the *buraku* would be hard put in its dealings with the outside, for his verbal ability is great and his influence strong."[10] Today all communities must maintain relations with the higher levels of government on diverse matters ranging from taxation, rice delivery quotas, licenses to do business or carry on an occupation, to the allocation of funds from the national treasury for schools, road repair and the like. Elsewhere we have tried to show that formalized impersonal relationships are still inadequately developed in Japan. This means that when individuals and local communities have dealings with government agencies, the negotiations are likely to be greatly facilitated if the local leaders can provide the necessary liaison. In other words, one of the functions of the

[9] Paul S. Dull, "Mano Tokuichi: a Case Study of a Political Boss in a Japanese Town," mimeographed. (A paper read at the Far Eastern Association meeting in New York, April 13, 1954.)

[10] Norbeck, *op. cit.,* p. 118.

yuryokusha is to serve as a link between the formal government and the people.

A third factor, not mentioned by Norbeck, has to do with the adjudication of local disputes. In many Western countries, the administration of justice is one of the important functions of government. In Japan, however, the tradition is to avoid taking disputes before the legally constituted authorities for settlement. The practice, still true to a surprising degree, is to effect a compromise through mediation, usually provided by someone prominent in the local community. This is one reason why, as we have already noted, the legal profession is relatively underdeveloped in Japan.

Concluding Remarks

The formal structure lays down certain rules for policy-making and execution. The more important rules have been mentioned here on the assumption that they would tend to work to the advantage of some groups in the power structure and to the disadvantage of others. Another assumption that has been made is that these rules would also tend to encourage certain types of political processes to develop.

A third assumption we have made is that the formal structure does not tell the whole story. The formal structure may sometimes serve as a façade for decisions arrived at by the application of a different set of rules. It was this consideration that led us to the examination of informal government. But the phenomenon of informal government in Japan is sufficiently variegated and complex to warrant a full-length study. The purpose of the brief description in the foregoing paragraphs is not to provide a detailed and well-rounded analysis, but merely (1) to call attention to its existence, and (2) to point out certain important features which help explain the nature of the political process in Japan.

PART **II** *Political Forces*

Chapter 5

Business

During the past century a marked change has come over the ethos with reference to businessmen and business enterprise. There was a time when businessmen were relegated to the bottom of the social heap, ranking lower, in theory, than the peasant and the artisan, to say nothing of the haughty samurai. Money and money making were tainted, and respectable people shunned the frank and open pursuit of wealth. The historical record contains examples of merchants who brought the wrath of the ruling groups upon their heads by their ostentatious display of wealth, with the result that they lost it all through confiscation by the state.

Even after the doors were thrown open to Western influences in the 1850's, this negative, if not hostile, attitude toward money making persisted in many circles. It was this state of affairs which led Shibusawa Eiichi, a descendant of a samurai family who found business enterprise more congenial and later became a leading financier, to write a book "harmonizing" morality and economics. "Morality and economy," he wrote, "primarily were meant to walk hand in hand. But as humanity has been prone to seek gain, often forgetting righteousness, the ancient sage anxious to remedy this abuse zealously advocated morality

on the one hand, and on the other warned people of profit un-
lawfully obtained. The later scholars misunderstood the true
idea of their predecessor and made the hasty conclusion that
righteousness and gain are incompatible, that 'if one be virtuous
he cannot be rich; if rich cannot be virtuous'; and that one
loses righteousness if he obtains profit; and he loses profit if he
approaches righteousness. They forgot that productiveness is a
way of practicing virtue." [1]

Such an apologia for the pursuit of profit would be out of
place in contemporary Japan. Today those who engage in commerce and industry are considered the pillars of the community
and find easy entry into the most respected levels of society.
Seekers of wealth no longer need be apologetic, for their number
is legion. The change in the ethos is but one measure of the
rise of business to a position of dominance in the national life.

COMMERCE AND INDUSTRY IN THE ECONOMY

There are other measures of the rise of business. In contrast to agriculture where productivity, whether measured in
terms of per capita or per acre output, has increased relatively
little over the decades, commerce and industry have made remarkable gains. This can be readily seen by taking a look at
almost any index of economic activity—steel production, hydro-
electric power generated, ton-miles of freight carried by the
railroads, and so on.

Another indication is the distribution of national income.
According to calculations made by the Economic Counsel Board,
in 1952 agriculture's share of the national income came to about
19.5 per cent, while commerce and manufacturing (excluding

---

[1] Quoted in Kyugoro Obata, *An Interpretation of the Life of Viscount Shibusawa* (Tokyo, 1937), p. 266.

construction, public utilities, and transportation) accounted for about 40.1 per cent.[2] These statistics provide another rough measure of the relative importance of commerce and industry.

Physical Volume of Output in Major Industries
in Japan Proper, 1895–1939
(1910–14 = 100)

YEAR	TOTAL	TEXTILES	METALS, MACHIN- ERY	CHEMI- CALS, CERAMICS	FOOD PROD- UCTS	MINING
1895–99	37	41	25	—	80	28
1905–09	69	70	61	53	85	68
1915–19	160	152	162	186	123	138
1925–29	313	270	355	453	193	157
1935–38	582	466	950	835	189	227

Source: William Lockwood, "Industrial Development," in *Japan* ed. by Hugh Borton (Ithaca, 1950), p. 72.

The State and Economic Enterprise

Lockwood comments that "The tempo of industrialization sustained in modern Japan over half a century or more is unequaled in the Western world."[3] The question arises: how was Japan able to achieve such rapid industrialization? Although different observers are apt to put a different weight on the contribution of the Japanese state to economic development, all agree that it was important if not essential. During the formative period of modern Japan, the state took an active lead in industrialization because Japan was technologically backward compared to the Western nations, and her capital accumulation was small. The state channeled capital into industry; it hired hundreds of foreign advisers and technicians, sent students

[2] Keizai Shingicho, *Nihon keizai to kokumin shotoku* (Japanese economy and national income) (Tokyo, 1954), pp. 34–5.
[3] William W. Lockwood, "Industrial Development" in *Japan,* ed. by Hugh Borton (Ithaca, 1950), p. 64.

abroad, established model factories, built arsenals and foundries, laid railroad lines, and gave subsidies to private entrepreneurs interested in establishing new enterprises. In certain lines of activity the state has continued to operate to this day. For example, railroads and communications systems are for the most part government owned and operated, and tobacco and salt are government monopolies. In other lines of economic activity, the state divested itself of direct interest by selling factories, mines, shipping lines and the like to private companies at reduced prices, thereby providing the foundation for some of the industrial combines or *zaibatsu* firms which eventually came to dominate the economy.[4]

Almost from the very beginning there was a tacit partnership between the government and certain business families. At a crucial point in the Restoration movement, some merchant families lent substantial sums to the newly created Meiji government in order to enable it to meet its most urgent financial obligations. Among these families was the house of Mitsui, which later served as a fiscal agent of the government and which became a leading *zaibatsu* firm.[5]

With the passage of years, many of the business companies became strong enough to dispense with the sustained support of the state; nevertheless they continued to enjoy the largess of the government in one way or another. It has been contended, for example, that commerce and industry enjoyed tax benefits because the income tax law of 1887 applied only to individuals and not to legal persons.[6] Another important consideration was

---

[4] Cf. Thomas C. Smith, *Political Change and Industrial Development in Japan: Government Enterprise, 1868–1880;* William W. Lockwood, *The Economic Development of Japan* (Princeton, 1954), especially Chap. 10.

[5] Tsuchiya Takao, *Nihon shihonshugi no keieishi-teki kenkyu* (A historical study of entrepreneurs in Japanese capitalism) (Tokyo, 1954) shows on the basis of documents in the Mitsui archives and other materials the close ties between government and certain business firms.

[6] Hijikata Seibi, *Zaiseishi* (History of finance) (*Gendai Nihon bummeishi,* VI) (Tokyo, 1942), p. 373.

the availability of funds from the national treasury in case of need. Because of the "forced draft" character of economic development, Japan never went through a laissez faire period. Accordingly, the tradition of business firms turning to the state for loans and subsidies in times of business adversity became firmly established and remained a fixture.

In the early days business firms acted more or less as agents of the government. The larger companies maintained access to the government, and hence to government contracts, loans and opportunities to buy state-owned properties, through particular statesmen. Marquis Inouye Kaoru, a leading statesman of the Meiji era, was well known as a representative of the Mitsui interests in the government. Later as the political parties grew more influential, men who had intimate contact with big business sometimes assumed positions of leadership in the parties. Then in the 1930's as the power of the political parties waned, occasionally business executives came to participate directly in government. It also became a fairly common practice for important civil servants to retire before they reached the age of fifty and become associated with business firms.

Finally, the family connections that came to be welded between the leading business families and the political elite are impressive. The following is an excerpt from the report made by the mission on Japanese combines to the State and War departments in 1946:

Baron Hisaya Iwasaki is the head of the Iwasaki family and hence of the Mitsubishi combine. His second son is Takaya. A prominent personage in the Mitsui combine is Seihin Ikeda. The latter has been managing director of the Mitsui Bank, Governor of the Bank of Japan, Finance Minister, Member of the House of Peers, Member of the Privy Council, Chairman of the Board of Directors of Mitsui Gomei, formerly the top holding organization of the Mitsui combine. His daughter, Toshiko, is the wife of Takaya Iwa-

saki. Baron Hisaya Iwasaki's sister, Masako married Kijuro
Shidehara, the present Prime Minister of Japan. A niece of
Baron Misaya Iwasaki, Tokiko Kiuchi, married Viscount
Keizo Shibusawa. He is the head of the Shibusawa Family
and has been Chairman of the Board of Directors of the
Tokyo Savings Bank, Vice President of the Dai Ichi Bank,
President of the Finance Control Association, Governor of
the Bank of Japan, member of the House of Peers, Min-
ister of Commerce and Industry, Chief of the Wartime
Economic Bureau, Member of the Wartime Commodity
Price Investigation Council. He is at present the Minister
of Finance.

Baron Iwasaki's eldest daughter, Miki, married Renzo
Sawada. He has had a long career in the Foreign Office,
serving in various countries. . . . The Baron's nephew, Ju-
shiro Kiuchi, has also had a career in the Foreign Office,
serving in various legations and embassies. . . . His wife is
the daughter of Teizaburo Sekiya, an ex-Vice Minister
of the Imperial Household. Another nephew, Notalano [No-
butane?] Kiuchi, has had a long career in the Yokahama
(sic) Specie Bank. His wife is the daughter of Tetsujiro
Shidachi, former President of the Industrial Bank of Japan,
and interested in both Sumitomo and Mitsubishi concerns.

The Baron's sister, Haruji, married Komei Kato, former
ambassador to London, Prime Minister, and leader of the
Minseito political party. Her daughter, Misako, married Viscount Nagakage Okabe, a diplomat and politician now
lodged in Sugamo prison.[7]

The Report lists the names of other important business executives who have held government posts or who have family
connections with political leaders. It then goes on to say that
"The details of the zaibatsu and governmental connections of

---

[7] *Report of the Mission on Japanese Combines*, Part I (Washington,
1946), p. 16.

the individuals just named are merely instances to illustrate the common pattern. The web of such connections extends in all directions and has pervaded the government to an extent comparable to the industrial, commercial and financial spread of the older zaibatsu through the economic life of the country. Zaibatsu viewpoints and interests have had able and powerful representation in all governmental affairs, and the direction and execution of many governmental policies have been placed in the hands of members of their group." [8]

Although it is difficult to make a precise appraisal, available evidence indicates that the trend established before the war of business executives being linked through marriage and adoption to those holding posts in the higher echelons of government has continued in the post-war period.[9] Businessmen are also important in post-war political parties; but discussion on this point must be deferred.

The Structure of Business

We have spoken of the *zaibatsu* rather tangentially; but we may now take up the subject in somewhat more detail. *Zaibatsu,* literally "financial cliques," is a term that is applied loosely to refer to the big industrial combines. Sometimes it is used specifically to describe four large combines—Mitsui, Mitsubishi, Sumitomo and Yasuda; at other times it is used to refer to big business combines in general. The *Report of the Mission on Japanese Combines* listed 19 trusts.

---

[8] *Ibid.,* p. 13.

[9] Japanese are very conscious of family connections and many people make it a point to be informed on "who is related to whom." There are even books with elaborate charts showing family connections. See, for instance, Natori Giichi, *Sei-zaikaijin no meiun* (The fortunes of leaders in the political and financial world) (Tokyo, 1952), which shows the ties that exist at the present time.

The larger *zaibatsu* firms were engaged in a truly amazing variety of economic activities. It would take several long paragraphs to describe even briefly the ramifications of the Mitsui combine, one of the oldest and largest. An incomplete list of their activities would run something like this: banking, insurance, warehousing, foreign trade, logging, the manufacture of textiles, chemicals, electrical equipment, machinery, food processing, oil, shipping, etc. *Fortune* magazine once said the Mitsui was something like a combination of National City bank, Prudential Life Insurance, Westinghouse, Youngstown Sheet and Tube, Allied Chemical and Dye, Anaconda, American Woolen, Celanese, International Paper, American Sugar Refining, Anheuser-Busch, U.S. Rubber and "scores of lesser subsidiaries." [10] The vast economic empire, controlled through a complicated system of subsidiaries and holding companies, was ultimately responsible to the House of Mitsui, itself divided into 11 Mitsui families, whose activities were regulated by the Mitsui house law administered by a family council.

Not all *zaibatsu* firms were organized exactly in the same way; there were different types of organization, but we need not go into the details. The important point here is that a few *zaibatsu* firms managed to account for a large portion of the total production. According to the *Report of the Mission on Japanese Combines,* 15 companies accounted for 51 per cent of the coal production for Japan proper, 69 per cent of the aluminum production, 52 per cent of paper, 19 per cent of rayon, and so on. [11]

It is within the last one hundred years or even less that the *zaibatsu* companies have come to occupy such an important role in the economic picture. The concentration of economic power in their hands was a result, in part, of their becoming agents for the execution of the economic policy set by the Meiji government. Indeed, George Allen believes that "A concentration

[10] September, 1936, p. 127.
[11] Page 9 gives a detailed table.

of this sort is likely to occur whenever a country with a hitherto primitive economy begins a career of industrial development, especially when the initiative in this process rests with the State." [12]

Specifically, students of the *zaibatsu* attribute their growth to several factors. First, the nature of Japanese corporation law and its enforcement was such that few restraints were placed on the scope of corporate activity. "There has never been any movement in Japan strong enough to produce a Sherman Act, a Commissioner of Corporations, a Money Trust Investigation, a Federal Trade Commission, or a Securities and Exchange Commission such as developed in the United States, nor a series of Royal Commissions to amend the Companies Act such as Great Britain produced. The partnership between business and government in Japan is evident throughout the fabric of Japanese law. . . ." Second, succession laws and customs affecting inheritance favored accumulation of family fortunes under the control of the male head of the house. Third, the Japanese government "affirmatively encouraged group action by business interests for the fixing of prices, allocation of raw materials, division of markets and similar matters." [13]

Although there was keen rivalry and competition among *zaibatsu* concerns, there was also a good deal of cooperation affected through interlocking directorships, joint investment in enterprises, and investments in each other's companies. For these reasons, the word *zaibatsu* came to symbolize monopoly, especially from the point of view of the small businessman. To be sure, companies like Mitsui and Mitsubishi were particularly active in those sectors of the economy which required the investment of large amounts of capital and the use of technical skill of a high order; but they also competed with small firms. Against *zaibatsu* competition the latter were practically in a

[12] George C. Allen, *A Short Economic History of Modern Japan* (London, 1946), p. 126.

[13] *Report of the Mission on Japanese Combines*, pp. 21, 14, and 15.

hopeless situation, for the *zaibatsu* firms controlled through their banks the system of credit, they controlled the sources of raw materials and markets, and, lastly, through their financial power and prestige they were able to "pirate" key personnel and employees from smaller business enterprises. It is therefore not surprising that many independent businessmen were eventually absorbed by the *zaibatsu* or found themselves placed under their domination. The latter took the form of thousands of small factories and back-alley workshops producing under a subcontract arrangement with the *zaibatsu* firms.

In order to create a more competitive economy, the Occupation ordered the dissolution of the *zaibatsu*. Toward this end, shares of *zaibatsu* holding companies were put in the custody of a liquidating commission with the hope that these stocks would be sold to the public; many leading figures in these companies were purged and removed from their posts; holding companies were ordered broken up; and a fair trade commission was established to prevent the revival of monopoly. As a result of these measures, the *zaibatsu* were to some extent dissolved in theory and in practice. However, since Japan achieved her independence, the trend has been unmistakeably in the direction of their revival. The press contains frequent references to firms re-amalgamating; and in many instances these new firms which are being created as a result of mergers are assuming the prewar *zaibatsu* names. The dissolution of the *zaibatsu* was probably one of the least successful of the Occupation measures.

A phenomenon perhaps peculiar to Japanese economic development is the survival of small industries in the face of industrialization and the growth of monopoly. One clue to the structure of the economy is the way in which the labor force is distributed among factories.

Unfortunately, the statistics for 1930 and for 1951 are not strictly comparable; but if we take the plants with 99 employees or less we find that in 1930 such plants accounted for three fourths of the plants and that even in 1951 they comprised as much as

three fifths. These figures show that small plants still predominate insofar as numbers of workers are concerned.

Distribution of Industrial Plants by Size of Plants, Classified by Number of Employees

1930		1951	
SIZE OF PLANT, BY NO. OF EMPLOYEES	PER CENT OF ALL INDUSTRIAL PLANTS	SIZE OF PLANT, BY NO. OF EMPLOYEES	PER CENT OF ALL INDUSTRIAL PLANTS
Less than 5	55.2	Less than 5	12.51
5–29	11.9	5–29	30.81
30–99	8.3	30–99	17.61
100–499	10.8	100–199	7.30
500–999	4.7	Over 200	31.77
Over 1000	6.0		
Government works	3.3		

Source: Tokutaro Yamanaka, "The Nature of Small Industries," *The Annals of the Hitotsubashi Academy*, IV (October, 1953), p. 2.

The persistence of small industries may be explained in part
by the dual character of the Japanese economy. As Professor Yamanaka, a well-known authority, put it, the process of industrialization in Japan was "double-faced." "To begin with, it was
transplanted from abroad by the Government as part of its policy
to maintain the independence of the national economy. . . .
Secondly, there were some departments of traditional industry
which were not endangered by competition with American and
European productive powers. Among them were silk, textiles,
porcelain, lacquered wares, tea and fancy mats though produced
under the economy of isolation, they turned into export industries with the opening of Japan to foreign trade." [14] It was the
latter that helped pay for the technical assistance and imports of
machinery which made modern large-scale industries possible.

[14] Tokutaro Yamanaka, "Japanese Small Industries During the Industrial Revolution," *The Annals of the Hitotsubashi Academy*, II (October,
1951), p. 32.

Another important point is that consumer tastes and habits have persisted along traditional lines to a remarkable degree, so that there is a domestic market for traditional types of housewares, food products, clothing and the like which can be met by small industries. Finally, the existence of small industries is linked to the depressed state of Japanese agriculture. Chronic overpopulation in the rural areas provides a source of cheap labor, without which small industries could not operate.

Owners of small businesses and industries have never been able to exert the kind of influence, either economically or politically, commensurate with their numerical strength. It is fairly easy to guess why this should be so. The crux of the matter is that they have not been able to organize effectively to make their potential power felt. Geographically they are scattered over the land. Even more important, small businessmen face intense competition among themselves, as well as competition with big business. Finally, many of them operate on a shoestring, and hence their energies must necessarily be concentrated on making a day-to-day living, leaving little margin for the consideration of larger and long-term issues. Although prophecies of their eventual disappearance which were frequently made have not been fulfilled, small business occupies an unhappy position in the general economic picture.

BUSINESS ORGANIZATIONS

Business, like other groups, has its organizations which seek, among other things, to defend its interests. Historically, the emergence of organizations representing business may be traced to the years following World War I. No doubt their development at this time was associated with the tremendous expansion that occurred in commerce and industry as a result of the war boom, and symbolized the fact that Japanese business had reached its maturity.

It is common practice to distinguish two general types of organizations: those which have legal standing because of legislative sanction, and private organizations. The prime example of the former is the Chamber of Commerce and Industry. A Japanese work on business organizations published in 1926 described the Chamber of Commerce as follows: "The Chamber of Commerce exists today as a result of government encouragement and leadership; it is an advisory body of merchants and industrialists to the government, and an organ representing their views."[15] Among private organizations, there were a number of trade associations, e.g., the Japanese Textile Federation, the Association of Japanese Shipowners, the Federation of Coal Mines, etc., and several organizations with a broader base, such as the *Nihon Kogyo Club* (Industrial Club of Japan) formed in 1917, which represented the interests of large industrialists.

These organizations performed a number of functions on behalf of business interests. Many of them had small research staffs and they tried to keep their members informed of developments which were of interest to the business community. Another purpose was to present a united front to demands from organized labor. Finally, these organizations served as an agency for applying pressure on government agencies and legislative bodies.

Post-War Organizations

Of the business organizations which are active in the post-war period, two deserve special mention: *Nihon Sangyo Kyogikai* or Japan Industrial Council and *Keizai Dantai Rengokai* or Federation of Economic Organizations. The Industrial Council is the successor to the wartime Council of Important Industrial Organizations, one of the agencies through which the state exer-

[15] Morita Yoshio, *Waga kuni no shihonka dantai* (Organizations of capitalists in our country) (Tokyo, 1926), p. 15.

cised control over the economy, and "has embraced almost all of
the important enterprises. There are both zaibatsu firms and
enterprises that were formerly dominated by state capital." [16]

The Industrial Council, in turn, is the prime mover in the
larger Federation of Economic Organizations; and the close connection which exists between the two organizations is attested to
by the fact that the president of the Council, Ishikawa Ichiro, a
chemical company executive, is also the president of the Federation.

The Federation has three types of members. It has corporate members like the Japan Industrial Council, the Council of
Financial Organizations, the Japan Foreign Trade Association,
and others. Second, 97 large business firms are represented in the
Federation; and, finally, some 700 business firms hold associate
memberships. A prominent adviser to the Federation is Ichimada
Hisato, former Governor of the Bank of Japan, and more recently
Minister of Finance. Other officers and directors of the Federation are drawn from the leading banks and industrial firms, and
a list of their names reads like a who's who of Japanese business.

According to an article written by Ishikawa, the organization has a three-fold objective.[17] First, it seeks to work with the
government to try to bring about a revision of its economic policies. From time to time the Federation invites leading political
figures to meet with its representatives to discuss current economic problems. On at least one occasion it has issued a strong
statement addressed to all political parties. This statement, published in conjunction with two other economic organizations, on
May 13, 1953 urged the parties to become more aware of the
"crisis" that was threatening the economic world and to establish

---

[16] Hisha Kimpachi, *"Keizai dantai no uchimaku"* (Behind the scene
of economic organizations), *Toyo keizai shimpo*, Bessatsu, no. 7 (March,
1952), pp. 67–8.

[17] Ishikawa Ichiro, *"Shin Keidanren no shimei"* (The task of the
new Federation of Economic Organizations), *Jitsugyo no Nihon* (Industrial
Japan), LVI (January 1, 1953), pp. 36–7.

a basic over-all economic policy to deal with it. As the Federation saw it, the need was for a policy that would embrace industry, foreign trade, finance, and labor.[18]

Second, the Federation seeks to influence public opinion by collecting information and undertaking research. Third, it seeks to bring about better relations with the United States through personal contact and other means. On the last point, one account states as follows: "In discussions with officials of General Headquarters [of SCAP], the Federation has occupied a pivotal position; and it has also served as a host for receptions welcoming people who have come from over there [i.e., the United States]."[19]

One way to get some understanding of how economic organizations make their influence felt is to take a specific instance and study it in some detail. The activities of the Coal Mine Association in connection with a bill to put coal mines under state control provides an interesting case study of pressure group tactics.

The Coal Mine Bill

Shortly after the Socialists formed a coalition government with the Democratic party in the spring of 1947, the Socialists introduced a bill designed to place coal mines under state control. Although the Socialist party hoped for eventual nationalization, it was at this point willing to settle for limited state control since it did not wish to antagonize the Democratic party with which it was in coalition. Naturally there was strong opposition from coal mine operators who were apparently able to persuade a number of Democratic representatives to act contrary to the party caucus and refuse to go along with the coal control bill.

[18] *Asahi shimbun,* May 13, 1953.
[19] Hisha, *op. cit.,* p. 68.

Because of opposition, the bill was bottled up in the Mining and Industry committee, and after it was forced on to the floor of the lower house its provisions were watered down through a series of amendments. The amended bill was finally passed in December, 1947; but, as one author says, the Socialists "had gained an empty victory, since the provisions of the law not only were far removed from their original proposals but also were in many cases so vague and left so much to the discretion of the Minister of Commerce and Industry that a change in the cabinet could be expected to have serious effects on the scope and vigor of the law's enforcement." [20]

The *Nihon Sekitan Kyokai* or Japan Coal Mining Association, a voluntary association of coal mine operators, formed the spearhead of opposition to the Socialist-sponsored bill. The Association appears to have put stress on applying pressure in key places. It sent members and delegations to talk to cabinet members, heads of the various Ministries, and leaders of all the political parties.[21] Coal mine operators in Kyushu created a war chest of three and a quarter million yen by assessing a 10 yen contribution for every ton of coal mined. A part of this fund was used to pay travel expenses and per diem to operators going to Tokyo to lobby against the bill.

The Mining and Industry committee in the lower house, to which the bill had been referred, became a key target of the Association and coal mine operators. Ito Ushiro, chairman of the committee, later testified in an investigation on lobbying in connection with this bill that the tactic of the opposition was to keep the bill in the committee. He said he received tens of threatening

[20] Evelyn S. Colbert, *The Left Wing in Japanese Politics* (New York, 1952), p. 227.

[21] This account is based on testimony before the Diet investigating committee which looked into the lobbying activities of the coal mine operators. See *Futo zaisan torihiki chosa tokubetsu iin kaigiroku* (Proceedings of the special investigating committee on illegal property transactions). Second session of the National Diet, 1948.

letters and over 200 telegrams opposing the bill. Some telegrams purportedly came from labor unions, he said, but an investigation revealed that they were signed by ficticious individuals. The Association, moreover, had a useful ally within the committee in the person of Nishida Takao, a Democratic representative from Fukuoka. Nishida was an owner of a coal mine and a director of the Association. Yamakawa Ryoichi, president of the Japan Coal Mining Association, has testified that he had many conversations with Nishida concerning the bill.

The Association also made some attempts to influence public opinion, although this does not appear to have been its principal tactic. The Association contacted newspaper and magazine writers and editors, and tried to persuade them to oppose the pending legislation. It also distributed a book and other literature on the coal mine issue to newspapers. According to reports, some small magazines and newspapers printed anti-coal mine control articles and later called on coal mine operators asking for monetary contributions.

At least two individual coal mine owners urged the Association to undertake a broader campaign to influence public opinion, but the Association appears to have been somewhat reluctant to do so. In the end, the two owners, Tanaka Shoji and Hida Rikichi, proceeded on their own responsibility to provide 50,000 yen each to three small political societies, *Nihon Kaiho Domei* (Japan Emancipation League), *Sekitan Kokkan Hantai Domei* (League to Oppose State Control of Coal Mines) and *Shin Taishuto* (New Mass Party), presumably in order to enlist their aid in the fight against the coal mine control bill. Tanaka also spent 200,000 yen for 60 to 70 placards, for 2,000 posters, and 4,500 leaflets.

The opponents of the bill almost succeeded in getting it pigeon-holed in the Mining and Industry committee where there was considerable sentiment against it; but at this point the Socialist government, which was anxious to get the measure passed in the few days that remained before adjournment, managed to get it placed on the agenda of the plenary session by resorting to parliamentary steamroller tactics. The opposition Liberal party, which had opposed the bill from the beginning, and dissident factions of the Democratic party together with a few dissident Socialists, then took to delaying tactics, and the National Diet became the scene of fist fights, heckling and general disorder. A contemporary newspaper account described the situation as follows:

The National Diet, which started pompously under the democratic Constitution with the mission of rehabilitating defeated Japan, has finally turned into a fighting scene. Not only at the plenary session on 20 November but also at the plenary session and in the Mining-Industry Committee on the following day, fights occurred one after another. Paper balls were hurled at the Speaker by some members while others snatched the microphone, shouted, brawled and vociferated, until Ubukata, who got drunk, went so far as to urinate into a spitoon, saying boastfully that he was probably the first to pass water on the floor of the Diet. Thus the Diet members made an ugly scene, like a lawless mass of racketeers.[22]

The Socialists have charged that coal mine operators were behind these disorders in the National Diet. A newspaper reported that "At the meeting of the Socialist Party Diet members held on 24 November, Nogami, Naruse, Morita, and Tanaka, Orinoshin brought up the fact that coal mine operators were threatening Representatives supporting the bill within the sacred walls of the National Assembly and acting as a serious oppression upon the Representatives in the fulfillment of their duties. By this, it became clear that the confusion, violence and drag-out

[22] Translated from the *Tokyo Tomin Shimbun*, November 24, 1947, in Allied Translator and Interpreter Section, *Press Translations and Summaries* (hereafter cited as ATIS *Press Translations*) November 24, 1947.

tactics employed by the Liberal Party within the Diet since 20 November were all part of a prearranged plan. Moreover, it is clear that these actions were conducted under the close supervision of the coal mine operators." [23]

[23] Translated from *Tokyo Mimpo*, November 26, 1947, **in ATIS** *Press Translations*, December 2, 1947.

Chapter 6

Labor

The emergence of a capitalist economy and the growth of industry on a substantial scale have brought about changes in virtually every sector of Japanese life. Of these changes, one of the most important has been the creation of a working class, owning little or no property and dependent upon wages for its livelihood. The creation of such a class can, at least potentially, bring about far-reaching modifications in the political structure. Presumably, since the mode of life and economic interests of workers are different from those of other groups such as the peasantry and the business class, their political attitudes too would be different. And if all workers could unite behind a single political program they could—one would suppose—become a potent political force.

One of the basic assumptions made by the Occupation was that labor could become a bulwark of democracy. A policy statement on trade unions issued by the Far Eastern Commission in 1946 noted, among other things, that "Japanese workers should be encouraged to form themselves into trade unions for the purpose of preserving and improving conditions of work, participating in industrial negotiations to this end, and otherwise assisting the legitimate trade union interests of workers, including organized participation in building up a peaceful and democratic Japan. . . . Where practicable and while not interfering with their normal operations trade unions and their officials should take an active part in the process of democratization of Japan and should be encouraged to participate in measures taken to achieve the objectives of the occupation such as elimination of militaristic and monopolistic practices and the democratic reconstruction and development of a peaceful Japan." [1]

Partly because of the encouragement given it by the Occupation, Japanese labor has acquired in the post-war period more power than it ever had before. Nevertheless, the position of labor in the over-all political picture is still a minor one and it has not won political victories which are in keeping with its potential strength. A succinct summary of the situation is a remark attributed to an official of the International Confederation of Free Trade Unions that Japanese trade unions "have no arms, but want to shake their fists." It is pertinent to inquire why Japanese labor should be so weak.

THE LABOR MOVEMENT

Historically, the Japanese labor movement began around the turn of the century. The movement was started by a small group of intellectuals of middle class origin who were attracted to socialist doctrines. Organized labor remained small and ineffectual, and although it began to grow after the end of World War I, it never became a major force either in economic or political affairs. In 1936, the peak year, trade union membership stood at

[1] Quoted in Miriam S. Farley, *Aspects of Japan's Labor Problems* (New York, 1950), p. 245–6.

420,000, representing only 6.9 per cent of non-agricultural workers. After 1936 and until the close of World War II, union membership and activity declined, owing, among other things, to government suppression.

A number of explanations have been put forward to account for the relative weakness of Japanese labor in the pre-war period. First, the existence of surplus labor in the countryside and the inability of urban industry to absorb the surplus population have created a situation in which the supply of labor has almost always exceeded the demand. This, of course, has put labor in a weak bargaining position. Second, the structure of Japanese industry has made it difficult for labor to become organized. It will be recalled that structurally Japanese industry was such that a large number of small firms existed side by side with the large industrial combines. "Hence labor unions," says Miriam Farley, "found that most employing establishments were either too big to challenge with success, or too small to organize effectively." [2]

Third, paternalism has characterized labor relations. The relationship between employer and employee, particularly in the smaller establishments, has involved more than the payment of a wage in return for a certain amount of work done. The relationship has been a highly personal one, in which the employee was expected to work faithfully and loyally in return for which the employer assumed the obligation to look after the welfare of the worker. A recent survey shows that employers in small plants still prefer to hire relatives or persons who have been recommended to them by relatives or friends. Employers apparently feel that workers recruited in this fashion will be more reliable, both in terms of political views and willingness to work hard. Also the belief is that such workers will stay with the firm longer because they will feel a certain sense of obligation to the person who served as the intermediary. It has been argued that so long as employers prefer to follow such recruitment methods, the role

[2] "Labor Relations," in *Japan*, ed. by Hugh Borton, p. 95.

of labor unions as employment agencies will be greatly circumscribed.[3]

Fourth, labor unions have, except for a brief period under the Occupation, operated in a hostile atmosphere. Union activity was looked upon as being somewhat subversive. Persons of conservative political disposition felt that labor unions had no place in the traditional social system, and that they were an embodiment of class conflict which clashed with the ideal of social harmony. The very fact that from the very beginning the labor movement was closely associated with left-wing parties and politics no doubt helped to make it less respectable in the eyes of solid citizens. It is therefore not surprising that for a long time labor unions were hounded by the police and that labor leaders were forced to spend time in prison. The revival of unions in the post-war period must be seen against this background.

The Post-War Scene

It has been mentioned that at least in the beginning, the Occupation favored a strong and healthy labor movement. This meant that union leaders were now no longer on the defensive, but had the backing of the highest political authority. The intellectual and social ferment which came in this period and which forced many people to question the validity and usefulness of old ideas and institutions also provided a background favorable to the growth of trade unions. Within a short time, unions sprang up almost everywhere. In some instances, old-line leaders emerged to form unions. In other instances, enthusiastic young men without previous experience in the labor movement pushed forward to establish unions. And there were even cases where unions were formed at the suggestion of employers, the idea apparently being

[3] Ujihara Masajiro, *"Waga kuni ni okeru dai koba rodosha no seikaku"* (The characteristics of workers in large plants in our country) *Shakai-teki kincho no kenkyu,* p. 240–2.

that if the formation of unions was inevitable, it would be better to have these unions led by men who were fundamentally friendly to the employer.

The number of workers who could be brought into unions was substantial. According to the 1950 census, there were a little more than 35.5 million men and women over 14 years of age who formed the working force of the nation. Of this total, a little less than 14 million or roughly 39 per cent were wage and salary earners. The distribution of these wage and salary workers among the major industries is shown in the following table:

Distribution of Wage and Salary Workers Among Industries

	NUMBER OF WORKERS	PER CENT
Agriculture	525,000	3.8
Forestry, hunting, lumbering	185,000	1.3
Fishing, fisheries	308,000	2.2
Mining	564,000	4.0
Construction	971,000	7.0
Manufacturing	4,415,000	31.6
Wholesale and retail trade	1,381,000	9.9
Finance, insurance, real estate	339,000	2.4
Transportation, communication & other public enterprises	1,703,000	12.2
Service	2,056,000	14.7
Civil service	1,508,000	10.8
Not clear	12,000	0.1
Total	13,967,000	100.0

Source: *Nihon rodo nenkan,* edited by Ohara shakai mondai kenkyujo, 1954 edition, p. 15.

If we compare the foregoing figures with statistics tracing the growth of the labor movement in the post-war period, the following picture emerges:

Growth of Labor Unions and Union Membership, 1947–52
(as of end of June of each year)

NO. OF UNIONS		UNION MEMBERSHIP	PER CENT OF WAGE WORKERS
1947..........	23,323	5,692,179	46.8
1948..........	33,926	6,677,427	54.3
1949..........	34,688	6,655,483	55.7
1950..........	29,144	5,773,908	45.9
1951..........	27,644	5,686,774	42.6
1952..........	27,851	5,719,560	40.2

Source: *Nihon rodo nenkan,* edited by Ohara shakai mondai kenkyujo, 1954 ed., p. 61.

On the face of it these figures are impressive, for, as can be seen, union membership has ranged between 5.5 million and 6.5 million, representing 40 to 50 per cent of the total number of wage workers.

Not all industries, of course, are unionized to an equal degree. In 1948, 91.5 per cent of workers in transportation and communications were union members, while 55.1 per cent of workers in manufacturing industries were organized.[4]

The foregoing statistics tell us something about the magnitude of organized labor in Japan, and give us an inkling about its potentialities as a political force. But unless one probes a little deeper, he is likely to misjudge the power labor is able to exert in the political arena. Labor is weaker than it might be, and the chief cause, it would appear, lies in its fragmentation.

THE FRAGMENTATION OF LABOR

Labor does not speak as one voice and act as one unit. We can cite several reasons why this should be so. One cause, we may

[4] Suehiro Gentaro, *Nihon rodo kumiai undo shi* (History of the Japanese labor movement) (Tokyo, 1950), p. 175.

surmise, is the way in which unions are organized. An unusual feature of organized labor in Japan is the preponderant position occupied by "enterprise" unions. As the name implies, an enterprise union is one in which all employees of a mine, shop or factory, or of a company which owns several factories, including clerical and even some supervisory employees, come together to form one union. Nearly 80 per cent of all local unions, which account for about 80 per cent of all unionized workers, are organized on this basis.[5] It would follow from this that Japanese unions are on the whole small in size.

Size of Japanese Labor Unions, 1946–50

YEAR	LESS THAN 50 MEMBERS	50–100 MEMBERS	101–500 MEMBERS	501–1000 MEMBERS	1001– MEMBERS	TOTAL
1946	26.3	21.2	40.5	7.4	4.6	100
1947	37.2	20.3	32.9	5.3	4.3	100
1948	42.9	19.6	29.2	5.0	3.3	100
1949	44.3	18.6	29.1	4.9	3.1	100
1950	43.4	18.7	29.6	5.0	3.3	100

Source: Okochi Kazuo, *Nihon rodo kumiai ron*, p. 114.

Quite clearly the trend has been in the direction of an increase in the percentage of unions with less than 50 members. This reflects the fact that unions were formed first in the larger companies and as unionization spread to the smaller firms, the number of small unions organized on an enterprise basis increased. Thus in 1950 more than 90 per cent of all the unions had less than 500 members.

Some of the enterprise unions have remained independent, while others have affiliated with national unions. Some of the national unions in turn have affiliated with large national federations. According to one account, "The affiliation of locals with

[5] Solomon B. Levine, "Prospects of Japanese Labor" *Far Eastern Survey*, XXIII (May, 1954), pp. 66 ff.

national unions, and of these with national federations, has been erratic, tenuous, and incomplete. Many locals have remained unaffiliated, and both local and national unions have changed their allegiance frequently with shifting political tides in the labor movement." [6] There are also instances of multiple affiliation and of a local affiliating with a federation even though its national union is not affiliated with the federation.

National Federations

There were, as of 1954, three major national federations: *Sodomei, Sanbetsu,* and *Sohyo. Sodomei,* short for *Nihon rodo kumiai sodomei* (Japanese federation of trade unions) is relatively conservative and has pursued a cautious policy. *Sanbetsu* or *Zen Nihon sangyo betsu rodo kumiai kaigi* (Congress of industrial unions of Japan) stands to the left, is militant and has come under communist influence. *Sohyo* or *Nihon rodo kumiai sohyo kaigi* (General council of trade unions of Japan) was born in 1950 when several left-wing unions seceded from *Sodomei* and *Sanbetsu.* At present *Sohyo,* the largest, has more than 3 million members and includes about one-third of the local unions of the country. In addition to these three national federations, there are some independent groups.

Some idea of *Sohyo's* scope may be gained from the list of unions, national and local, which are affiliated with it.

Unions Affiliated with Sohyo
(Number of members in parenthesis)

Japan Coal Miners' Union (265,000)
All Japan Federation of Metal Miners' Unions (55,000)
All Japan Metal Workers' Union (60,000)
Japanese Federation of Iron and Steel Workers' Unions (125,000)
All Japan Automobile Workers' Union (25,000)
Federation of Chemical Industries Unions (38,000)

[6] Levine, *op. cit.,* p. 66.

Japanese Federation of Synthetic Chemical Workers' Unions (80,000)
Japanese Federation of Textile Workers' Unions (360,000)
All Monopoly Labor Union (37,000)
All Japan Federation of Movie and Drama Workers' Union (1,500)
All Printing Bureau Workers' Union (8,000)
Japan Radio Broadcasting Workers' Union (7,000)
All Communications Workers' Union (160,000)
All Japan Electrical Communications Workers' Unions (106,000)
All Wireless Workers' Union (3,000)
Japanese Electrical Industries Workers' Union (95,000)
National Railway Workers' Union (370,000)
Japanese Federation of Private Railways Workers' Unions (120,000)
Federation of Municipal Traffic Workers' Unions (39,000)
All Japan Seamen's Union (80,000)
All Japan Federation of Maritime Workers' Unions (4,000)
All Japan Harbor Workers' Union (20,000)
All Japan Express Workers' Union (93,000)
Japan Teachers' Union (520,000)
All Japan Federation of Waterworks Workers' Unions (6,000)
Japanese Federation of Government Personnel on Financial Affairs (20,000)
Federation of Ministry of Finance Personnel Unions (2,000)
All Ministry of Agriculture and Forestry Personnel Union (80,000)
All Japanese Federation of Local Government Personnel Unions (180,000)
All Japan Garrison Forces Labor Union (75,000)

Source: *Nihon rodo nenkan* edited by Ohara shakai mondai kenkyujo, 1954 edition, p. 469.

Sohyo, as the list shows, includes under its tent a large variety of labor unions in such diverse fields as mining, industry, communications, entertainment, teaching, and government. Since *Sohyo* contains within it a number of unions in key industries like coal mining, electricity and communications, it is potentially in a position to wield great economic and political power.

But *Sohyo,* as well as other major unions, is not a cohesive monolithic organization, but is composed of factions which try to hang together to achieve common ends. Takano Minoru, an important personage in *Sohyo,* is identified with the left-wing faction. *Sohyo* also contains a right-wing faction and some neutral factions.

The machinery for getting cooperation among these factions appears to be the executive committee of the union which acts in the interval between national conventions. Although posts are not necessarily distributed evenly, major factions are represented on the executive committee. Since *Sohyo*'s officers are leaders of important constituent unions and are in a position to withdraw, taking their unions with them, they enjoy a certain amount of bargaining power.

An important test of the ability of a major union like *Sohyo* to remain intact is the national convention, when a lengthy policy statement must be agreed to. Transcripts of the proceedings of national conventions would seem to show that quite often strong objections are raised by representatives of constituent unions to portions of the policy statement drafted by the executive committee, that compromises on wording are made, and that unity is thereby achieved.[7] Some observers believe that one technique used to increase the possibilities of agreement is to "taboo," by a kind of mutual understanding, certain statements and questions that might prove troublesome. One example, in the case of *Sohyo*, would be criticism of left-wing Socialists.[8]

Such devices may have salutary effects in keeping down disruptive pressures, but their effectiveness in the long run must be discounted. The post-war history of major unions shows that they are able to remain intact only for short periods and that splinter groups soon secede and join with other groups to form new unions.

Ostensibly unions break up as a result of ideological differences. A left-wing faction, for example, may propose policies which the rest of the union feels are too radical and as a result

[7] *"Sohyo taikai sokkiroku kara"* (From the transcript of the proceedings of the Sohyo convention), *Shakai undo tsushin* (Report on social movements), nos. 388, 389 (August 5, 12, 1953).

[8] Yakabe Katsumi, *"Sohyo no tatteiru chiten"* (Where Sohyo stands), *Chuo koron*, September, 1953, p. 72.

the proposal is rejected. The left-wing faction then may argue that it has no alternative but to withdraw. It may be true, too, as some people believe, that factional strife is accentuated by the preoccupation of unions with politics.[9] Since unions have become closely identified with left-wing political parties, factional conflicts within parties are almost bound to be reflected in the unions and vice versa.

Important as are ideological differences, it would appear that they are not the basic cause of instability. William T. Moran has commented that "This splitting and re-grouping of Japanese labor organizations have developed, on the surface at least, between 'left-wing' and 'right-wing' factions, and have arisen out of differences of opinion as to effective tactics. . . . Any analysis based on this explanation alone is bound to be superficial. For one thing, rivalries between individual leaders who command loyalties of rank and file sections play a part that has special importance in a nation like Japan."[10]

One is inclined to believe that Moran has come close to the nub of the problem. In Japanese organizations, including labor unions, the real issue is: who is going to be the leader? An interesting facet of modern Japanese culture is the emphasis it puts on achievement. Every school boy is exhorted to climb the ladder of success through diligent effort. Fame, fortune, and high social status are looked upon as worthwhile goals; and thus many people aspire to become leaders. The rewards which accrue to leaders are, of course, obvious. They include such things as higher income, greater security, status, prestige, and power. An important reward in Japanese culture appears to be the fawning deference of one's followers. For some reason, many Japanese derive a large measure of psychological satisfaction from this.

[9] Ota Kaoru, "*Rodo sensen toitsu no shin hoko*" (A new departure in the unified labor front), *Chuo koron*, March, 1954, p. 130.

[10] William T. Moran in Farley, *Aspects of Japan's Labor Problems*, pp. 219–20.

It is clear that not everyone can be a leader, for the number of positions at the top must be necessarily limited. The issue, therefore, comes down to this: is it better to take one's chances and strive to become the leader of a big organization, or be content with being the leader of a small organization? The Japanese preference is with the latter, presumably because this would enable more people to become leaders.

Those who are followers also seem to prefer many small organizations to a few large ones. It has been pointed out elsewhere that Japanese prefer highly personalized and enduring human relationships to formalized impersonal relationships. It is evident that the former could be best achieved in small organizations.

We may now return to the main theme of this section, which is the fragmentation of Japanese labor. For various reasons, Japanese labor is divided and hence is unable to exert the kind of pressure commensurate with its strength in numbers. "The Japanese unions are still groping for a basis on which to unify and mobilize the wage-earners. Their leaders are divided on both objectives and strategy; the rank and file is not certain which leaders to support."[11]

UNIONS AND LEFT-WING PARTIES

A close tie between the labor movement and the Socialist party has existed from the very beginning. As has been mentioned, the first labor unions were organized by Japanese Socialists at the turn of the present century. Since then, Socialists and also Communists have actively sought the support of labor unions, and labor leaders in turn have identified themselves with the left.

[11] Levine, *op. cit.*, p. 65.

This association has continued into the post-war period. Some, but not all, of the unions which sprang up after the end of the war were organized by pre-war Socialists and Communists, and these men naturally assumed positions of leadership. The influence of pre-war Socialists was particularly strong in the *Sodomei*, while young men without previous experience in the labor movement took control of many of the unions which affiliated with the *Sanbetsu*. For a time *Sanbetsu* came under strong Communist influence, but this was gradually eliminated through the formation of "democratization leagues" which were organized within various unions to combat Communist infiltration.

An obvious link between labor organizations and the Socialist party is the overlap in personnel. Local labor leaders have often been elected to prefectural assemblies and even the National Diet on the Socialist ticket. Those with political ambitions often find labor union work a useful steppingstone to political office.[12]

The identification of labor unions with the Socialist party, however, is not without its drawbacks. For one thing, even though the leaders of a union like *Sohyo* may throw their support to the left-wing Socialists, as they have done in the past, there is no assurance that the rank and file will necessarily follow the political advice of their union leaders. Without doubt when it comes to voting, many union members cast their ballots for conservative party members rather than for Socialists. On the other hand, if the Socialist party openly becomes a class party, representing primarily the interests of the working class, it will be unable to win the support of other classes within the nation. There is some reason to believe that the Socialist party has just about reached the outer limits of its potential strength. "If we assume," says one commentator, "that the rise of progressive forces through the power of organized labor has already reached its limits, the

[12] See chart in *Shakai undo tsushin,* no. 379 (May 6, 1953).

progressive forces must go a step farther and change from an organized labor party to a national party." [13]

There seems to be sentiment among some labor leaders in favor of separating the labor movement from Socialist party politics. Labor unions, so the view goes, should concentrate on striving to improve labor conditions and should remain neutral insofar as politics are concerned. Although there are obvious advantages to be gained from changes in this direction, the probabilities of such changes being achieved on a large scale do not appear to be high at this moment. At least three reasons may be cited in defense of such a view. First, despite the rise of organized labor in the post-war period, power within the National Diet and in the government generally has been in the hands of conservative political forces which are basically hostile to labor. Under the circumstances, the tendency is for labor to look upon any action which the government may take with suspicion; and labor will probably never feel fully secure until it has managed to attain more political power than it has to date. Second, many important economic questions are intimately related to political decisions. Taxation and inflation—to mention two—directly affect the economic position of labor, yet both belong fundamentally in the political sphere. Third, many of the big employers are government corporations such as the National Railways, and hence the best way to bring pressure on such corporations is through political means. For these and other reasons, Japanese labor is not likely to leave the political area.

[13] *"Ima no mama de wa Sa-ha shinshutsu ni genkai ga aru"* (If present conditions continue there are limits to the rise of the Left-wing Socialists), *Shakai undo tsushin,* no. 379 (May 6, 1953).

Chapter 7

Agriculture

In his classic work, *Japan, a Short Cultural History*, the British historian, Sir George Sansom, comments that the Japanese state thought highly of agriculture but not of agriculturalists. Sansom was writing about the 17th and 18th centuries, but his apt remark could very well apply to the 20th century.

Behind this paradox lie a number of considerations—historical, economic, and social—which help explain the role agriculture plays in Japanese politics. One of the purposes of this chapter, therefore, will be to show why this paradoxical situation exists.

AGRICULTURE—THE BASIS OF THE STATE

The notion that agriculture is the basis of the state is a recurring theme in Japanese political writing. One would have no difficulty in compiling a small encyclopedia of such writings; but for our purposes two illustrative examples should suffice. The first is a passage from the writings of Ogyu Sorai, an eminent 17th century philosopher: "To value the root and not value the branch—this was a principle adopted by the ancient sages. By the root, one means agriculture, and by the branch one means commerce and industry." [1] A more recent example is taken from the writings of Tachibana Kozaburo, one of the theorists of the ultra-nationalist movement of the 1930's. He wrote: "So long as we have the bright sun over our heads, and the good earth under our feet, the human world will be eternal. . . . Indeed, it is only when agriculture is its basis that a country will have eternal life. This is particularly true in the case of Japan." [2]

It takes no great insight to see why at one time agriculture should have been so esteemed. After Japan adopted a policy of isolation from the world in the middle of the 17th century, she was compelled to rely entirely on her own resources. Under the circumstances, the production of food in sufficient quantity to feed her population became an overriding consideration, for the alternative was starvation on a large scale.

This situation no longer obtained after the 1850's when Japan rejoined the community of nations. But for different reasons, agriculture continued to receive emphasis. One of the objectives pursued by Meiji leaders was for Japan to remain self-sufficient in food as long as possible. This was related to their overriding ambition to make Japan a military power. It was believed that dependence upon other countries for food would be detrimental to the attainment of such power.

Another reason was more intangible, but no less real. Leaders, especially of the conservative variety, have always looked upon the agricultural way of life as the repository of traditional moral values. It has been widely held that the sense of duty, of obligation, of loyalty—indeed all of the virtues—are best preserved in the farm households and villages. According to this view, agriculture helps counteract the corrupting influences of the big cities, where individualism runs rife; it acts, in other

[1] Quoted in Sakurai Takeo, *Nihon nohonshugi* (Agriculture as the basis of the state in Japan) (Tokyo, 1935), p. 75.

[2] Quoted in Maruyama, *Nihon fasshizumu no shiso to undo*, pp. 126–7.

words, as a kind of balance wheel, bringing stability to society. An example of this point of view is the following passage taken from a book published in 1944 urging the preservation of the farm population:

> All Japanese have behind them the history of their families and the history of their nation. This can be seen particularly well when we look at the peasants. It is in the farm village that solidarity of the family is most pronounced, for the family is based exclusively on the natural ties of parents and children; the family is composed of 3 to less than 10 members, it undertakes production and consumption as a unit, it preserves life and property on a cooperative basis, and it makes progress cooperatively. It cannot be denied that it is the pursuit of agriculture that makes them so. But is it not even more basic that they are the embodiment of the true Japanese mind and history? [3]

AGRICULTURE IN THE NATIONAL ECONOMY

The policy of the state with respect to agriculture has been guided by certain principles, not all of which are necessarily mutually compatible. Two of them have already been mentioned: the achievement of self-sufficiency in food for purposes of national power, and the preservation of agriculture for purposes of social stability. A third consideration was the use of rural youth in the armed forces. Experience showed that young men raised in the farm areas made the best soldiers. All of these aims involved the protection of agriculture.

But there were at least two other aims which conflicted with those just cited. First, a disproportionate share of the cost of in-

[3] Kanzaki Hiroyoshi, *Noson jinko ijiron* (On maintaining the agricultural population) (Tokyo, 1944), pp. 81–2.

dustrialization was put upon the agricultural population. In the Meiji era the land tax formed the backbone of the tax system, and even when other sources of taxes later came to be tapped, the landed class continued to bear a heavy burden, partly because of the tendency for local taxes to rise sharply. The following table gives some idea of the proportionate tax burden for the year 1931:

Rates of Taxation on Farmers, Merchants, and Manufacturers, by Income Levels

(Merchants = 100)

	¥300	¥500	¥1000	¥1200	¥2000	¥3000	¥5000
Landlord	—	373	389	348	391	323	328
Owner-cultivator	279	229	186	181	170	—	—
Merchant	100	100	100	100	100	100	100
Manufacturer	92	139	97	130	108	93	119

Source: Yagi Yoshinosuke, *Beikoku tosei ron*, p. 58.

Second, there was a desire, felt particularly strongly by business and industrial groups engaged in the export trade, to keep food prices at a reasonable level. Rice was an important item in the average household budget, and particularly in the budgets of urban workers. The wage level was therefore partly tied to the price of rice.

Obviously the state could not pursue all objectives mentioned here at the same time; and what happened in practice was that compromises were made. In these compromises the agricultural population more often than not came out second best.

Agriculture and Industrialization

It has been suggested that agriculture was caught between conflicting policies of the state. But this does not completely explain the malaise that has afflicted Japanese agriculture for a long time. During the last one hundred years or so, Japan has become the most industrialized country in Asia; yet this industrialization has occurred without producing far-reaching changes in the basic structure of agriculture. Commercialized agriculture based on large-scale operations with the extensive use of labor-saving machinery and representing the investment of large amounts of capital has not accompanied industrialization. Agriculture in Japan is still a family enterprise much as it was a century ago.

A number of implications follow, and a recital of a few salient facts at this point should serve to sketch in the general picture. First, farms are minute in size; throughout the years at least two thirds of the farms have been one *cho* (2.45 acres) or less in size. There has been a long-term tendency for the size of the farms to become stabilized at a level where they can be worked with the labor force of an average family, consisting of three adults or equivalent. When each farm unit is as small as this, investment in expensive labor-saving machinery is uneconomical; hence farming operations are dependent on human labor, with the result that productivity per worker remains low.

Second, the number of families dependent upon agriculture for all or part of their livelihood has not changed substantially. Over the decades, the number of farm families has varied somewhere between five and a half million and just under six million. Incidentally, there is a correlation between the number of people on the farms and the business cycle; in periods of depression, the sons and daughters who had taken employment in urban industries drift back to the rural areas, thereby aggravating the economic distress in the farm areas.

Third, farm productivity in terms of the amount of rice harvested from every acre of land has risen somewhat over the long term. For example, the average yield of rice per *tan* (.245 acres) of land was 1.431 *koku* (1 *koku* equals 4.96 bushels) for the five-year period, 1887–1891; in the period 1946–1950, the yield had risen to 2.007 *koku* a year, representing an increase of about 40 per cent.[4] Compared to the increase in productivity achieved in the other sectors of the economy, this increase was small. Because of the low level of productivity, wage levels in the farm areas lagged behind those in the industrialized urban areas. There is reason to believe that the discrepancy between the two became marked since about the end of World War I, and the relative

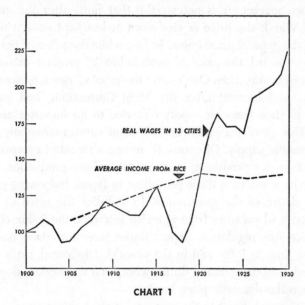

CHART 1

Real wages in thirteen cities and the average income per farm family from rice cultivation, taking the year 1900 as 100.

Based on statistics in Nihon Gakujutsu Shinkokai, *Beika no choki hendo* (Tokyo, 1935), pp. 44–5.

position of the farm population remained unfavorable throughout the interwar period. Chart 1 compares real wages in 13 cities and the average income per farm family from rice cultivation, taking the year 1900 as 100.

The conclusion to be drawn from this is that agriculture,

[4] Figures taken from *Japan Statistical Yearbook*, 1949 and 1950 editions, published by the Bureau of Statistics, Office of the Prime Minister.

which quickly reaches a point of diminishing returns, has had to support too many people, and consequently the average income per head has not risen appreciably.

We have been speaking of long-term trends; but the position of agriculture vis-a-vis the other sectors of the economy in any particular year is determined by the price that rice will bring on the open market. It is noteworthy that until after the end of World War I, the price of rice more or less kept pace with the rise of the general price index. In fact while the price of rice was moving upward, the price of some industrial products moved in the opposite direction. One reason the price of rice rose was that population increased after the Meiji Restoration, and caused Japan to shift from an exporter of rice to an importer around 1895. This gave rice producers a kind of natural monopoly over the domestic supply. Of course there was a threat of competition from other rice-producing areas in Asia whose production costs were even lower than those prevailing in Japan. But owing partly to the desire of the government to stabilize the price of rice, and partly to pressure from agrarian interests, the influx of foreign rice was regulated. Import duties were levied on rice for the first time in 1905, and in the years that followed, rates were adjusted, and on occasion duties were even suspended, depending upon the domestic price level.

The real threat to the price structure, however, came from another source, namely from competition provided by rice grown in the colonies, Korea and Formosa, where the cost of production was lower than in Japan proper. In 1915 imports from these colonial areas amounted to 4.4 per cent of domestic production, and these percentages gradually rose to 9.7 per cent in 1925 and 24.6 per cent in 1935.

Agrarian interest groups tried to check this inflow of rice grown in the colonies, but industrial and commercial groups favored reasonably low prices for rice. There was also the fear that restrictions on the importation of Korean and Formosan rice would fan the feeling of discontent among the colonial peo-

ples.[6] Starting in 1915, therefore, the government launched a price
support program which provided for the purchase of rice when
prices were depressed and sale when prices rose. Cynics have
maintained that price supports were set just high enough to
maintain the owner-cultivator class in the countryside. In any

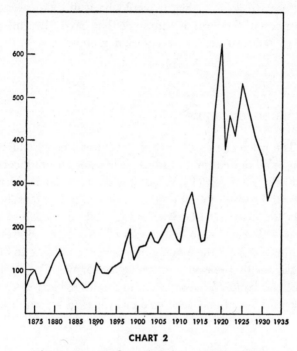

CHART 2

Fluctuations in the price of rice, 1873–1934.
Price of rice for 1879 equals 100.

Based on statistics in Nihon Gakujutsu Shinkokai, *Beika hendo to keiki hendo* (Tokyo, 1938), p. 8.

case, it is clear that price supports and other practices were not
always successful in keeping prices stable. Chart 2 shows the
fluctutation in prices.

[6] E. F. Penrose, "Rice Culture in Japanese Economy," in *The Industrialization of Japan and Manchukuo, 1930–1940,* ed. by Elizabeth
Schumpeter (New York, 1940), pp. 145–6.

As can be seen from the chart, prices rose phenomenally during the war period and then broke sharply after 1925, declining continuously until 1932. As a result of this price drop, farm income decreased substantially, and an economic depression of great magnitude hit the rural areas, giving rise to political agitation. But before we go into this, it would be well to survey several other aspects of the farm picture since they have a bearing on the nature of political action by agrarian groups.

CLEAVAGES IN AGRICULTURE

The price of rice and other agricultural commodities is of concern to all agricultural producers; but not all producers have an equal stake in it. Briefly stated, it is the large landholder, with a substantial surplus to put on the market, who is intensely interested in the price his rice will bring; while the small producer who has little surplus to sell is more likely to be interested in other things—one of them being his chances of adding to his land holdings. For this reason, the struggle over who is to get what share of the limited amount of farm land has been at the basis of important social and economic cleavages in agriculture.

The Pattern of Land Tenure

There has never been any degree of equality in land ownership—at least in modern times. It is customary to distinguish three general types of landholders: landlords, who cultivate part or none of their holdings and who have surplus land to rent to others; owner-cultivators, who own the land they cultivate; and tenants, who cultivate land rented from landlords. There are of course combinations of these, a common one being "owner-cultivator—tenant," that is, an agriculturalist who cultivates his own land and in addition rents some land from a landlord.

A relatively small percentage of the more than 5 million farm families can be classified as "landlord" families. If we assume, somewhat arbitrarily, that a family owning 3 or more *cho* would in the Japanese context be considered a landlord, we find that in 1935 about 7.5 per cent fell in this category. This rather small minority of landlord families owned 44.1 per cent of the cultivated land.

Percentage of Families Owning Land and the Size of Their Holdings, 1935

SIZE OF HOLDINGS	PER CENT OF ALL FAMILIES	PER CENT OF TOTAL AREA OWNED BY SUCH FAMILIES
3– 5 cho	4.3	14.1
5–10 cho	2.2	12.8
10–50 cho	0.9	12.5
50 cho or more	0.1	4.7
	7.5	44.1

Source: Nochi Kaikaku Kiroku Iinkai, *Nochi kaikaku temmatsu gaiyo* (Tokyo, 1951), p. 598.

At the other end of the spectrum, about 28 per cent of the farm families in 1941 were tenants, owning no land whatever, while another 40 per cent were partial tenants, owning only a part of the land they cultivated. The long-term trend, incidentally, has been for the two extremes to diminish in size, resulting in a slight increase in the middle group. What has happened is that excess land owned by the wealthier landed families was sold to tenant farmers and smaller landholders. This development was probably related to the growth of alternative outlets for capital. Capital invested in land probably returned somewhere between 3 and 5 per cent. Much more attractive returns were possible in banking, business, and in the stock market.

But, as these figures show, as late as the 1930's over two

thirds of the families rented land, and for these families rent reduction and acquisition of more land had high priority. Owing to intense competition for land, rents have been traditionally high. As a rule rents were payable in kind and amounted to about one half of the crop. There was, moreover, little security of tenure since most lease agreements were verbal and could be broken by the landlord if he so desired. Understandably peasants, under these circumstances, aspired to own their land. But rent reduction and the acquisition of land could only be achieved at the expense of the landlord class; and thus there existed within the agricultural community actual or potential conflict over these two questions.

One index of the conflict between the landed and the landless is the number of tenancy disputes. In the period between 1921 and 1941 there were anywhere from 1,500 to 6,800 tenancy disputes every year. Their frequency was roughly in inverse ratio to the price index. As the price of rice went down the number of disputes rose. This would suggest that in a period when agriculture as a whole might have taken concerted action to get prices raised, it was also beset with internal cleavages, making such action more difficult.

Land, Status, and Power

If we were to take almost any list of officials at the village level—village headmen and members of the village council—and compare it with another list of landowners in that village ranked according to the size of their holdings, we would probably find that most of the names on the first list would also appear in the upper part of the second list. Landholding and power are associated—at least to the extent that power holders are also landowners. In Japan, as in other countries which are still unindustrialized or which have been industrialized only recently, land is regarded as something more than an economic asset. Land is, to be sure, a symbol of economic security, being fixed and tangible; but it confers social status on its owner. He who owns land is likely to be highly regarded in his community, and is looked up to by his neighbors.

Obviously in a country where land is a scarce commodity, a landowner enjoys economic power and is in a position to translate it into political power if he so desires. But one must not jump to the conclusion that the formula, land equals economic power equals political power, is necessarily valid. At least two other factors must be associated with land: education and family history. Landownership can provide economic surplus which enables its owner, or his sons, to acquire more education than others less fortunate. The expectation of rural inhabitants is that those who are better educated and better informed should provide leadership. Hence the better educated find themselves being consulted on important local issues, and even being pushed into positions of leadership. As for family history, it is important because Japanese rural society is still one of ascribed-status rather than achieved-status. One's social position tends to be governed by the social position of the family from which he comes rather than by what he has achieved. Prominent families with a long history in a locality enjoy social prestige and power. By the same token, newcomers and upstart families are looked down upon even though they may own considerable amounts of land. It may take several generations for such upstart families to acquire status.

Political power at the local level, then, has been traditionally exercised by a small class of landholding families which have deep roots in that area. Since political power has been buttressed by social and economic power it has been relatively stable, and changes in leadership have occurred only slowly.

AGRICULTURAL INTEREST GROUPS

There are several farm organizations functioning more or less on a national scale which have become the channels of pressure group activities for agrarian interests. It is perhaps characteristic of modern Japanese history that the initiative for establishing some of these organizations came from the government. It is important to bear this in mind when we come to examine the history, organization and tactics of several of these organizations.

The *Teikoku Nokai*

This organization, whose title means the Imperial Agricultural Association, was in the pre-war period the spokesman of Japanese agriculture. The beginnings of the *Teikoku Nokai* go back to the late 1870's when the government took steps to form small discussion groups for the purpose of exchanging information about better agricultural techniques. This led to the formation of the *Dai Nihon Nokai* (Greater Japan Agricultural Association), which was an organization composed of some leading government officials, who served as its officers, and local discussion groups led by landlords. In 1894 the *Zenkoku Nojikai* (All Japan Agricultural Affairs Association), a group separate from the *Dai Nihon Nokai*, was established. Its objective was to form agricultural associations in the villages and towns and to bring them together into a nation-wide organization. These organizations enjoyed official standing, in that their existence was recognized by law. In 1910 the *Zenkoku Nojikai* became the *Teikoku Nokai*. Because of its historical background, the *Teikoku Nokai* had as one of its functions the encouragement of activities that would increase agricultural productivity. Its other important function was to serve as a channel of communication to government agencies concerning farm matters. On a number of occasions the *Teikoku Nokai* applied pressure on the government to raise the price of rice. In the 1920's it became very much concerned with tenancy disputes and began to pay attention to legislation affecting tenancy practices.

In terms of structure, the *Teikoku Nokai* was a national federation of agricultural associations organized on several levels. At the lowest level were the village, town, and city agricultural associations. These came into being when two thirds or more of those who owned land or engaged in agriculture (but excluding tenant farmers cultivating less than 1 *tan* of land) in a district agreed to establish a local association and secured permission from the government. Once such a body was organized, all farm- ers and landowners in the district were compelled to join and pay dues. Officers of these local associations were elected by the membership for 4-year terms. At the next level were *gun* (county) associations composed of the heads of the local associations plus special members appointed by the government. The latter, how- ever, were not to exceed one third of the total membership. At the third level were prefectural associations composed of *gun* organizations, and finally at the top of the pyramid was the *Teikoku Nokai*. In 1932 the number of organizations at each level was as follows:

Number of Nokai *at Various Levels*

Prefectural Nokai	47
Gun Nokai	560
City Nokai	92
Town Nokai	1,505
Village Nokai	9,866

Source: Sawamura Yasu, *Nogyo dantai ron* (Tokyo, 1936), p. 51.

A well-known authority on Japanese agriculture notes that the higher one got in the various levels, the stronger became the influence wielded by large landlords. He also notes that the higher levels were primarily concerned with political matters, while the lower levels were more interested in technical matters connected with agricultural production.[7] In the light of our pre-

[7] Tohata Seiichi, *Nihon nogyo no tenkai katei* (The development of Japanese agriculture) (Tokyo, 1939), p. 115.

ceding discussion of landlord leadership in agricultural affairs, it should not be surprising to learn that the *Teikoku Nokai* acquired the reputation of being a landlord-dominated organization.

The Sangyo Kumiai

Like the *Teikoku Nokai*, the *Sangyo Kumiai* (industrial cooperatives, or more accurately, rural cooperatives) was a national federation of local organizations. These cooperatives came into being toward the end of the 19th century, and represented a marriage of traditional forms of mutual aid and European cooperatives, especially the German variety. The early cooperatives, set up under government initiative, were primarily concerned with supplying credit to farmers. As mentioned earlier, Japanese statesmen wished to preserve the owner-cultivator class for purposes of political and social stability; and hence were anxious to make credit facilities available to help such farmers, especially now that the land tax was made payable in money. The basic legislation regarding cooperatives was enacted in 1900, the law providing for voluntary membership and election of officials.

Other types of cooperatives were established in the years that followed. There were established cooperative associations for marketing farm crops and later for storing grain, for purchasing seeds, fertilizers and other farm necessities, for food processing, and for the joint use of farm equipment. In time the local cooperatives became affiliated with large central institutions. For example, a central cooperative bank was created, with the government providing a substantial portion of its capital. There was also a central wholesale association to handle purchases made by the local cooperatives.

Some idea of the growth of the cooperative movement may be gained from these figures: by 1940 there were 15,101 cooperative societies with more than 8 million members. It is said that

about 64 per cent of all rural households had joined one cooperative or another by the mid-1930's.[8]

The *Sangyo Kumiai,* like the *Teikoku Nokai,* came to be
regarded as a landlord-dominated organization. An examination
of the membership reveals that it included farmers from all
strata, with the wealthier farmers somewhat overrepresented
and the tenant farmers somewhat underrepresented.[9] In terms
of the amount of business done through the cooperatives, the
landlords who accounted for about 5 per cent of the membership
did about 15 per cent of the business. The landlords made up
about 38 per cent of the officials.[10]

Nihon Nomin Kumiai

Given the cleavages that existed in agriculture, it was inevitable that sooner or later there should emerge organizations
representing the interests of the lower social strata in the rural
areas. Beginning in the early part of the 20th century, a few local
groups which called themselves "tenant unions" began to spring
up here and there; but it was not until after the end of World
War I that they became numerous and significant enough to
attract attention. The *Nihon Nomin Kumiai* or Japan Farmers'
Union, was founded in Kobe in 1922 by two Christian socialists,
Kagawa Toyohiko and Sugiyama Motojiro. Soon local tenant
unions which had been established or were being established
affiliated themselves with the Japan Farmers' Union and by 1925
the organization boasted 675 affiliates and over 50,000 members.[11]

In the beginning the *Nihon Nomin Kumiai* put its emphasis

[8] John L. Cooper, *Development of Agricultural Cooperatives in Japan,* SCAP, October, 1949, p. 2; Sengoku Kotaro and Shimada Hideo,
Nihon noson sangyo kumiai no tembo (The outlook for Japanese agricultural
cooperatives) (Tokyo, 1936), p. 7.

[9] Sengoku, *ibid.;* p. 233 gives the breakdown.

[10] *Ibid.,* pp. 247–8.

[11] Nochi Kaikaku Kiroku Iinkai, *Nochi kaikaku temmatsu gaiyo* (A
report on the land reform) (Tokyo, 1951), p. 1040.

on the reduction of land rents. As one account says, "Its demand for a 'permanent 30 per cent reduction in rent' was very appropriate for the times, and within a short period it made great strides; from Hokkaido in the north to Kagoshima in the south there were no areas where the flag of the Farmers' union could not be seen." [12] But within a few years its emphasis began to shift from rent reduction to the socialization of land, and from economic questions to political issues. This shift was accompanied by a split within the leadership of the Farmers' Union between the right-wing and left-wing factions and there eventually emerged two organizations. Since this is not intended as a political history of that period, the details of this split need not concern us here. Instead we can turn our attention briefly to the activities of the local affiliates.

In many instances, the main issue at the local level was the amount of rent which tenants had to pay their landlords. In areas where the tenants were organized into unions, the union would send a committee to negotiate rent reduction with the landlords or with a committee of the landlord association. A reduction in rent would be refused and sometimes the landlords would counter by bringing suit to force their tenants to give back the land. At this point the union would resort to demonstrations, would withdraw its members from the local fire fighting squads, or would even take to physical violence. In the end a compromise settlement would be reached; and it appears that where the farmers' unions were well organized the tenants were able to get favorable terms. An interesting survey of five villages which were the seat of tenancy disputes shows that the price of land in these villages dropped following a reduction in land rents.[13]

[12] Matsuoka Saichi, *Nihon nomin shiso no hensen ni tsuite* (On changes in the ideology of peasants in Japan), in *Shiho kenkyu* (Study of the administration of justice) published by the Ministry of Justice, XVII (March, 1933), p. 97.

[13] Kyochokai, *Kosaku sogichi ni okeru noson jijo* (Conditions in areas which were the scene of tenancy disputes) (Tokyo, 1934).

Tenancy disputes of the kind described here were led and financed locally, although sometimes the National Farmers' Union sent lawyers when court procedure was involved. It would seem that fundamentally there was a difference in the goals envisaged by the national headquarters and the local affiliates. The former was staffed by men who had been associated with urban labor movements and who ideologically were inclined to the left in varying degrees. Their ultimate aim was a modification or destruction of the capitalistic system, and hence they were impelled to put their stress on political action. In contrast, the local units were primarily interested in rent reduction, and so long as this could be achieved through local pressure without resorting to political methods they were not likely to be terribly interested in politics at the national level. This helps explain the weakness of the Japan Farmers' Union and other tenant organizations and their eventual disappearance from the political arena in the late 1930's.

FARM ORGANIZATIONS AS PRESSURE GROUPS

Subsidies to Agriculture

While it is true, as already noted, that agriculture was forced to bear a disproportionately heavy tax burden, it is also true that this was to some extent counterbalanced by an outward flow of funds from Tokyo. After all, tax money was used for a number of purposes which benefited, directly or indirectly, the entire population. But over and above that, there were funds which came back to the farm villages in the form of subsidies. These subsidies were paid for sundry activities whose objective was the promotion of agriculture and related industries, such as forestry and sericulture, and for public works. The payment of these subsidies was the business of the Ministry of Agriculture and Forestry, and, in the years 1929 to 1949, they ranged from 35 per cent to just under 70 per cent of its budget.

These subsidies were seldom given directly to producers, but rather were channeled through farm organizations, the most important of these being the *Teikoku Nokai*. According to Tohata, "A certain amount of the agricultural subsidy was used for expanding local government offices and farm organizations, and for adding personnel." [14] Thus we see that the close connection between the government and farm organizations which had developed in the beginning continued down through the years. In one sense, this was an advantage—at least to some sections of agriculture—in that agricultural groups had good access to government agencies. But there was a disadvantage, as Tohata points out. When farm organizations became so closely identified with the Ministry of Agriculture and Forestry, they could no longer function as constructive critics of government policy. "There were some advantages when prefectural agricultural associations and local affiliates of the central cooperatives had their offices in the local government building, and local officials and officers of these associations got together and cooperated in their work; but there was some doubt about the advisability of their being one and the same thing." [15]

Cooperatives and the Rice Control Bill

Throughout the 1930's the supply of rice exceeded the demand, partly as a result of the increasing importation of rice from Formosa and Korea. Instead of shutting out this flow of rice from the colonies, the government adopted a policy of government buying and selling through the Rice Control Act of 1921 (amended in 1933). In 1935 legislation strengthening the rice control act and giving farm organizations, particularly the cooperatives, a more important role in the stabilization program was introduced in the 67th session of the Imperial Diet. It immediately became the focal point of contention among several in-

[14] *Nihon nogyo no tenkai katei*, p. 152.
[15] *Ibid.*, p. 154.

terest groups: the rural organizations favoring it, and the rice dealers and urban consumer groups standing firm against it. Since the bill was still pending in the upper house when the 67th session came to an end, it never became law; but there is some merit in considering it here because it provides an excellent case study of the way in which pressure groups operate in the Japanese political scene.

Spearheading the forces in favor of the proposed legislation was the *Zenkoku Noson Sangyo Kumiai Kyokai* (All-Japan Association of Rural Cooperatives), an organization formed in 1933 to combat an anti-cooperative movement that was sponsored by business firms. Toward the middle of February, 1935, a mass meeting was held in Tokyo to denounce the proposed rice control measure. According to a contemporary newspaper account, some 20,000 rice dealers (out of a total of about 200,000) assembled in Tokyo. Some of them carried banners with slogans like "It is a matter of life and death," "Mass meeting to express absolute opposition to the rice control bill," "Down with the wicked bill," "Who is depriving us of our livelihood," etc. During the 6-hour meeting, 48 speakers rose to denounce the bill, and the meeting passed a formal resolution against it.

Because of fear that violence might break out or that the crowd might hold a demonstration in front of the Diet building, about one thousand policemen were on hand. "The police in the Tokyo area," according to the account, "prevented probably thousands from attending the meeting. Police boarded incoming trains and forced out all delegations to the meeting which they could recognize (or thought they could) as such. Many dealers from out of town, foreseeing such police tactics, traveled alone or in groups of no more than three are [sic] four. Several thousand from adjoining prefectures escaped police vigilance by making the trip in motorcars." [16]

In order to counteract the effects of this meeting, the All-

[16] *Trans-Pacific*, February 14, 1935.

Japan Association of Rural Cooperatives sent the following instructions to all its affiliates:

1. When the government presents the rice control bills to the Diet, we will inform our branch organizations by wire. Preparations should be made by the branch offices and the League [of rural cooperatives] as well as other persons in the electoral district to send telegrams and letters to the members of the House of Representatives from the rural areas, seeking their support for the bill.

2. When the special committee in the lower house on the bill approaches its decision, we may repeat the campaign indicated above, particularly with reference to areas from which the committee members come. Depending on the circumstances, we may also ask the heads of the League, and the directors of the All-Japan association from the areas concerned to come to Tokyo.

3. We would like branch organizations, in consultation with the League, to submit petitions to the members of both houses asking them to pass the bills for strengthening the rice control law as soon as possible.

4. We would like other appropriate measures to be taken.[17]

After the bill was introduced in the lower house, the All-Japan Association of Rural Cooperatives called a meeting in Tokyo on March 4, and the more than 1,200 delegates who were present adopted a resolution, the text of which was sent to the Ministry of Agriculture and Forestry, the Ministry of Commerce and Industry, and the political parties. This was followed by another meeting on March 11 to which 6,000 delegates came, and more resolutions were passed.

Meanwhile, a number of local branches held meetings to

[17] Zenkoku Noson Sangyo Kumiai Kyokai, *Dai rokuju-shichi gikai ni okeru beikoku san-ken ryo-hoan o meguru sangyo kumiai to sho-undo* (The activities of the rural cooperatives with reference to two bills on rice and raw silk in the 67th session of the Diet) (Tokyo, 1935), p. 69.

indicate their support for the bill. Finally, the youth auxiliaries of the cooperatives were mobilized and some delegates from these organizations met in Tokyo to pass a series of resolutions.

Despite these efforts on the part of the cooperatives, the bill died in the upper house. In reflecting on its defeat, the Association came to the following post-mortem conclusion:

> What this political battle made clear is that insofar as the cooperatives are concerned, our influence in the lower house, to say nothing of the upper house, is very weak. The number of representatives who are connected with the cooperatives is certainly not small; this is even more true in the case of representatives from the rural areas. Nevertheless, the fact that these two bills, which form the heart of the agricultural policy, were presented by the government and did not get the absolute support of these representatives clearly indicates that the goals governing their political actions do not lie in the cooperatives nor in agrarian problems.[18]

THE POST-WAR SCENE

The Farmer in the Post-War Era

War, defeat, and occupation brought in their train serious economic dislocation. Traditional sources of raw materials and outlets for manufactured goods in the colonial areas were lost, many of the major industrial centers lay in ruins, and the outlook for the future was unclear, making long-range planning difficult if not impossible. The farmer had his share of trouble, but at least he had a roof over his head and rice in his fields. In these respects, he was often better off than the urban factory worker.

Furthermore, the relative position of the agriculturalist vis-a-vis those in other occupations was enhanced by the critical

[18] *Ibid.*, p. 2.

food shortages that came in the early years of the occupation. Food was at a premium; and although the farmer was forced to sell a certain portion of his crop to the government at fixed prices, he was able to sell any surplus on the black market. At the same time, debts which the farmers had accumulated during the depression years were for practical purposes wiped out by the inflation which saw the value of the yen drop to a small fraction of its former worth. One should not get the impression that life in the countryside became easy all of a sudden; but it is true that the farmer's position rose relative to that of the city dweller. It has been estimated that in the pre-war period, if the level of consumption in the urban areas was taken as 100 the level in the rural areas was 48; in 1949, however, the ratio was 100 for urban areas and 95 for the countryside.[19]

The Land Reform Program

Another development which had far-reaching consequences in the rural villages was the land reform program put through by the Occupation as an integral part of the attempt to democratize Japan. At the time that the program was launched in 1946, General MacArthur indicated his conviction that it would "finally and surely tear from the soils of the Japanese countryside the blight of feudal landlordism which has fed on the unrewarded toil of millions of Japanese farmers."

The main provisions of the land reform program were as follows: Absentee landlords were compelled to give up their entire holdings. Resident landlords were allowed to retain one *cho* (4 *cho* in Hokkaido) of land which they did not cultivate. No person was allowed to own more than 3 *cho* (12 *cho* in Hokkaido). Absentee landlords and others with landholdings in excess of the amount allowed by law were forced to sell such land

[19] Okawa Kazushi and Noda Tsutomu, "Measurements of the standard of living in Japan," *Keizai kenkyu* (Study of economics), II (January, 1951), p. 84. (This is an English abstract of a longer article in Japanese in the same issue.)

to the state at fixed prices plus a subsidy which the state provided. First chance to purchase land taken over by the government was given to the tenant farmers who had been cultivating it. In order to make it easy for such tenants to buy land, they were given long-term loans extending to 25 years. Even with this redistribution of land, tenancy was not completely wiped out; and in order to protect tenant farmers, a maximum rent of 25 per cent on paddy and 15 per cent on dry fields was set. Moreover, rent which was traditionally payable in kind was now made payable in money. The land reform program was administered by local land commissions, composed of 5 representatives of tenant farmers, 2 of owner-cultivators, and 3 representatives of landlords. In some instances, these representatives were chosen by local elections, and in other instances they were selected by a caucus.

This was indeed an epoch-making program and an undertaking of great magnitude and difficulty. By the time the main portion of the program was completed in 1949, some 1,122,000 *cho* of rice land and 775,000 *cho* of non-paddy land or a total of 1,897,-000 *cho* had changed hands. The change that came over the pattern of land-holding may be seen in the following figures: in 1941 53 per cent of the land was cultivated by tenant farmers, but in 1949 this figure had dropped to 14 per cent. As a result of the land reform measures, absentee landlords and large landholders disappeared, and Japan became a country in which about 86 per cent of the land was cultivated by its owners.

It is safe to say that the most important consequence of the land reform was political rather than economic. Conceivably farm productivity might rise somewhat because owners are likely to take better care of their land, but improvements in this direction are bound to be limited. In the final analysis, the old problem of two many people trying to make a living off a limited amount of land remains as acute as ever. Politically, however, the reform brought a measure of stability—even if only temporary —to the countryside, and it siphoned off discontent which under some circumstances might have been channeled into revolutionary action. In China, the Communists rode to power on the hunger of peasants for land; in Japan the Communists were denied this opportunity. It is reported that even Communist party members bought land contrary to the wishes of the Japanese Communist party, which favored nationalization of land rather than its distribution to cultivators.[20]

The land reform program had another political effect, in that it altered the nature of local leadership. Since conditions varied from village to village it would not be wise to be dogmatic, but certain patterns of change are discernable. In those areas where the landlord-tenant relationship was based on kinship, as it was in many districts in northern Japan, and where there was accomodation between the two on a give and take basis, the power structure remained basically intact.[21] But elsewhere the larger landholders seem to have been put on the defensive and their power has been challenged by tenant farmers. On the whole, however, the conservative forces led by the larger landholders are still in power, although this has sometimes been achieved at the cost of putting non-farmers, such as priests and school teachers, into office. Indeed, it is quite possible that this trend will continue in the future and that more and more local offices will be filled by professionals who seek careers in local government service.[22] If this occurs the way will be open for forces other than those represented by wealthy landed families to make their influence felt in local affairs.

Changes in Farm Organizations

The early years of the occupation saw the resurgence of the left-wing farm organization, *Nihon Nomin Kumiai* or *Nichino* (Japan Farmers' Union). A few months after the end of the war

[20] Kawai Etsuzo, *Noson no seikatsu* (Life in the farm villages) (Tokyo, 1952), p. 64.

[21] Furushima Toshio, *Kaikaku tojo no Nihon nogyo* (Japanese agriculture in the process of reform) (Tokyo, 1949), p. 98.

[22] See Royama Masamichi, *Noson jichi no hembo*, pp. 396, 399–400.

in 1945, Socialists, both of the left-wing and right-wing variety, called a preparatory conference, and in February, 1946, the organization was formally established. The *Nichino's* campaign to organize tenant farmers was quite successful and by 1947 it boasted well over a million members and several thousand local affiliates scattered throughout the country. The *Nichino* was particularly active in those areas which had been the scene of tenant disputes before the war, and in many instances, it took the lead in pushing through the land reform program, by giving advice to tenant farmers, by getting its members elected to the local land commissions, and by running its men in local elections.

For several years the *Nichino* managed to ride the crest of the wave of change that swept over the rural areas as a result of the land reform, but starting about 1948 its popularity rapidly waned. At least two reasons may be cited to explain its decline. First, almost from the very beginning there was a struggle between the Socialists and Communists within the *Nichino* organization. In July, 1947, Hirano Rikizo, a well-known right-wing Socialist took his followers and seceded from *Nichino* and formed *Zenkoku Nomin Kumiai* (All-Japan Farmers' Union). Then in April, 1948, at the second convention of the *Nichino,* the Socialist and pro-Communist factions split, each faction holding its own meeting. The second, and perhaps more fundamental reason for the decline of the *Nichino* was the fact that the chief plank in its program—land for the landless—lost its appeal once tenant farmers got land as a result of the land reform program.

Unlike the *Nichino,* which frankly seeks to represent the interests of the poorer farmers, the *Nogyo Kyodo Kumiai* or Agricultural Cooperative Association, tries to represent all classes in the rural areas. The Cooperative Association is the successor to the *Nogyokai* or Agricultural Association formed in 1943 as a result of the amalgamation of all farm organizations including the Imperial Farmers' Association. Legislation adopted in 1947 called for the abolition of the wartime Agricultural Association and its replacement by the new Cooperative Association.

The principal functions of the Cooperative Association lie

in credit, buying and selling, storage, insurance, food processing and rural welfare. But since about 1949 the Association has turned its attention to politics as witnessed by the fact that in March, 1949, representatives of the organization met and passed a resolution on taxes on farmers. The post-war Association has some wealthier farmers in titular positions and about 15 per cent of its officers are men with experience in pre-war farm organizations. Nevertheless, observers believe that the landlord influence in the post-war organization has declined considerably and that the present organization is much more aggressive than its predecessor. It is also clear that the Agricultural Cooperative Association is not so radical as the *Nichino*.[23]

Concluding Remarks

Politically, the importance of Japanese agriculture is to be found in the fact that (1) it, despite industrialization, continues to support between forty and fifty per cent of the population, (2) it is the repository of traditional social values, and (3) it provides the basis for conservative political organizations. In its economic aspects, Japanese agriculture has not kept pace with commerce and industry. In an effort to redress economic disadvantages, farmers have attempted, mostly through their organizations, to achieve political solutions to some of their problems. On the whole, they have not enjoyed spectacular success, partly because of cleavages within the agricultural community itself. It may be said in conclusion that Japan continues to think highly of agriculture but not of agriculturalists.

[23] *Nochi kaikaku temmatsu gaiyo*, pp. 1031 ff.

PART **III** *The Political Process*

Chapter 8

The Bureaucracy

"All realistic study of government," says Friedrich, "has to start with an understanding of bureaucracy (or whatever else one prefers to call it), because no government can function without it." [1] As the range of governmental activities increases—and it seems to be increasing everywhere—the power of the bureaucracy is inevitably enhanced. The decisions made by bureaucrats make their influence felt in diverse fields, such as economic growth, social welfare and the distribution of the national income. Indeed, it may be said that the bureaucracy forms the core of modern government.

The bureaucracy has occupied a peculiarly strategic position in the Japanese political system. Japanese bureaucrats have never been hampered by a set of values which holds that the less there is of government the better. Japan has no legacy of a laissez faire period. On the contrary, ever since the Meiji Restoration (and even prior to that) the people have acquired a habit of looking to a paternalistic government for leadership and assistance.

[1] Carl J. Friedrich, *Constitutional Government and Democracy* (Boston, 1941), p. 57.

WHO ARE THE BUREAUCRATS?

The Beginnings of the Civil Service

The personnel of the early Meiji regime was determined largely by historical circumstances. It was inherent in the nature of the Meiji Restoration that the first bureaucrats in the new Meiji regime should be drawn from those people who had been most active in overthrowing the Tokugawa Shogunate. The roster of government personnel, therefore, included a strong representation of lower samurai, with a sprinkling of court nobles. In terms of geographical origins, an unmistakeably strong position was held by officials from the old fiefs of Choshu, Satsuma, Tosa, and Hizen.

With the passage of years, however, a more systematic method of recruitment had to be adopted. Late in 1885 a civil service based in theory upon a merit system was established at the insistence of Prince Ito Hirobumi. Ito issued a directive to various ministers of departments outlining five steps to be taken on administrative reform: (1) definition of official responsibilities; (2) principles to be applied on making appointments; (3) multiplicity of official documents; (4) reduction of superfluous expenditures; and (5) official discipline.[2]

The section on the principles to be applied in making appointments specified that appointments and promotions should be based upon examinations. It was argued that the absence of a fixed system of choosing officials meant that appointments went to "friends of those already in office," that educated persons were often "deprived of all hope for advancement," and that it was "impossible to obtain the services of able and efficient men in public service."[3]

[2] Sterling T. Takeuchi, "The Japanese Civil Service," in *The Civil Service in the Modern State,* ed. by Leonard D. White (Chicago, 1930), p. 515.

[3] *Ibid.,* p. 516.

The first examinations were held in 1887 for officials of *sonin* (second) and *hannin* (third) rank, the first rank of *chokunin* officials being exempt. With the establishment of the Diet in 1890 the political parties applied pressure to get party men appointed to the exempt positions. When the first Okuma cabinet was formed in 1898, "party men, without due regard to their proper qualifications, filled the high posts of Chokunin rank, such as the posts of vice-ministers of departments, councilors, chiefs of various bureaus, governors of prefectures, and other important *Chokunin* posts, supervising and controlling *Sonin* and *Hannin* officials, who had been appointed by examination." [4] The spoils system, however, never took hold in Japan, for after the short-lived Okuma cabinet, new ordinances were promulgated which placed strict restrictions on qualifications for *chokunin* posts, making it difficult for party men to fill them. In subsequent years, the political parties tried to get these restrictions relaxed, but without too much success.

Composition of the Civil Service

The pre-war civil service had two basic divisions: the higher civil service, and the ordinary civil service. Each of the two basic divisions was subdivided into two sections. The higher civil service was composed of *chokunin* (first rank) officials, who held the top posts in the government, such as ministers and vice-ministers, ambassadors, bureau chiefs, and judges; and *sonin* (second rank) officials, who held the lower level policy-making posts. There were gradations, furthermore, within the *chokunin* and *sonin* grades. The ordinary civil service was composed of *hannin* (third rank) officials and *yatoi* or unclassified officials. As is to be expected, the *chokunin* and *sonin* officials represented but a small fraction of the total body of civil servants.

[4] *Ibid.*, p. 520.

Grouping of the Pre-War Civil Service

RANK	1913 NO. OF OFFICIALS	PER CENT	1930 NO. OF OFFICIALS	PER CENT
Chokunin	649	0.31	1,347	0.28
Sonin	8,045	3.8	14,057	2.9
Hannin	69,745	33.7	111,591	23.4
Yatoi	128,352	62.19	348,631	73.42
	206,791	100.00	475,626	100.00

Source: *Nihon tokei nenkan,* 1914 and 1931 editions.

Except for technicians, entrance into the higher civil service was through competitive examinations held annually in Tokyo. Off hand this would seem to be a democratic system which would make it possible for the ablest young men from all corners of the social world to attain policy-making positions in the government. But actually, it resulted in a tightly knit and self-perpetuating bureaucracy. The civil service examinations were controlled by a 90-man committee, composed almost entirely of the Law Faculty of Tokyo Imperial University (now Tokyo University), and were largely legal in character. Although thousands of aspiring young university graduates took the examination every year, only a few hundred passed. Those who were successful in the examinations, moreover, were not automatically assured of a job. The actual appointments were made from the list of those who had qualified by passing the examinations. And when it came to making the appointments, "Sons or brothers of leading officials or of those who had influence with the officials received preferential treatment. Letters of recommendation from prominent persons were presented in support of applications, and not infrequently a candidate resorted to the giving of 'gifts.' " [5]

[5] Maynard N. Shirven and Joseph L. Speicher, "Examination of Japan's Upper Bureaucracy," *Personnel Administration,* July, 1951, p.49.

For several reasons the scales were tipped in favor of graduates of the old Tokyo Imperial University. First of all, they were likely to be better trained than graduates from the private universities. Second, since the examinations were mostly prepared by the Tokyo Imperial University faculty, it was natural that their students should do better than students from other universities. Third, since the Tokyo Imperial University had numerous alumni in government service, it had many personal connections which were invaluable when appointments were made. As a result, the upper bureaucracy came to be dominated by graduates of this university. This situation, incidentally, still exists. A good illustration is the personnel in the Minister's Secretariat within the Ministry of Finance in 1953:

Minister's Secretariat, Chief, Morinaga Sadaichiro
    (Tokyo Imperial University)
  1. Secretarial Section, Chief, Yoshioka Eiichi
      (Tokyo Imperial University, class of 1938)
  2. General Affairs Section, Chief, Murakami Kazu
      (Tokyo Imperial University, class of 1937)
  3. Accounts Section, Chief, Kimura Hidehiro
      (Tokyo Imperial University, class of 1937)
  4. Local Affairs Section, Chief, Ota Genzo
      (Tokyo University of Commerce, class of 1937)
  5. Research Section, Chief, Tanimura Hiro
      (Tokyo Imperial University, class of 1938)

As can be seen, all but one of the six men in this bureau within the Ministry of Finance are graduates of Tokyo Imperial University.

The examinations for the ordinary civil service, that is the *hannin* rank, were geared to high school graduates and were given in various localities when deemed necessary by the government. Since there was a sharp distinction between the higher and the ordinary civil service, officials of *hannin* rank were treated as second class citizens and were seldom promoted to *sonin* rank. Although they were without prestige and status, it was the *hannin* officials and those in the unclassified civil service who carried on the great bulk of the day-to-day administration. Some American observers are inclined to believe that it was the corps of lower officials, together with the police which had extensive functions, that kept the government going. "The technical officials, along with the thousands of lower administrative officials and clerks who were not university graduates, or who had attended the wrong schools or come from the wrong families, carried on the day-to-day work of administration which kept the system from collapse." [6]

THE WAYS OF THE BUREAUCRACY

Officialdom and the Public

The relationship between the bureaucracy and the people is sometimes described by an old and often repeated phrase, *kanson minpi*, which literally means, "official exalted—people despised." Years ago, a well-known political figure, Tani Kanjo, wrote that when he saw the way in which local officials and police officials treated the people, it looked as if "they were holding down a conquered territory." "The abuse of power by petty officials," he continued, "is particularly severe. They do not realize that it is their duty to do their best for the welfare of the people since they owe their livelihood to the taxes paid by them. On the contrary, they look upon the people as if they were slaves." [7]

Before the war, civil officials owed their loyalty and allegiance to the Emperor. Each official was, in theory, vested with a segment of the Imperial authority, with those in the upper ranks of the hierarchy having more and those in the lower reaches having less. In their training and indoctrination, officials

[6] Shirven and Speicher, *ibid.*, p. 50.
[7] Quoted in Tsuji Kiyoaki, *Nihon kanryosei no kenkyu* (A study of the Japanese bureaucracy) (Tokyo, 1953), p. 186.

were never encouraged to think of themselves as existing for the good of the public.

The situation has changed somewhat in recent years, and there are even signs that some agencies are becoming aware of "PR" or public relations; [8] but it is true to say that as yet the notion that the bureaucrat is a "public servant" is somewhat alien to the Japanese mentality. When an individual becomes an official, he has, according to the prevailing scale of values, achieved status and prestige, and he tends to show it. By the same token, the expectation which seems to prevail among the general public is that bureaucrats are an arrogant and haughty lot who look with scorn upon the citizenry. Although there is a good deal of grumbling about the supercilious way in which officials are wont to treat the public, the average citizen finds it more expedient to bow low and assume a humble air when approaching officials.

Status Consciousness

A strong sense of hierarchy prevails within the Japanese bureaucracy. As already mentioned, a wide gap separated the higher civil servants from the lower civil servants. A former bureaucrat relates that higher officials got tables with green table cloth, a swivel chair and a telephone. One day a lower official who aspired to become a higher official brought a green table cloth from his home; but this became a subject of much discussion in the office, and his superiors finally made him get rid of it.[9]

A bureau chief was given a separate office, four book shelves and 10 chairs for guests; a section chief got, in addition to a table with a green table cloth, 2 book shelves and 3 to 5 chairs for guests; while lower civil servants had no chairs for

[8] See *Asahi shimbun,* January 9, 1955.
[9] Imai Kazuo, *Kanryo, sono seitai to uchimaku* (Bureaucrats, their mode of life and behind-the-scenes activities) (Tokyo, 1953), p. 57.

guests. In the days when telephones were more plentiful, higher officials were given a home telephone, and those of *chokunin* rank were entitled to government-owned cars. The sense of hierarchy was even carried over into private life. An official was once transferred because his child who was in the same class in school as his superior's child got better grades.[10] Promotions were based to a large extent on personal connections, and on the year in which officials were graduated from college. The feeling for status was so strong that it was not considered proper, for instance, to keep a person as a section chief when his classmates had already risen to bureau chief positions.[11] It is true that all bureaucracies are hierarchically organized; but one gets the impression that the sense of hierarchy is particularly acute in the Japanese instance.

Legalism

The Japanese bureaucracy is highly legalistic in its approach to administrative problems. The average bureaucrat likes to have every official act authorized in advance by a specific regulation or statute. When confronted by a situation that calls for a decision, the official usually runs to the bookshelf where the regulations and manuals are kept and starts to thumb through the pages looking for a law or ordinance that would cover the particular case. If no statute can be found, and if there are no precedents, which are a great arbiter of Japanese administrative practice, decisions are likely to be postponed. According to an American observer of Japanese administration, "The difficulty of securing decisions, a chronic plague of large organizations, severely afflicts the Japanese government." [12]

Superficially, one might interpret this addiction to legal-

---

[10] *Ibid.*, p. 58–61.

[11] *Ibid.*, p. 88.

[12] Milton J. Esman, "Japanese Administration—a Comparative View," *Public Administration Review*, VII (Spring, 1947), p. 105.

ism as showing a preference for "government by law." But if we adopt this interpretation we come to a paradoxical situation: Law and legal institutions are underdeveloped in Japanese society and culture; yet administrators prefer "government by law." A plausible explanation of this paradox may be found in the character of Japanese social relations. We have repeatedly emphasized that Japanese feel comfortable when social interaction takes place on a highly personal basis. When a bureaucrat transacts official business with a friend or someone who has been introduced to him through mutual friends he can behave according to the dictates of social custom. However, when an administrator has to deal with a total stranger, he is confronted with an impersonal formalized social situation; and it is under these circumstances that he seeks refuge in the "law." Resort to law in the Japanese context, therefore, is not the attainment of justice, but a retreat from difficult social situations.

Fragmentation

When the Occupation began to apply pressure to reform the administrative system, it found that first of all the structure of the upper levels of the civil service had to be clarified. "Surprising though it may seem to one accustomed to the American practice of charting organizations and work operations, the Japanese had not, prior to the Occupation, attempted to chart their vast and complex organizations of government." [13] In order to create this chart showing the functional relationship of ministries and administrative agencies to each other, to the Prime Minister and Cabinet, and to the legislature and the judiciary, the staff was "faced with the problem of digging necessary data out of unindexed official documents, and facts from officials whose concepts of organization were often vague." [14]

[13] SCAP, *Political Reorientation of Japan,* I, p. 256.
[14] *Ibid.*

Accounts by people who have held posts in the Japanese government are pretty much agreed that the governmental structure was terribly fragmented. Each section, each bureau, and each ministry was highly jealous of its prerogatives and there was relatively little coordination of governmental activities. Pertinent documents, which are often vital if intelligent decisions are to be made, were kept by individual officials who often refused to show them to other administrators.[15] On this point a former official, Imai Kazuo, relates his personal experiences:

Shortly after I assumed my position in the government service, I was sent to the next section to borrow some documentary materials. As I recall it, they had to do with statistics which had been collected from every prefecture in the country. It seemed that the next section no longer had much need for these documents since the study it had been making based on them was now completed; but they put up a lot of arguments and refused to lend them to me. I still remember the parting words of the man in charge of the section with whom I had negotiated since they were out of this world. He said, "if this data is so essential, why doesn't your section send letters to the prefectures and get them."[16]

Whenever a section or a bureau worked up a proposal which impinged upon the work being done by other agencies, it had to get the approval of all those affected. The necessary documents were circulated so that the needed seals (which take the place of signatures) could be affixed; but bureaus and sections were not inclined to hurry and cases are known where it took as much as three years for the process to be completed. In case of urgent matters, an official took the papers and walked from ministry to ministry, bureau to bureau, and section to section collecting the necessary seals. Various techniques were

---

[15] Tsuji, *op. cit.*, p. 188–9.
[16] Imai, *op. cit.*, p. 142.

evolved to overcome the tendency of individuals or sections to put up road blocks; some bureaus, for example, would draft the document but would hold up its circulation until the last minute. Then the bureau would put pressure to rush it through explaining to the other agencies that "if we don't get this completed in time for tomorrow's cabinet meeting, we won't be able to present it to the next Diet." There was also a certain "etiquette" involved in "walking the papers." The ministries and their subdivisions were arranged in a hierarchical order, and the accepted procedure was to go first to the lowest section and proceed upward. Sometimes officials would refuse to affix their seals for one reason or another. Imai tells about an incident in which one section chief refused to affix his seal because another section chief had already approved the document.

> He had no complaint whatever to make against the proposal, but he was displeased that I had gotten section chief B to affix his seal. He refused to affix his. When I explained that in my view this document affected both of them about equally, he reprimanded me, saying, "You don't know the regulations concerning departmental organization." I argued with him a little, but I was unable to get his seal that day . . . The following day, a more experienced and able official went in my place and by begging or something got the matter straightened out. I learned later that the two section chiefs got along as well as the proverbial cats and dogs, and this was the reason for the difficulty.[17]

Gekokujo: "the Lowers Dominating the Uppers"

The conventional charts on Japanese governmental organization show a series of boxes arranged vertically and connected with solid or dotted lines indicating the flow of authority.

[17] Imai, *op. cit.*, p. 150.

The lines point downward suggesting that the upper levels issue orders which are carried out by the lower levels. This may be true insofar as the structure of formal authority goes; but in practice this is not always the case. It has been said that in a government office, "the superiors do not use their inferiors, but rather the inferiors use their superiors." [18]

One reason for this state of affairs was the high rate of transfers in the civil service. An American observer has reported that "It was not at all uncommon for a man with twenty years of service to have held twenty different positions." [19] Under these circumstances it was well-nigh impossible for a man to become an expert in his job. Indeed it was maintained that a man who held an important administrative position did better if he did not know too much about his job. [20] His primary responsibility was not to run his bureau or ministry but rather to deal with other important officials on matters of policy, budget, etc.

On many important matters, therefore, substantial influence was exercised by the lower levels of the bureaucracy. In many instances the center of gravity was at the level of section and bureau chiefs who appear to have exercised a good deal of de facto power. Historical documents which have recently become available on political developments in the 1930's show that quite often the minister was unable to control his ministry. A typical example is the following entry in the diary kept by Harada Kumao, who served as Prince Saionji's secretary:

> On September 4, I met Finance Minister [Inoue]. He said: "The War Minister [Minami] on the whole was in complete accord with me on the army reorganization plan, and the matter was agreed upon between us. However, upon re-

[18] Imai, op. cit., p. 104.

[19] Foster Roser, "Establishing a Modern Merit System in Japan," Public Personnel Review, XI (October, 1950), p. 201.

[20] Adachi Tadao, Kindai kanryo-sei to shokkai-sei (Modern bureaucracy and job classification) (Tokyo, 1952), p. 153.

turning to the War Ministry, he was severely criticised by the Military Affairs Bureau Chief, Koiso Kuniaki, and the Intendance Section Chief for having agreed with me on the matter. Consequently, he returned to me later and said: 'I previously agreed with you on the matter, but I find it difficult to get the members of the staff to give their consent to the agreement. . . .' For this reason the matter is back to where we started." [21]

The foregoing quotation shows the lower echelons exercising veto power; but it is also true that in many instances the lower officials took the initiative in important matters. It appears that at hundreds of points within the bureaucracy proposals regarding policy, new statutes and regulations, administrative actions and the like were drafted and sent upwards, where they were rejected, pigeon-holed, or approved in their entireties or in modified form. The Japanese government had little in the way of high-level machinery for coordinating administrative action. For example, in budgetary matters, once the annual budget was adopted, the work of the bureau of the budget was virtually finished for it exercised no control over the administration of the budget, the disposition of funds being completely under the control of the spending agencies.[22] One could state without doing too much violence to facts that the Japanese government was virtually a government without a clearly defined and effective head.

Inefficiency

A common complaint directed against the bureaucracy by the general public is that it is given to "slow motion." Japanese bureaucrats, like their counterparts in many other countries, do

[21] Harada Kumao, *Saionji Ko to seikyoku* (Prince Saionji and the political situation) (Tokyo, 1950), II, pp. 44–5.
[22] Esman, *op. cit.*, p. 107.

not endeavor to get things done in a hurry. Many foreigners who have gone into Japanese government offices are impressed by the tea drinking and gossiping that goes on. Much time seems to be wasted; and it is, of course, the taxpayer and the public who pay for it in the end.

Another sight which impresses the foreigner is the large number of officials and clerks who are found in almost every government office. Many people believe that Japanese business firms are terribly overstaffed; and the same thing is true of government agencies. In 1953 there was provision in the budget for 1,528,259 central government employees, divided into the following categories:

Number of Government Employees Provided for in the Budget

National Safety Agency	123,153
General Accounts	416,816
Special Accounts	340,098
Government Corporations	648,192
Total	1,528,259

Source: *Japan Statistical Yearbook,* 1953 edition.

If we exclude the National Safety Agency which is the embryonic army and navy, we get a figure of a little more than one million four hundred thousand. However, there are in addition, a large number of government employees who do not appear in the budget at all. These are "temporary employees" who are denied tenure and retirement benefits, but often work side by side with regular staff members and do the same kind of work. Their salaries are paid out of funds appropriated for "supplies," and therefore do not appear as personnel expenses in the budget. Their exact number is not known, but it is estimated that it reaches between 600,000 and 1,000,000, if we include both central and local governments. "It is strange," commented the newspaper,

Asahi, "that there should be such a large number of temporary staff members when the existence of too many regular public officials is always complained of. A public office is certainly a place which ordinary men of common sense can hardly understand." [23]

Attempted Reforms

The Occupation, in attempting to bring about a series of changes in Japanese society and culture, did not overlook the bureaucracy. But its activities in this area were hampered by at least two considerations. Very early the Allied powers decided to avoid direct military occupation and to work instead through the existing Japanese government. This meant that the Japanese government, and particularly the bureaucracy, was to become an instrument for effecting changes in the Japanese political and social structure. The Occupation authorities, therefore, were caught in a dilemma, since, on the one hand, they were dissatisfied with the undemocratic composition and methods of the administrative system, and yet on the other hand needed this system to carry on their work. Second, the bureaucracy was very well entrenched, and resistant to change. The Occupation recognized that reform was necessary, but it also "recognized that an institution so pervasive and so firmly established as the Japanese bureaucracy could not be reformed by summary measures, that superficial tinkering would produce only superficial results." [24]

Several Japanese government agencies saw that it would be impossible to maintain the status quo in face of Occupation pressure, and came up with their own proposals for "reform." One of these involved a request for the importation of American experts to advise on civil service reform; and this led eventually to the creation of the United States Personnel Advisory Mission, which went to Japan in November, 1946, to study the existing per-

[23] *Asahi Evening News,* March 21, 1955.
[24] *Political Reorientation of Japan,* I, p. 247.

sonnel system and to make recommendations. After detailed study, the Mission came up with a series of recommendations calling for: (1) creation within the Japanese government of a central personnel agency; (2) enactment of a national public service law, providing for service-wide standards of personnel administration; (3) creation of a civil service division within SCAP to advise on reforms in this field.

As a result of these recommendations, the National Diet passed the National Public Service Law in October, 1947. The law was, according to one observer, a "thoroughly and completely emasculated instrument compared with that which had been recommended by the Mission," but still it represented a beginning toward the development of a merit system.[25] Under the provisions of this law, the principle of job classification was adopted, the *Jinji-in*, or National Personnel Authority was created, and examinations for higher administrative personnel were decreed.

In 1948 a basic training course in personnel administration was given to some 400 trainees drawn from the staff of the National Personnel Authority and representatives of various ministries. The National Personnel Authority, with the help of American advisers and Occupation authorities, worked out a job classification scheme consisting of about 450 distinct occupations. The jobs were classified by the kind of work, e.g., typing, and the difficulty of work, e.g., Typing I, Typing II, and so on.

In accordance with the law, the National Personnel Authority held examinations in 1950 for higher civil servants, i.e., vice-ministers down to section chiefs. "On the morning of January 15, 1950, in various Japanese cities, numerous limousines drew up to university buildings and while newspaper cameras clicked, their occupants dismounted, bade their chauffeurs to wait or return at specified times, and entered classrooms (many for the first time in more than 20 years) to take a test."[26] Two types of

[25] Roser, *op. cit.*, p. 201.
[26] Shirven and Speicher, *op. cit.*, p. 48.

written tests were given; one to measure administrative ability, and the other to test technical knowledge. The tests covered more than 2,600 positions, which were grouped in 60 occupational categories. In addition, each position was placed in one of four administrative levels. If the purpose of the examination was to weed out the old bureaucrats in order to pave the way for the infusion of new blood, it would appear that it was not particularly successful. In the end, 78.8 per cent of the incumbents were retained.[27]

But the higher civil servants felt humiliated and resented the fact that they had been forced to take the examinations; and the National Personnel Authority has never been forgiven by the bureaucracy for having held them. In recent years the National Personnel Authority has been pushed more and more into the background as a result of bureaucratic pressure. As for the job classification scheme which was established by the National Public Service Law, a Japanese writer has expressed doubt about its workability in Japan. He believes that a classification system based on specialization will not work in a bureaucracy which is not specialized and which rests on personal connections.[28]

It appears that the bureaucracy proved more than a match for the Occupation, and that the civil service reforms were one of the least successful of the reforms that were attempted in various fields. But this is not altogether surprising. Administration is not something that exists independently of the complex web of obligations and expectations which binds the community together. Administration, to be effective, must rest fundamentally on the system of values which prevails. Only when a change occurs in the prevailing values can we expect the bureaucracy to change its ways.

[27] Shirven and Speicher, *op. cit.*, p. 57.
[28] Adachi, *op. cit.*, p. 155.

THE BUREAUCRACY AND INTEREST GROUPS

Shortly after he took office late in 1954, Prime Minister Hatoyama Ichiro issued an order to all government agencies forbidding civil servants to play golf and mahjong with businessmen. Hatoyama's order elicited a favorable response from the press, and presumably the public. It is doubtful, given the nature of the relationship between government and interest groups, that Hatoyama's directive will have lasting results; but it did serve to focus official attention on certain unethical practices that had become rather conspicuous.

Bureaucrats and Businessmen

In Japan, as elsewhere, businessmen and others find it worth their while to establish personal and cordial relations with key figures in government agencies. The government, through its numerous activities, is in a position to affect the income and profits of business and agricultural enterprises. Every year, the government provides substantial subsidies to assist certain sectors of the economy—especially agriculture—and the flow of these subsidies may be modified by the application of pressure group tactics. The government, particularly the National Safety Agency buys billions of yen worth of goods and services annually; and since the government, unlike many private firms, always pays its bills promptly, businessmen leave no stone unturned to land a government contract. Finally, economic controls of one sort or another are still in force, which means that businessmen must get licenses or permits to carry on certain types of activities. Firms engaged in the import business, for example, must get dollar allocations before they can purchase goods from the dollar areas. Other things being equal, those who have an inside track to government agencies and officials enjoy tangible benefits.

There are several well-known techniques for establishing connections with officialdom. In the past some companies used to put retired bureaucrats on their payroll in order to take advantage of their personal ties with government officials. By custom, officials were expected to resign from government service in their forties and fifties, so officials usually began to cultivate business contacts in their middle age. "Enterprising business men offer comfortable posts—virtual sinecures—to pensioned officials in exchange for public favors arranged through their junior colleagues who remain in the service." [29] An attempt has been made to curtail this practice through a provision in the National Public Service Law which forbids an official for a period of two years from taking a post with a firm which had dealings with his agency. It is difficult to tell, however, whether the law is actually enforced.

Another technique used to win favors from government agencies is the age-old one of entertaining officials. The Ministry of International Trade and Industry, for example, is a prime target of businessmen, since it issues permits and licenses for foreign trade. In order to export and import goods and commodities, traders have to make the rounds of a multitude of bureaus and sections within the Ministry to get the necessary seals put on the documents. On the third floor of the building which houses the Ministry is found the Bureau of Trade which is the center of attraction; and the traffic here is so heavy that the third floor is popularly known as the "Bureau of Trade Ginza." According to the newspaper *Asahi*, "it is called this because so many executives of leading firms accompanied by beautiful private secretaries come and go." [30] *Asahi* quotes one trader as saying that if you want your application acted upon, "you have to become so friendly with officials that you can pick up the telephone and get section chiefs and bureau chiefs to act." [31]

[29] Hugh H. MacDonald and Milton J. Esman, "The Japanese Civil Service," *Public Personnel Review,* October, 1946, p. 223.

[30] *Asahi shimbun,* Dec. 12, 1954.

[31] *Asahi shimbun,* Dec. 31, 1954. Telephones are used extensively in the United States, but in Japan important matters are seldom discussed on the phone. This probably reflects the emphasis which is put on highly personalized, face-to-face relationship.

One common way to become friendly with officials is to entertain them. On Saturdays businessmen send their private cars to the Ministry to pick up officials and whisk them off to golf courses,[32] and in the evening lavish geisha parties would be given in some resort town like Atami. Businessmen often invite the lesser officials to mahjong parties where for some reason or other the guests are usually very lucky and manage to come home a little richer.

Other agencies which have a large clientele of individuals and interest groups are the Ministry of Agriculture, the National Safety Agency, and the Local Autonomy Board. The Ministry of Agriculture each year gives out billions of yen in subsidies for a variety of purposes—disaster relief, soil conservation and improvement, increase in food production and the like, and practically every village in the land would like to share in this outward flow of cash from the Ministry. Little wonder that numerous delegations beat a path to the Ministry of Agriculture, each armed with arguments—cogent or otherwise—telling why their locality should share in the largess.

The National Safety Agency, being a large purchaser of sundry items, ranging from socks to jet aircraft, naturally attracts to it thousands of eager suppliers. Because of the shortage of working capital, sellers may have to wait as long as six months for payment in ordinary business transactions; but when goods are sold to the National Safety Agency, payment is made quickly, sometimes within a week or ten days. Firms, therefore, work hard to get entree into the purchasing department of the National Safety Agency. "It is said," wrote a reporter in *Asahi*, "that the procurement plans of the purchasing department are clearly known to the more clever businessmen through the 'connections' that are established between the two." [33] According

---

[32] It should be mentioned that golf in Japan is an expensive form of recreation which only the rich can afford. Most officials could not afford to play unless somebody picked up the tab.

[33] *Asahi shimbun*, Dec. 29, 1954.

to one businessman a prospective call for bids is known a week or ten days before it is made public. The estimated price which the Agency expects to pay for goods is supposed to be a closely guarded secret; yet there have been instances when the estimated price and the bid matched exactly.[34]

The Autonomy Board is the focal point of delegations of local officials who come to Tokyo to seek funds to alleviate chronic deficits. An attempt was made under the Occupation to decentralize the government, with prefectural and village governments being given more functions and responsibility. Local governments, however, were not given sufficient tax revenues to enable them to pay for all of their new commitments, with the result that local governments generally operate in the red. Every year the central government turns back billions of yen in tax money to the local governments in various areas through the Local Autonomy Board. It is therefore not surprising that there is hardly a day when local delegations are not seen walking the corridors in front of the finance section of the Local Autonomy Board.

Gaikaku Dantai

A more permanent and institutionalized connection between an agency and its clientele is established through organizations known as *gaikaku dantai*. The Ministry of Agriculture is reputed to have about 300 such organizations attached to it. A typical example is the *Norin Bunka Kyokai* or Agriculture and Forestry Cultural Association. Essentially, these organizations provide liaison between the Ministry and the peasantry and provide certain services, such as publishing booklets and journals. An examination of the list of officers of these organizations will show many former bureaucrats as well as officials who still retain posts in the government. Another important function of *gaikaku*

[34] *Ibid.*

dantai is to serve as a steppingstone to elective office. When a bureaucrat decides to resign from the civil service and run for an elective post, he often seeks the support of these organizations with which he has had close contact while serving as an administrator.

The *gaikaku dantai* which were attached to the police acquired such an unsavory reputation that they had to be abolished. For a number of years, the Tokyo Metropolitan Police headquarters had a "Federation of Police Supporting Associations" which raised money to supplement funds provided by the Tokyo Municipal government and assisted the police in law enforcement. Funds provided by the Association, for example, were used to compensate police officers who were injured or killed while on duty. Eventually, however, local political bosses and racketeers got control of many of these associations and used them to influence the police, leading to a number of scandals involving high-level police officials. As a result, these organizations were ordered abolished.

But it appears that the police (as well as other agencies) cannot function effectively without their auxiliary organizations; in the spring of 1955 it was reported that new organizations have been set up to assist the police. For instance, there is the Tokyo Metropolitan Police Round-Table Association, headed by Takahashi Ryutaro, a former Minister of Transportation, which collects ¥10,000 (about $27) each from 120 large firms in Tokyo.

Another organization is the Crime Prevention Federation which is said to have a membership of 1,300,000 with 92 branches in the city of Tokyo. "The federation is engaged largely in education campaigns and other movements fostering the idea of crime prevention among Tokyo citizens." Finally, the Mothers' Associations Federation, with 350,000 members in 53 branches, devotes its efforts to preventing juvenile deliquency.[35]

[35] "Tokyo Police HQ Probes Financial Supporters," in *Asahi Evening News*, April 29, 1955.

Chapter 9

Political Parties

When the Democratic party was formed in the autumn of 1954 as a result of the amalgamation of the Progressive party and dissident elements of the Liberal party, a reporter with a sense of history is said to have gone to the Progressive party headquarters and asked to see the collection of name plates. His thought was that as this was the fourth change in the name of the party since the end of the war, a collection of name plates showing the successive changes in the party would be found there. He learned, however, that there was only one thin name plate with the words, "Progressive party." What had happened was that every time the party was reorganized, the old name was shaved off the wooden plate and a new one painted on. This story provides a fitting introduction to this chapter on parties for it illustrates at least two of their characteristics—the rather cavalier attitude parties sometimes take toward party labels, and the lack of stability of party organization.

Before entering into an analysis of party structure and related matters, it is useful to take a brief look at the historical development of parties.[1] The first parties were organized in the 1870's, and from these beginnings there eventually evolved by the 1920's two so-called bourgeois parties—the *Seiyukai* and the *Min-*

[1] The best work on party development is Robert Scalapino's *Democracy and the Party Movement in Prewar Japan* (Berkeley, 1953).

seito. The former appealed more to the rural and agrarian elements, while the latter was more urban and pro-business in its outlook. With the granting of universal manhood suffrage in 1925, the way was paved for the emergence of left-wing parties based in varying degrees on Marxian principles.

The rise of the military and ultranationalism following the Manchurian invasion in 1931 increasingly put the parties on the defensive until they were forced to dissolve on the eve of World War II. Although parties were banned, informal and personal groupings of politicians continued to exist, and these groupings provided the nucleus of new parties which were formed soon after the termination of hostilities in 1945. It was characteristic of the disorganized state of affairs that in the beginning hundreds of political clubs, societies and so-called parties were founded; but before long four principal parties emerged. The Liberal party (*Jiyuto*) and the Progressive party (*Shimpoto*) were both conservative and traced their roots in a very general way to the *Seiyukai* and *Minseito* respectively. The Socialist party (*Nihon Shakaito*) was made up of men who had been active in the pre-war proletarian parties, notably the *Shakai Minshuto,* the *Nihon Musanto* and the *Nihon Ronoto.* Being composed of socialists of varying political hue, the Socialist party has been plagued by internal bickering and factionalism. The Japanese Communist party (*Nihon Kyosanto*), acquiring legal status for the first time, came to be led by Communists who had either been released from prison or had returned from exile.

Of all the major parties, the Communist party and the Liberal party (until its amalgamation with the Democratic party in 1955) enjoyed the longest continuity, although it is true that individual Liberal party members sometimes shifted party affiliation. Thus the Liberal party's first leader was Hatoyama Ichiro who was succeeded by Yoshida Shigeru when the former was purged by the Occupation; but later Hatoyama led the rival Democratic party, while Yoshida lost his position as leader of the Liberal party. Party men have shifted from one party to another from time to time, usually between conservative parties, but on occasion between conservative and radical parties. In 1948 the newspaper *Shin Hochi* carried an article which stated:

Recently, people are surprised to see how often politicians change their party affiliations.

On 15 April, the central executive committee of the Socialist Party decided to admit the membership of Diet-member Kagetsu, Junsei, who belonged to the Liberal party until a short time ago, while Socialist Moriyama, Takehiko bolted his party and came over to the Democratic-Liberal Party. Mrs. Nakayama, Masa of the Democratic party changed her party three times, from Democratic to Democratic-Liberal and back to Democratic.[2]

The party which has undergone the largest number of reorganizations is the present Liberal-Democratic party which began as the Progressive party (*Shimpoto*) in 1945, changed to the Democratic party (*Minshuto*) in 1947, became the National Democratic party (*Kokumin Minshuto*) in 1950, took the name of Progressive party (*Kaishinto*) in 1952, changed to the Democratic party in 1954, and amalgamated with the Liberal party to become the Liberal-Democratic party in 1955. The Socialist party, which split into a Right-Wing Socialist party and a Left-Wing Socialist party with separate headquarters and separate local organizations as a result of disagreement over the San Francisco peace treaty, was reunited in 1955 after lengthy negotiations.

PARTY STRUCTURE

The Conservative and Socialist Parties

In Japan, as in other countries, interested citizens are free to join political parties of their choice. Except for the Commu-

[2] April 20, 1948, and translated in ATIS *Press Translations*, April 24, 1948.

nist party, which looks into the ideological orientation of prospective members, parties do not maintain rigid entrance requirements, although some like the Socialist party have a rule that a new member must be recommended by two party members. Actually, however, relatively few people go to the trouble to join a party, pay dues regularly, and take part in its activities. The core of Japanese parties, therefore, consists of professional politicians, especially members of the National Diet.

All parties have some kind of machinery to keep things running, and structurally, there are no substantial differences between the conservative parties and the socialist parties. In theory the party convention, usually held annually, determines party policies and chooses the more important officers. According to the rule set forth by the former Liberal party, the convention is the highest decision-making body within the party, and it, among other things, elects the party president for a 4-year term. In practice, however, conventions do not exercise much choice in the selection of a party leader; and they usually rubber-stamp proposals and policies advanced by the leading officials of the party. One gets the impression that Socialist party conventions exercise more control over party affairs than do the conventions of the conservative parties; but it is difficult to establish whether the differences are of a significant magnitude.

Whether or not one agrees with the statement of a Japanese writer that "it is after all a few executive officials who sit in the inner council and really control the party," [3] there is no question that party leaders are able to exercise a powerful influence.

Japanese newspapers and political commentators often speak of the "three party officials." In the case of a conservative party like the old Liberal party, they refer to the

(1) Secretary-General (*kanji cho*) who keeps the party

[3] Inagaki Tatsuo, *Gendai seito ron* (Contemporary parties) (Tokyo, 1949), p. 46.

machinery running, and who has charge of the activities of the various divisions, such as the youth division, the industrial division, the labor division, the agricultural division, the publications division, and so on;

(2) Chairman of the Policy Research Committee, which is responsible for formulating party policies. The Policy Research Committee of the Liberal party issued pamphlets and other material outlining party policy on various political issues;

(3) Chairman of the Executive Committee, which oversees the work of the Policy Research Committee, the Budget Committee, and a host of lesser committees, and the work of the Secretary-General. These three officials, plus the president of the party, together with party advisers, make up the *hombu* or the party headquarters.

The "three officials" of the Japanese Socialist party are the Secretary-General (*shoki cho*), the Chairman of the Policy Deliberation Committee, and the Treasurer. The Socialist party does not have a president, and his functions are taken over by the Chairman of the Central Executive Committee.

The headquarters of all the parties are located in Tokyo; but parties also maintain a certain number of local offices in other cities and in the prefectures. Structurally, the local parties duplicate the headquarters organization, but on a much smaller scale. It may be said that particularly in the case of the conservative parties the local party organizations are not well developed. The conservatives can count on the support of local political leaders and hence can dispense with an elaborate local organization. A great many of the local parties are skeletal organizations, and become active only as elections approach.

The Socialist party organization, when compared to the conservative parties, is much more tightly knit. The local party organizations seem to maintain closer contact with the Tokyo headquarters. Those who have had experience with party affairs at the local level say that headquarters often seeks the views of the lower echelons, that is, the local organizations, before it formulates party policy; but it is difficult to determine just how much voice the rank and file have in party decisions. Some idea of the difference between the conservative parties and the left-wing parties with reference to local organizations may be obtained from the following table:

Number of Members and Branches of Political Parties, 1949

PARTY	MEMBERS	BRANCHES	MEMBERS PER ONE DIET MEMBER
Liberal	67,047	702	251
Democratic	20,327	283	290
Socialist	95,251	1,172	2,027
Communist	87,186	3,406	2,422

Source: *Sengo Nihon no seiji katei* (Post-war Japanese politics) (*Nihon Seiji Gakkai nempo*, 1953), p. 38.

The Communist Party

The Communist party differs from other parties in that its primary objective is not to gain power through parliamentary means but to affect basic changes in the social, economic, and political order through revolutionary action. Since it is a revolutionary party, it wants as its members a relatively small number of people who are ideologically pure, so to speak, and who are willing to dedicate themselves to the cause and submit to party discipline. The Communist party, therefore, is a much more monolithic party; but it, too, like most Japanese organizations, has been plagued by factionalism.

The structure of the Japanese Communist party is similar to that of Communist parties elsewhere; and hence we need not go into it in detail here. Theoretically, the Party congress is all-powerful, but in fact power is lodged in the Central Committee. The most prominent official of the party is the Secretary-General, who heads the Central Committee. Party discipline is entrusted to the Control Commission, which can, in extreme cases, expel "undesirable" members.

The Communist party has a hierarchy of local units, and one of the most important of these is the "cell." According to a Japanese Communist publication, "Cells are created in shops, agrarian communities, schools, and residential areas. These cells, each of which has a definite, independent character, serve as the nuclei of Party activity." [4]

The strategy and tactics of revolutionary action vary from time to time depending upon the policy set by the international Communist movement. During periods when a militant policy is in the ascendency, the government in turn tightens its controls, and this usually leads the Communist party to go partly underground. When this occurs, a part of the party continues to function openly, publishing newspapers and pamphlets, and even putting up candidates for elections, but the most important part of the party disappears from public view.

PARTY LEADERSHIP AND COMPOSITION

Party Leaders

Since the primary purpose of political parties (except the Communist) is to get its leaders into office, and since the largest single block of elective posts is found in the National Diet, it is natural that Diet members should carry great weight in party affairs. Nowadays most of the party leaders are members of the House of Representatives.

Occasionally, however, influence is wielded by men who hold no official post and who appear in the party roster under some innocuous title like "adviser." One such individual was the late Tsuji Karoku, of the Liberal party, who was described in the press as a "kuromaku" or "black curtain" since he stayed

[4] Quoted in Rodger Swearingen and Paul Langer, *Red Flag in Japan* (Cambridge, 1952), p. 97.

behind the scenes and pulled strings. The following excerpt from a newspaper account published in 1948 gives us a picture of Tsuji:

Tsuji is 72 years of age. . . . In his youth, he went to China and once met Sun Yat sen. He has had no experience as a government official or as a politician but he has engaged in business. It is an interesting fact that he has been active only behind the political scenes. . . .

People wonder why such huge amounts of money pour into Tsuji's pocket. Since he was helped liberally during his youth, he is willing to help others. The people who have been helped by him willingly give him money. And he distributes this money liberally.

Sometimes, certain people take advantage of him. However, he forgives them if they apologize for their faults. At New Year's Eve he spends the whole night at his house so that he may be able to lend to any follower in need.

He is very fond of political chat. Although his relationship with the Liberal Party is close, he speaks highly of Katayama among recent Premiers, and is highly appreciative of the Socialist Party.

At the formation of the Katayama Cabinet, he was disappointed when he heard that the Liberal Party had not joined it. Judging from the above, it seems that his power in the Liberal Party is not so strong as is rumored.

His house is always beset by various visitors including bosses, state Ministers, bureaucrats, domestic and foreign journalists; and he receives them all cordially. Of these visitors, he is most fond of politicians.[5]

If men like Tsuji wield influence (the extent of which must vary from individual to individual) without holding a govern-

[5] *Mainichi shimbun,* April 20, 1948, and translated in ATIS *Press Translations,* April 24, 1948. Tsuji is also mentioned in testimony before a Diet investigating committee. See *Futo zaisan torihiki chosa tokubetsu iinkai giroku,* no. 11 and no. 12 (Second session of the Diet).

ment or a party post, there are also those who hold posts but
are essentially figureheads. This comes from the fact that parties
find it to their advantage to put forward men with established
reputations as their leaders, and so prominent men are sometimes approached to take posts as party presidents. Harry Emerson Wildes reports in his book, *Typhoon in Tokyo* that men like
the late Marquis Matsudaira Tsuneo, ex-ambassador and Court
official, Admiral Kichisaburo Nomura, and Sato Naotake, ex-
ambassador and President of the House of Councillors, all declined invitations to head post-war parties.[6]

This is not to imply, however, that party presidents are
necessarily figureheads. Former Prime Minister Yoshida acquired a reputation for running his Liberal party with an iron
hand, and came to be referred to as "one man" Yoshida. The
veteran Hatoyama Ichiro, who left the Liberal party to become
president of the Democratic party when it was organized in 1954,
was something of a figurehead in the beginning, yet acquired
a good deal of power after he led the party to victory at the
polls in the general elections in the spring of 1955.

One of the striking features of party leadership and composition is the relatively large number of men who are carry-
overs from the pre-war period. Political upheavals are usually
registered in the makeup of the political elite, and the fact that
the Japanese political elite managed in a remarkable way to
weather war, defeat, and Occupation attests to the essential
continuity of Japanese political life.

A full decade separated the 1955 general elections from the
surrender; yet in the Democratic party, which won a plurality,
only 34.4 per cent of the successful candidates had begun their
political careers during the Occupation period, all the rest having
had pre-war experience. The ratio of newcomers in the Liberal
party, however, was much higher, for some 61.6 per cent of the
successful Liberal party candidates had entered national politics

[6] New York, 1954, p. 108.

in the post-war period.[7] The figures for the Socialist party, which has for the first time in Japanese political history secured enough of a following to pose a threat to the monopoly of power long enjoyed by the conservative parties, are illuminating. Of those who ran for office under the Socialist party banner, about one-half of the Right-Wing Socialists, and one-sixth of the Left-Wing Socialists had participated in pre-war politics. In his study of Japanese Socialist leadership, George Totten says: "When one considers, for example, the dozen or so top leaders in each wing, the proportion of prewar leaders is striking: only one of the Right Wing was not a party functionary before the war, while only one-fourth of the Left were not. The observation that even today's Japanese Socialist leadership stems largely from the prewar generation is borne out by the fact that 70 percent of the Right and 45 percent of the Left are over fifty years old, and of the dozen top-rank Right Wing leaders, all except Sone are close to or over sixty."[8]

Thus except for the Left-Wing Socialists who have developed younger leaders, Japanese political parties are faced with a serious problem of recruiting new and energetic leaders. Since the future of party government hinges on the quality of leadership, this is a matter which is worth considering further. It would appear that the problem is in part related to the channels of leader recruitment.

For the conservative parties there are four major roads to party leadership:

(1) The Bureaucracy: Before the war when parties were weak, career civil servants were able to become cabinet members; but under the new Constitution the majority of cabinet members must be drawn from the National Diet. Ambitious bureaucrats who wish to get to the top, therefore, must leave the

[7] Kenneth Colton, "Conservative Leadership in Japan," *Far Eastern Survey*, XXIV (June, 1955), pp. 92–3.

[8] George Totten, "Problems of Japanese Socialist Leadership," *Pacific Affairs*, XXVIII (June, 1955), pp. 160–1.

bureaucracy and carve out a niche for themselves in a party hierarchy. Partly because of its long tenure in office, the old Liberal party had the largest representation of bureaucrats; in 1949 almost one out of every five Liberal party members in the House of Representatives had a bureaucratic background.[9] If the parties become more stabilized, and if any one party manages to stay in power for an extended period, that party will very likely attract to it an increasing number of bureaucrats. After all not many bureaucrats are going to make the jump from a secure civil service position into the maelstrom of party politics unless they feel that the future of parties affords some promise.

(2) Business: One of the striking changes that has occurred in the composition of the Diet during the last 50 years is the decline of landowners and their gradual replacement by businessmen and people in the professions. Most of the businessmen in the post-war Diets have been drawn from the small and medium-sized enterprises and from the middle ranks of big business.[10] Those who can draw income from their business enterprises have an advantage in that it generally takes money to win an election, and once in office, entertainment costs and other outlays can easily exceed the salary received.

(3) The Professions: There are more lawyers and journalists holding seats in the Diet than there are university teachers, doctors, and dentists. Lawyers and law-making form a natural combination. Moreover, lawyers are in a happy position of being able to maintain a law office while holding a post in the Diet. Journalism and writing enable individuals to become known, and some can capitalize on this to get into politics.

(4) Local Politics: An increasing number of men are coming to the National Diet with previous experience and training in local politics. Today the Diet contains men who have served as governors of prefectures, mayors of cities and towns, members of

[9] Oka Yoshisato in *Sengo Nihon no seiji katei*, p. 36.
[10] Colton, *op. cit.*, p. 95.

prefectural assemblies, and members of city and town councils. Local politics holds promise of becoming one of the important channels of advancement into party leadership.

The Socialists also recruit leaders through the above mentioned channels, although the proportion of bureaucrats and businessmen is much smaller than that of the conservative parties. Indeed, one of the serious obstacles to further expansion of the Socialist party is the inability of the socialist movement to attract to it, in sufficiently large numbers, men who have influence and standing in their communities. The big difference between the conservatives and the Socialists, especially the Left-Wing Socialists, is the position of labor union officials. A number of labor leaders are getting into national politics through the socialist party.

Speaking of conservative leadership, Kenneth Colton makes the point that recruitment of new leaders is more difficult now than before the war because youth is more attracted to socialism, the length of Diet sessions makes it difficult to combine politics with some other career, and the channels of recruitment tend to postpone the age at which an individual can embark on a political career.[11] Undoubtedly, these are all factors; but one wonders whether there are not more basic causes impeding leadership recruitment.

Highly competitive societies face the problem of choosing and elevating individuals to leadership positions in such a way as to keep bickering and group tensions to a tolerable level. Competition is never unbridled, for if it were the group would soon be torn asunder. There are always explicit or implicit "rules of the game" which regulate competitive situations. One device sometimes used before the war was to reserve certain positions for members of the Imperial house, or for men from aristocratic families, thereby removing such positions from the reach of commoners. This, of course, was no permanent solution since

[11] Colton, *op. cit.,* p. 96.

such aristocrats almost never made the decisions, power being in fact held by others who worked behind the scenes. The struggle for power for the top post was thus eliminated, but not for posts in the next level.

A device commonly used in many cultures to reduce jealousy and group dissension is to choose leaders on the basis of seniority. Age as a criterion for selecting leaders has the advantage of being unambiguous, and since everyone grows old, the young who are left out of the selection are generally willing to wait their turn. The Japanese are often able to reduce group tension by allocating leadership positions to the aged.

Perhaps the most fundamental reason that new leadership has not emerged is the factionalism which permeates Japanese parties. It is no exaggeration to say that Japanese parties are in effect working coalitions of a number of political leaders, each with his following. By the judicious distribution of party posts and committee chairmanships, cabinet posts (when the party is in power), and material rewards, several factions can be kept together under one party banner. When there is a conflict of personalities or political principles, one or more factions may break off and join another party or several factions may come together and form a new party. The relationship between the leader and his followers may not be as solid as the Rock of Gibralter, but neither is it something that is fleeting and casual. The free lancer, the man unaffiliated with some faction, is not likely to get very far within the party, and so the pressure will be on him to join one faction or another. And it will probably require a long time after he first joins a faction for him to work into a position of prominence within it. If the personal relationships within a party were more fluid and if there were, as a consequence, more "free lancers," a newcomer would have much more chance to rise to the top quickly. The existence of factions and their structure tend to impede the development of new leadership.

A somewhat exceptional situation exists at present with respect to the left wing of the Socialist party. The left wing clearly has younger members and younger leaders.[12] The answer may be that many Left-Wing Socialsits have come to the party via trade unions; and since it was only in the post-war period that trade unions developed on a fairly large scale, the situation is more fluid, permitting younger men to come to the fore. It will probably turn out that as the union movement becomes more mature the leadership will become more fixed.

THE SOCIAL BASIS OF PARTIES

Parties and Social Classes

If parties are to enjoy stability and continuity they must have some meaningful relationship to social classes and groups; otherwise parties would be nothing more than coteries of individuals which would most likely come together and break up in a bewildering fashion. As has been suggested in the preceding pages, the personal element looms large in Japanese parties; yet it would be a mistake to conclude therefrom that Japanese parties are completely divorced from social groupings.

On the basis of public opinion polls and other data, we can get some idea of the social basis of Japanese political parties. The results of a survey made by the newspaper *Asahi* in the spring of 1950 may be summarized as shown in the table on page 179.

The conservative parties draw support from various occupational groups, with somewhat stronger support coming from businessmen and farmers. The left-wing parties, on the other hand, are preferred by members of the working class, and get substantially less support from the business community and from farmers and fishermen. It is interesting to note, however, that in the 1955 elections a number of labor union leaders ran under the Left-Wing Socialist banner in rural areas and managed to get

[12] Totten shows the differences in age between the left wing and the right wing in his article, p. 161 (footnote).

Party Support, by Occupational Status

PARTY	AVER-AGE	UNION WORKER	NON-UNION WORKER	SMALL & MEDIUM BUSINESS-MEN	FISHER-MEN, FARMERS	OTHER
Liberal	32.3%	32%	32%	41%	32%	29%
Democratic	6.0	5	4	7	7	6
Socialist	16.1	37	26	14	12	12
Communist	1.5	2	4	2	1	1
Peoples' Cooperative	0.7	0	1	0	1	0
Farmer-labor	0.5	1	0	0	1	1
Minor	0.8	0	1	0	1	0
No party preference	9.1	14	11	11	7	11
Don't know	33.0	9	21	25	39	40

Source: *Asahi shimbun*, April 23, 1950.

elected. In general rural areas are conservative, but in this instance it appears that many younger sons from farm families who had gone to the cities to work were able to influence the voting behavior of their kin who had remained in the countryside.[13]

More recent polls by *Asahi* show that roughly 40 to 50 per cent of salaried employees and 40 to 45 per cent of industrial workers support the Socialist party, while a third to a little over one half of those in commerce and industry, and in agriculture, forestry and fishing prefer the Liberal party.[14] These figures suggest that the conservative parties are regarded more as national parties in contrast to the Socialist party, which is basically a class

[13] Hirose Ken'ichi, *Saha Shakaito no jittai* (On the Left-wing Socialist party) (Tokyo, 1955), p. 84.
[14] *Asahi shimbun*, December 11, 1954.

party. The Socialists face a serious dilemma in that the more militant they become the more support they are likely to get from the class-conscious portions of the electorate; but at the same time they will frighten away the propertied classes with a stake in the capitalist order.

Barring some cataclysmic social and economic changes, the prospects of the Socialists coming to power in the near future appear to be remote. This is because those classes who now support the Socialist cause are still relatively small in number. According to the 1950 census, the total labor force was a little over 35.5 million. Of this labor force, a little over one fourth were "self-employed," and an additional one third were "unpaid family workers." Just under 40 per cent of the labor force were "employees." The structure of Japanese capitalism is such that the proportion of those who work for a wage is still relatively small. The census also shows that about one seventh of the labor force belong to the so-called white-collar occupations, i.e., professional and technical workers, managerial officials, and clerical workers. White-collar workers and unionized workers tend to vote for the Socialist ticket, but since they still represent a minority the Socialists cannot hope to become the leading party unless they are able to win more support than they have in the past from those in agriculture, industry, and commerce.[15]

Some interesting calculations have been made by projecting recent voting trends into the future. It is a well-known fact that in Japan those who have just reached voting age tend to cast their ballot for Socialist and other left-wing candidates, while the older age groups tend to favor the conservatives. At present about 1,700,000 individuals acquire the right to vote every year. This is offset by annual deaths which come to about 700,000, leaving a net increase in the electorate of about one million. Clearly the mathematics favor the Socialists since they are securing new supporters

[15] Statistics from *Japan Statistical Yearbook*, 1953 edition, published by the Bureau of Statistics, Office of the Prime Minister.

while the conservatives are losing their supporters through death. The net Socialist increase, however, will be reduced by the shift of voters from the socialist to the conservative side as they grow older. A rough calculation of the relative annual change in number of votes is as follows:

	DECREASE	INCREASE	NET INCREASE
Conservatives	600,000 (death)	900,000 (shift)	300,000
Radicals	900,000 (shift)	1,700,000 (new)	800,000

According to these calculations, the left-wing will get about 500,-000 a year stronger. In the 1955 elections, the conservatives enjoyed a margin of some eleven million; hence if the present trend continues (and long-range projections are not always accurate) the conservative and Socialist forces will become equally balanced in about twenty years.[16] These projections, however, leave out one important variable, namely the effect of education. Formal education seems to make individuals incline toward Socialism; and since the educational level of the nation is rising, the Socialists will be able to benefit from this and will probably gain supporters at a faster rate than is indicated here.

PARTIES AND LEGISLATION

The Legislative Process

The prime function of a party is to get its leaders into office; once it gets control of the government by achieving victory at the polls, a party is in a position to carry out a legislative program embodying at least a part of its campaign promises.

The new Constitution declares that the Diet "shall be the highest organ of state power, and shall be the sole law-making organ." Laws enacted by the Diet may originate from several

[16] *"Aru keisu-jo no ketsuron"* (A certain statistical conclusion), *Shakai undo tsushin* (Report on social movements), no. 448 (February 23, 1955), pp. 1–2.

sources. Individual Diet members, Diet committees, policy research committees of the parties, and the Cabinet can introduce bills for consideration by the Diet.

When an individual member wishes to introduce a bill, in drawing up the measure he may seek the assistance of the legislative reference service of the National Diet Library and of other specialists provided for the purpose. But before he can submit it to the Diet, the bill must have the approval of 20 or more members in the lower house and of 10 or more members in the upper house. In case the bill calls for the appropriation of funds, the number is increased to 50 and 20 respectively.

When a bill is submitted, the Speaker of the House of Representatives assigns it to the appropriate standing committee. On bills of general interest, and on those which require appropriations, the committee will hold public hearings at which interested individuals and representatives of organizations may appear to present their views on the bill in question. Individual committee members are empowered to offer amendments. If the bill is approved by the majority of committee members, it can then go before the plenary session of the House of Representatives. If it gets a majority vote in the House of Representatives, it goes before the House of Councillors. The proportion of member-sponsored legislation is small. During the first to the tenth Diet sessions, 1,276 laws were enacted, of which 218 or 17 per cent were sponsored by Diet members. Recently the number of bills ostensibly introduced by members has increased; but in many instances these are actually government bills introduced by an individual member at the request of some government agency.[17]

The great majority of legislative measures are those that concern the operations of government agencies. A section or a bureau in one of the ministries will draft a bill; and it will be

[17] Yoshimura Tadashi, *"Giin rippo no kompon mondai"* (The basic problem of member-sponsored legislation), *Senkyo* (Elections), V (October, 1952), p. 1; see also Hattie Kawahara Colton, "The Working of the Japanese Diet," *Pacific Affairs*, XXVIII (December, 1955), pp. 363–72.

discussed at lower levels and eventually in ministry conferences. If the bill has the backing of the Ministry it will be presented to the Cabinet. Many important proposals are submitted to advisory committees for advice. Sometimes advisory committees may be asked to draw up the detailed provisions of the proposed measure. The membership of these committees consists of scholars, government officials, and representatives of various groups. Before the war, Diet members also served on advisory committees, but this has more or less ceased in the post-war period.[18]

At the beginning of each Diet session the Cabinet compiles a list of bills which each ministry wants to get approved. If a bill has been carefully drawn up, and if there is no strong opposition from other government agencies, it will usually stay on the list and be introduced in the lower house. Occasionally if a bill is dropped from the list, it may turn up later as a bill sponsored by a Diet member.

Bills sponsored by the Cabinet fall into two broad categories. First, there are bills intended to carry out party policy, or to carry out administrative action of some bureau or agency. The latter type is numerically most important. Second, there are bills for adjusting or modifying existing laws.[19]

Because many legislative proposals originate with the bureaucracy, some Japanese observers are inclined to minimize the role of parties. Since bureaucrats generally have more information and are more expert in these matters than party men, it is natural that they should exercise a good deal of initiative. But to conclude from this that parties exercise little influence on legislation is to overlook several salient points. Parties, in the first place, can exercise veto power; proposals coming from the agencies which go against party policy are likely to be pigeon-holed. For example, in the spring of 1955 the Ministry of Education was

[18] Sato Tatsuo, *"Horitsu ga umareru made"* (Until laws are made), *Horitsu jiho* (Law review), XXV (January, 1953), p. 45.

[19] Hayashi Shunzo, *"Rippo no doki oyobi kore ni kansuru jakkan no mondai ni tsuite"* (Motivation for legislation and several problems related to it), *Jiyurisuto* (Jurist), no. 35 (June, 1953), pp. 6 ff.

considering changes in the system of selecting textbooks for use in the schools. Prominent officials of the Ministry of Education were called before the Policy Research Committee of the Democratic party to explain the proposed changes; and if the party refused to go along the changes could not be made.[20]

Second, government agencies are likely to tailor their legislative proposals to what they believe is party policy. If the party in power indicates that it favors legislation advantageous to farmers, the Ministry of Agriculture will most certainly come up with a number of proposals. Third, the political parties can encourage government agencies to draft bills which they (the parties) want, and in this way shape the legislative program. Hence while it may be true that the actual drafting of legislation is often in the hands of bureaucrats, the parties are not mere bystanders in legislation. Certainly, the parties exercise decisive influence in determining the fate of bills. "Basic is the fact," writes Justin Williams, who was in charge of legislative matters in SCAP, "that political parties manage the Diet: every action is a party action, every vote a party vote, every decision a party decision. The individual member stands for nothing. Bills and resolutions, motions of any kind, speeches, interpellations, filibustering, even heckling and rowdyism, in committee and House sessions—all are products of political parties." [21]

Voting in the House of Representatives runs strictly along party lines. The decision to vote one way or another on a bill or resolution is arrived at in a party caucus, usually held in the caucus rooms in the Diet building. "Although major issues," says Williams, "are oftener than not resolved by the executive directors alone, rank-and-file members in caucus are privileged to express themselves as freely, as often, and as vehemently as they like; but once the party is committed, all members without exception either accept the verdict, resign, or are expelled." [22]

[20] See *Asahi shimbun*, March 17, 1955.
[21] "Party Politics in the New Japanese Diet," *The American Political Science Review*, XLII (December, 1948), p. 1163.
[22] *Ibid.*, p. 1165.

Although it is true, as has been suggested earlier and as Williams points out, that party policies tend to be set by a small number of leaders, the rank-and-file members are not entirely without power. Japanese party leaders, like leaders everywhere, could not consistently go against the needs and wishes of the rank and file and expect to remain in power for long. It is in the nature of leadership that the relationship between leaders and followers be a reciprocal one, albeit unequal.

One way in which individual Diet members can try to get more voice in party decisions is to organize semi-formal groups within the Diet. Freshmen Diet members of a party, for instance, will often form freshmen clubs and meet fairly regularly to exchange views. Because in the Japanese party system unanimous support of the party decision on legislation is required, cross-voting cannot occur. A Japanese political scientist believes, however, that a kind of substitute for cross-voting has been developed in the form of associations of Diet members which cut across party lines.[23] A recent example of this kind is the "Dietmen's League for the Promotion of Trade with Red China." The League worked actively, together with business groups and organizations interested in promoting closer relations with Communist China, in negotiations with a Chinese trade delegation which visited Japan in the spring of 1955. That the League contained members of left-wing parties is understandable, since the left-wing parties have favored closer relations with Communist China; but it also included some Diet members from conservative parties whose official policy has been to avoid rapprochement with Red China.

Parties and Interest Groups

It is inherent in the nature of parties that there should develop special relationships between them and interest groups of one sort or another. To stay in business, parties need funds and votes; and for understandable reasons parties will pay special

---

[23] This was brought to the attention of the author by Professor Kyogoku Jun'ichi of Tokyo University in private conversations.

heed to the needs and demands of individuals and organizations which provide these two necessities.

Roughly speaking, the relationships between political parties and interest groups fall into two categories. There are certain types of problems which require legislation; and in order to get legislation enacted interest groups must bring pressure to bear on the party as a whole, or at least on its principal leaders. A recent example of activity of this kind is the movement on the part of ex-army and navy officers to get pensions, which had been abolished by the Occupation authorities, reinstated. In April, 1952 a group for the restoration of pensions was formed in Tokyo, and this group provided the basis for a national organization known as the "National Liaison Association for the Restoration of Pensions for ex-Officers" (*Kyu gunjin kankei onkyu fukkatsu zenkoku renraku kai*). The group held a meeting in Tokyo in September, 1952, which was attended by representatives from various localities. The group put pressure on the Liberal party, which was sympathetic to the idea of restoring pensions, probably—as the Socialists have charged—to facilitate rearmament. The Liberal party presented a bill restoring pensions, but the Diet was dissolved before it passed. When the Liberal party won the 1953 elections which followed the dissolution of the Diet, *Akebono* (Dawn), a magazine for ex-officers, made the following statement:

> The Liberal party which belongs to the conservative camp secured a strong position as a result of the elections, and we believe that its policies follow the lines we advocate. But until the results we wish are attained, we cannot relax our efforts. The "National Liaison Association for the Restoration of Pensions for ex-Officers" will strengthen its propaganda and educational activities with the objective of changing public opinion which is hostile to the restoration of pensions, and will lead a national movement for the purpose.[24]

Incidentally, an amendment to the pension law was passed in 1953, thereby restoring pensions to ex-officers.

[24] *Akebono,* II (June, 1953), pp. 53–4.

The second type of relationship between parties and interest groups involves individuals, business firms, and local government groups. It attests to the power of the parties that the number of individuals and delegations appealing to the parties for assistance has increased substantially. Sometimes as many as 4,000 persons appear in one day at the House of Representatives to request interviews with Diet members, and the number of written requests submitted to the House of Representatives is said to be more than ten times what it was before the war.[25]

The purposes of these visits and written requests vary; but one important objective is to seek the assistance of party members in approaching government agencies. Those who want special favors, such as the issuance of permits and licenses, the granting of funds, etc., from the government (which means in practice one of the ministries or agencies) find it helpful to use Diet members as intermediaries. A delegation which appears before a government bureau accompanied by a Diet member has a better chance of getting a hearing, for if such a delegation were abruptly turned away the Diet member would "lose face." Moreover, the establishment of 20-odd standing committees in the House of Representatives in the post-war period has served to strengthen the ties between Diet members and the ministries. The standing committees more or less parallel the ministries, that is, the foreign affairs committee corresponds to the foreign office, and so on, with the result that each ministry has acquired a kind of spokesman in the lower house. And by the same token, committees and committee members are in a position to get special treatment from ministries. Indeed, one of the important functions of Japanese political parties is to serve as a kind of link between the interest groups and the bureaucracy.[26]

Pressure groups and pressure group tactics appear to be

[25] See *Asahi shimbun,* June 20, 1953, for articles on interest group activities.

[26] Kyogoku Jun'ichi, *"Gendai Nihon ni okeru seiji-teki kodo-yoshiki"* (3) (Political behavior in modern Japan), *Shiso,* no. 342, (December, 1952), p. 82.

permanent fixtures of modern politics in Japan; yet they are often decried. The newspaper *Asahi,* for example, urged control of pressure group tactics in an article on December 15, 1954:

> We cannot make a blanket statement that lobbying activities (chinjo) are bad since they serve to reflect the popular will in politics. But the recent excesses in lobbying are too much. A conspicuous sight are local officials and members of prefectural, town, and village assemblies coming to Tokyo at government expense to plead before government agencies. Their presence affects efficiency in government offices and becomes the source of corruption. It also forces Diet members to neglect their main function, by making it necessary for them to act as intermediaries. . . . What we desire of the new [Hatoyama] cabinet which makes "clean politics" its watchword is to require that requests be submitted in writing and forbid people from directly approaching government agencies.

It is doubtful that any effective way can be found to prevent interest groups from applying pressure to get what they want so long as government is in a position to give subsidies, afford tax relief, grant licenses, etc. The public interest will usually come out second best, unless (1) there is an alert and militant public which urges its own interests, or (2) competing interest groups cancel each other out. It would seem that Japanese political parties, as presently organized, impede the latter situation from developing. The interests of capital and property tend to be served by the conservative parties, while labor and the propertyless tend to seek left-wing parties as their champions. Thus the parties cannot effectively serve as an instrument for bringing about accommodation between groups and classes.

Chapter 10

The Electorate and Electoral Behavior

The idea that legislators and other high officials should be chosen by the electorate, composed of the adult portion of the population, is to us a commonplace, having become a basic premise of the American political tradition. The American experience, however, should not blind us to the fact that in many parts of the world, this idea was for a long time considered revolutionary, and it was accepted with great reluctance if not with fear. The evolution of Japanese thinking on this subject provides an illustration of this thesis.

EXPANSION OF THE ELECTORATE

The first election law, adopted in 1889, governing the election of members of the House of Representatives, rested on the principle of a highly restricted electorate. The ballot was limited to men 25 years of age and over who paid 15 yen in direct national taxes, either in the form of a land tax or income tax. A further qualification was made in the provision that the land tax should be paid for a period of at least one year, and income taxes for at least three years. Finally, the voter was required to have resided in the electoral district for a year or more. A practical consequence of these restrictions was to limit the electorate to the larger landowners, a few businessmen, and high officials, and to exclude intellectuals and a large section of the urban population.

It was not long before the socialists began to agitate for a radical expansion of the electorate. The Manifesto of the short-lived Social Democratic party organized in 1901 argued that the party could achieve its aims once it gained a majority in the Diet, then, in its view, an organ of the "landlords and capitalists." "Once the right to vote passes into the hands of the majority of the people, the most important obstacle to attaining the interest of the majority will be overcome." The following year, the League for Universal Manhood Suffrage (*Futsu senkyo domei kai*) was formed under the auspices of the socialists.

In 1900 the tax qualification was reduced from 15 yen to 10 yen, thereby increasing the number of men with the right to vote from 453,474 to 501,459. It is doubtful that this step had anything to do with agitation from the left; rather its motivation lay in more practical considerations. In the beginning the suffrage had been limited to landowners and other taxpayers on the theory that they were the pillars of conservatism and hence would not upset the political status quo. But the domination of the landed interest in the legislature also had its disadvantage in that the Diet was relatively unsympathetic to legislation intended to stimulate industrial development, especially when such development might take place at the expense of agriculture. The expansion of the electorate in 1900, therefore, came largely as a result of pressure from the urban districts and from commercial and industrial interests.

Three years later, in 1903, a bill calling for universal manhood suffrage was introduced in the Diet but failed to pass. Another bill was approved by the lower house in 1911, but this was rejected by the House of Peers. During the debate in the House of Peers, a spokesman for the government argued against the bill in the following terms:

The government wishes to indicate that it is absolutely opposed to the present bill. . . . The ideal of universal suffrage grew out of the theory of natural rights which was in vogue in Europe at one time. I believe that it is based on the very faulty and dangerous view that all people are born with the right to vote. At the present time this theory no longer has influence, and it goes without saying that people are not born with such rights. It is a gift which the state bestows. . . . If such a system is adopted, the knowledge [possessed by] the voters may decline, but it will never rise, and so I believe that it will have unfavorable results in selecting representatives of the people. We fear that in the end the majority of lower class people will override the minority of upper class people, and hence the government is absolutely opposed to this bill.[1]

The next expansion of the electorate came in 1919 when the tax qualification was again reduced, this time from 10 yen to 3 yen, thereby giving the vote to small landowners. But the tax qualification, small as it was, served to exclude the urban proletariat and some intellectuals in urban areas. Despite the reduction in the tax qualification, sentiment in favor of universal manhood suffrage remained strong, fanned by the worldwide spread of Wilsonian ideals. Despite the fact that even Hara Kei, the first commoner to become premier, remained hostile to the expansion of the electorate on the ground that such expansion would destroy the class system which was the basis of stability, the proponents of universal suffrage—intellectuals, the big city press, and the left generally—eventually won the day after a spirited campaign. In 1925 the universal manhood suffrage act was passed, taking effect in the 1928 national elections. As is well known, the next large extension of the electorate occurred in the post-war period, when, as a result of Occupation pressure, women were

[1] Quoted in Suzuki Yasuzo, *Nihon seiji no kijun* (The basis of Japanese politics) (Tokyo, 1941), pp. 175–6.

granted the right to vote for the first time. The following table provides a summary of the increases in the size of the electorate:

Increase in the Size of the Electorate, 1912–47

YEAR	QUALIFIED VOTERS	VOTERS PER 1,000 POPULATION	VOTERS PER 1 REPRESENTATIVE
1912	1,503,650	29.2	3,947
1915	1,546,341	28.8	4,059
1917	1,422,118	25.7	3,733
1920	3,069,787	46.3	6,616
1924	3,288,368	55.6	7,087
1928	12,409,078	199.7	26,629
1930	12,813,192	198.8	27,496
1932	13,095,621	200.3	28,102
1936	14,303,780	206.5	30,695
1947	40,907,493	520.3	87,784

Source: *Japan Statistical Yearbook*, 1949 edition.

Today Japan enjoys universal suffrage; yet it is evident that neither the hopes of the early socialists nor the fears of the conservatives have materialized. Undoubtedly the alteration of voting procedures has modified the mode of politics and the ways in which power is gained and exercised; nevertheless, it has not, by any stretch of the imagination, revolutionized Japanese politics. Voting as an idea appeared to have revolutionary implications; yet in practice it did not lead to a fundamental change in the social order. This was because, as we shall see, it was to a considerable degree incorporated into the existing political system.

ELECTORAL BEHAVIOR

Japanese journalists and scholars often speak of the three "ban" in connection with elections. In their view, elections are governed by *kamban* or signboard, *jiban* or foundation, and *kaban* or satchel. The three *ban* by no means account for all of the complex factors that are associated with voting but they do serve to highlight the more striking features of electoral behavior in Japan.

Kamban

Kamban, literally signboard, poster, billboard, etc., refers to the candidate's reputation and standing in the community. Those who run for office, particularly in local elections, are expected to be men of some prominence or achievement. One man may have a local reputation for physical strength and stamina, another for ability in accounting, and still another for skill in negotiation. When individuals who have a reputation aspire for elective office, they are likely to get votes without the benefit of too much active campaigning. Robert Ward reports that "Various campaign techniques, perhaps appropriate in the individualistically organized societies of the West, are not approved in the family-centered and cohesive communities of rural Japan." "The writer," he continues, "knows of one case in which a villager, most anxious for office, confined his entire public campaign— aside from a few discreet contacts with relatives in other *buraku* —to the utterance at a meeting of his own *buraku* assembly of a single sentence: "Kondo tatte imasu kara, do ka yoroshiku onegai shimasu (Since I am standing [for election] this time, please do what you can)." [2] Undoubtedly, the candidate in this instance had standing in his village, for if he had run for office without it, he would have been a laughing stock of the community.

Much the same thing can be said for national elections, particularly for members of the House of Councillors representing the nation at large. There has been a tendency in recent years

[2] Robert Ward, "The Socio-political Role of the *Buraku* (hamlet) in Japan," *American Political Science Review,* XLV (December, 1951), p. 1035.

for two types of candidates to get elected to the upper house: men who had been prominent in the pre-war period, for example, former Admiral Nomura Kichisaburo and General Ugaki Kazushige, and leaders of labor unions organized on a nation-wide scale. In these cases, *kamban* rather than issues, political ideology, or party affiliation, is the important consideration.

If a candidate feels that his *kamban* is not big enough to attract votes he sometimes tries to increase its size, as it were, by getting prominent leaders to make speeches on his behalf in his district. But a veteran campaigner has warned that nowadays the masses are intelligent enough to be able to compare the *kamban* with the candidate's real ability, and are not easily fooled. The same politician notes that before the war, an individual who had headed a ministry (and therefore had *kamban*) was almost certain to get elected if he ran for office, but today this is no longer the case.[3]

We can, on the basis of fragmentary data, make a crude estimate of the extent to which candidates get votes because of their personal qualifications. In a survey made just before the 1949 national elections in an industrialized section of Tokyo, voters were asked to indicate whether they voted for a candidate or for a political party. The results can be seen in the following table:

Basis for Voting: Candidate vs. Party

AGE OF VOTER	CANDIDATE	PARTY	BOTH CANDIDATE AND PARTY	DON'T KNOW	OTHER	TOTAL
20–24	22% (33%)*	30% (41%)	25% (21%)	23% (5%)	(0)	100%
25–29	25 (33)	31 (47)	2 (20)	11 (0)	(0)	100
30–39	33 (39)	39 (40)	21 (19)	7 (1)	(1)	100
40–49	52 (34)	17 (42)	20 (21)	11 (3)	(0)	100
50–	48 (37)	15 (33)	20 (9)	17 (12)	(10)	100

* The figure in ( ) shows percentage for workers as distinguished from the population at large.
Source: Ukai Nobushige, *"Koba rodosha no tohyo kodo," Sekai*, no. 84 (December, 1952), p. 93.

[3] Tsuji Kan'ichi, *Jingasa* (Rank and file) (Tokyo, 1953), pp. 37–42.

According to these figures, between one fifth and one half of those questioned say they vote for candidates. The general tendency—less marked in the case of workers—is for older age groups to put the emphasis on candidates and disregard party affiliation. It has been suggested that the percentage of workers voting for party affiliation is stable despite age differences because of the existence of left-wing parties which avowedly represent the interests of the proletariat.[4]

Another test of the extent to which individual candidates are able to rely on personal reputation in getting votes is provided by the case of Hirano Rikizo, a member of the Diet from Yamanashi prefecture. Hirano, a veteran in the pre-war socialist movement, ran under the Socialist party banner in 1947 and got 58,916 votes to head the list. He was then purged for his wartime activities, and hence was unable to be a candidate in the 1949 elections. He returned to political life in 1952, when he ran on the Kyodo-to or Cooperative party ticket and won 47,183 votes. Considering that the Cooperative party polled only 1.2 per cent of the vote at the national level, we must conclude that the party label was not an important factor in the Hirano vote. Then in 1953 he ran as a Right-Wing Socialist, getting 40,727 votes. However, he failed to be reelected in the 1955 national elections when he campaigned as a candidate of a minor party and got only 20,794 votes. Hirano's experience shows that a man who is well-known and has a following can change party affiliation and still manage to get reelected. It also shows that votes based on personal following are not always stable. In the years from 1947 to 1953 Hirano got between 40,000 and a little under 60,000 votes, but in 1955 it dropped 50 per cent.

The part played by personal factors may also be seen in the type of electoral behavior which is reminiscent of the "friends and neighbors" effect noted by V. O. Key in his study of southern

[4] Ukai Nobushige, *"Koba rodosha no tohyo kodo"* (Voting behavior of factory workers), *Sekai*, no. 84 (December, 1952), p. 93.

politics. The political vision of many people—especially in the rural areas—suffers from myopia, and such people are intensely interested in local matters but are little concerned with national issues and problems. A voter whose interest is focused on the local scene will vote for a candidate who comes from his area on the theory that such a candidate is likely to best represent local interests. A rather graphic illustration of the "friends and neighbors" effect is afforded by the votes cast for Kuriyama Chojiro, a Liberal party member from the 7th district, a rural section of the Tokyo metropolitan area. Kuriyama is a native of a small village located in Kita-Tamagun. The following table shows the distribution of votes cast for Kuriyama in the eight subdivisions of the 7th district:

Votes Cast for Kuriyama in the 1952 Elections for the House of Representatives

1. Hachioji	2,204
2. Tachikawa	2,155
3. Musashino	5,815
4. Mitaka-shi	4,155
5. Ome-shi	245
6. Nishi-Tamagun	723
7. Minami-Tamagun	5,832
8. Kita-Tamagun	21,218
Total	42,347

As the table shows, Kuriyama got almost one half of his votes in Kita-Tamagun where his home is located.

Thus the evidence suggests that the personal qualifications of the candidate, although not a decisive factor, enter into the picture much more than it probably does in American politics. But the "attraction" exerted by candidates as individuals is not the same for all voters. We have already seen that the older voters are more apt to vote for individual candidates while younger voters prefer to vote for political parties. In terms of occupational status, peasants, fishermen, and owners of small business enterprises tend to vote for individuals, while urban white-collar workers, government officials, teachers, students, and workers are more likely to put the emphasis on party affiliation.[5]

Jiban

Literally meaning base, foundation, or footing, *jiban* is often translated "constituency." A more functional translation might be "organized vote," or "political machine." A candidate who hopes to get returned to office election after election must build himself a *jiban*. There are certain time-honored ways of building a *jiban*, and when they are enumerated, students of American politics will see certain similarities with practices that prevail in the United States.

The first principle is to keep in good standing with prominent people in the electoral district in particular and with the voters in general; and this requires a willingness to attend to minute details. Tsuji Kan'ichi, a legislator from Nagoya, tells in an extremely frank account that he always carries a notebook containing about 400 names of individuals to whom he writes rather frequently. When he attends a gathering in his district, he has a photograph taken, and he tries to remember the names and faces of those present.[6]

There are other effective techniques. A politician must take every opportunity to appear before the public, either in person or vicariously. This means that he must take time out to attend public functions, he must put in an appearance during festivals and he must speak to groups of interested citizens, such as

[5] Nakamura Kikuo, "*Seito, jiban, senkyo*" (Parties, machines and elections), *Nihon seijigakkai nempo* (Annuals of the Japanese political science association), I (1950), pp. 95–6.

[6] Tsuji, *op. cit.*, p. 36.

women's clubs. He must also remember to send wreaths (on which his name is prominently displayed) to funerals of local dignitaries and to send flowers when a local businessman opens a new store.

The legislator who hopes to build a *jiban* must frequently dig into his pocket and make contributions to important local organizations, such as youth groups; and sometimes he must even send Japanese towels (on which his name is printed) to school picnics where they are distributed without charge. A favorite device for legislators from rural areas is to send thousands of picture postcards to voters when they go on trips, especially to foreign countries. As a rule, country folk get little mail, so a postcard from a Diet member is appreciated and remembered a long time. The following account describes the techniques used by Takagi Masutaro, formerly a representative from Tokyo:

> This man [Takagi] was very thorough in what he did for elections. During festivals he was the first to present an offering with his name inscribed on it. At school graduations, he distributed cake decorated with his name among students. Naturally he went around making calls during the New Year holiday season; and he always assisted at weddings and funerals. During the Diet sessions he always mounted the rostrum several times. Whenever the interests of the townspeople were involved, he would attend the committee sessions, even if he was not a member of that particular committee; and he would have a transcript of the meetings distributed among the voters.[7]

Another principle in building a *jiban* is to be the "servant of the people." Since many people vote for a legislator in hopes that he will bring benefits to the district, it is up to him to see that such voters are not disappointed. Any politician who hopes

[7] Washio Yoshinao (ed.), *Seikai gojunen, Kojima Kazuo kaiko-roku* (Fifty years in the political world: the memoirs of Kojima Kazuo) (Tokyo, 1951), p. 248.

to win elections must use his influence to get roads repaired and bridges built.

Legislators and others who hold elective office must also be willing and able to undertake a multitude of chores for their constituents. When the Diet is in session, numerous delegations of rural inhabitants and local bigwigs visit it. Many Diet members make it a point to take such delegations from their districts to lunch, buy them souvenirs in the several souvenir shops located in the Diet building, and even arrange sightseeing buses for tours in the Tokyo area. Sometimes politicians are expected to go beyond mere entertainment; they may be asked by a prominent constituent to find a job for some bright and deserving young man who lives in the district. Another important chore is to provide liaison between the citizens and government agencies. A taxpayer in trouble with the tax bureau will probably appeal to a Diet member to talk to the tax authorities; a businessman seeking an export permit might ask a legislator to put pressure on the Ministry of Trade and Industry to expedite matters. All of these chores are time consuming, but they often pay off at election time.

But no matter how active or conscientious a politician is in looking after the welfare of his constituents, he can come into direct contact with but a small fraction of the voters. He must therefore get at voters indirectly, in other words build an organization that will get out the vote for him when the time comes. A common way for a member of the House of Representatives to create such an organization is to acquire, through personal or financial ties, several followers who are active and influential in prefectural politics. Such followers are often found among members of the prefectural legislatures. The prefectural leaders, in turn, will have their own followers, usually at the city, town, and *gun* (county) level; and the latter may reach down into the village and ward levels. Officials of local groups and organizations, such as cooperatives, women's organizations, tradesmen's organizations and the like, are often important cogs in political machines of this kind. There will thus be a pyramid with a number of local politicians or "bosses" at the base and a member of the National Diet at the peak. Incidentally, two or more organizations may be interlocking at times.

Historical experience shows that once a *jiban* is built it possesses elements of stability because those who are in the organization enjoy benefits tangible and intangible. "It was the newcomer in politics," says Paul Dull, "who faced difficulties when he tried to construct a *jiban* without preliminary work in the organization. Inukai Tsuyoshi, who became president of the *Seiyukai* and premier, 1931–32, had the most effective *jiban* in Okayama prefecture. It was referred to as his 'iron constituency.' So loyal were the elements in his *jiban* that Inukai achieved a national reputation for spending less on an election than any other Japanese politician."[8]

Kaban

The third "ban" is *kaban* or satchel, signifying money spent on elections. Almost everywhere elections cost money, and Japan is no exception. To be sure, limits are placed by law upon the amount candidates are allowed to spend during an election campaign. The amount permitted is determined by dividing the number of registered voters by the number of representatives, and multiplying by 4 yen. But it would be naïve indeed to believe that anybody takes such legal limits very seriously. One legislator asserts that five or six times the legal limit should be enough.[9] By the very nature of things, it is difficult, if not impossible, to get accurate figures on amounts actually spent. A popular saying goes to the effect that a candidate who spends five million yen loses, but one who spends seven million yen wins.

[8] Paul S. Dull, "The *Senkyoya* System in Rural Japanese Communities," *Occasional Papers*, University of Michigan, Center for Japanese studies, IV (1953), pp. 32–3.

[9] Tsuji, *op. cit.*, p. 42.

Political parties and organizations are required to report sums received, and even on the basis of such reports, which by common consent understate the amount, it is evident that parties acquire substantial war chests. In 1953 the Liberal party reported its income to be more than 229 million yen, with 112 individuals and organizations contributing more than one million yen each. The following table gives the breakdown by party for 1953:

Income Reported by Parties, 1953

Liberal	229,260,000
Progressive	108,710,000
Socialist (Right-Wing)	29,270,000
Socialist (Left-Wing)	25,500,000
Farmer-Labor	1,070,000
Green Breeze	5,050,000
Communist	11,050,000

Source: *Asahi shimbun,* March 9, 1953.

As may be guessed, the conservative parties collect their campaign funds from wealthy individuals, mostly businessmen, large corporations, and trade associations, such as the Japan Shipowners' association, the Japan Coal Mine Operators' association, etc. Some business firms contribute to both the conservative parties and the Socialist parties; and some, particularly those interested in developing trade with Communist China, are known to have even contributed to the Japanese Communist party. Although the Socialists get funds from business firms, their chief source of funds is the labor unions, which often assess each union member at election time.

In addition to making contributions to party headquarters, individuals, firms, and unions provide candidates of their choice with funds. Over a thousand candidates ran in the 1955 general elections, and if we assume that each spent several million yen, the total, together with sums spent by the parties, comes to near astronomical figures. No wonder newspapers commented during the 1955 elections that money spent in connection with the election would help alleviate the economic depression which gripped the nation at that time.

How is all this money spent? There are the obvious expenses—the cost of maintaining election headquarters, rental for sound trucks which roam the streets calling out the candidate's name, the printing of posters and leaflets, food and drinks for supporters and friends and the like. Sometimes candidates will actually buy votes, either directly or through the so-called "election brokers." The price paid for one vote is said to range from two or three hundred yen to a thousand yen. Candidates are especially likely to resort to vote-buying when the race appears to be close and every vote counts. After every election, a few people are arrested and charged with buying votes, but probably vote-buying does not occur on a large scale simply because less crude methods are available for controlling the vote.

A substantial portion of the large sums that are spent for elections is absorbed, as it were, by the organization described above. Money is the lubricant which keeps the political machine going. A candidate running for the House of Representatives collects campaign funds from his friends and from the party. He keeps a part of it for his own expenses; the remainder he divides among his followers, usually prefectural leaders. The latter retain a portion of the money and pass it down to their followers who repeat the process. Thus, in the end, the sum originally raised by the candidate trickles down and passes into the hands of many people.

The Determinants of Voting

It can be said that the three "ban" remain prominent features of the political landscape because they work, however imperfectly. And they work, in the last analysis, because the man who goes into the polling booth is often influenced by them. We may, therefore, shift our attention to voters and to what makes them behave as they do.

Tradition is an intangible element, but it is always present, in varying degrees, in political situations. Some American voters will cast their ballot for the Democratic ticket or the Republican ticket merely because their fathers and grandfathers had voted that way. Compared to the United States, attachment to a party label is less strong in Japan; and in keeping with the Japanese mode of politics, loyalty seems to be focussed more on individuals. This is probably the reason a *jiban* can often be transferred from father to son, as it was in the case of Inukai Tsuyoshi to his son, Ken, from a man to his widow, or from a political leader to his chief disciple. Paul Dull quotes a leader in Okayama to the effect that "Inukai Tsuyoshi had done so much for him that he felt a *giri* to him so strong that it must be transferred to Inukai's son, Inukai Ken." [10]

A more rational way for a voter to choose a candidate or a party is on the basis of economic interest. Although the conservative parties do not openly espouse the interests of any one class, it is no secret that they are favorably inclined toward business and landowners. It is therefore not surprising that business executives, owners of business enterprises, bureaucrats, and the larger landowners (and ex-landlords) should tend to vote for the conservative parties. The left-wing parties, on the other hand, avowedly represent the interests of the working class and of the propertyless classes in general; and the question is whether these classes are more likely to vote for radical candidates than for conservative candidates. In a very broad way it seems that the answer is in the affirmative. The chief areas of Socialist strength are the more industrialized urban areas, while the rural sections form the strongholds of conservatism. The relationship between

[10] Paul Dull, *op. cit.*, p. 34.

party support and industry and agriculture may be seen by comparing the accompanying maps.

During the 1949 elections, Professor Royama and his associates tried to get data on the relationship between economic interest and voting behavior by the use of interview techniques. Their findings, presented here in chart form, are in line with what we have been saying about party support and economic interest.

As Chart 3 shows, businessmen quite consistently vote for conservative candidates, while some workers, by no means the majority, tend to vote for left-wing candidates. As might be expected, left-wing parties get more support from employees of large-scale enterprises than they do from those employed in medium and small business firms, where a more paternalistic relationship exists between employers and employees. And since

MAP 1

Prefectures where the agricultural population was 40 per cent or less (1950) are represented by dotted areas.

small enterprises still provide employment for a relatively high proportion of Japanese workers, a large increase in the size of radical party supporters does not seem likely to occur in the foreseeable future.

In addition to those who vote on the basis of tradition, or on the basis of economic interest, there are a substantial number of individuals who are in effect nothing but robots in the voting process. Such individuals, found most frequently in agrarian communities, exercise no independent judgment, but vote according to advice and instructions from others.

Voters in this category may be divided into two types. First, there are those who take a negative attitude toward politics —especially at the national level—and look upon it as something

MAP 2

Prefectures where the combined Right- and Left-wing Socialist vote was 35 per cent or more of the total vote in the 1955 National elections.

which is of little or no concern to them. Their attention is focussed on the well-being of their families and on local problems. Since they have little information about national issues, and little desire to know, they are easily persuaded by a local political leader or boss to vote for this candidate or that. Before an election, a local leader might invite people in for a drink and the

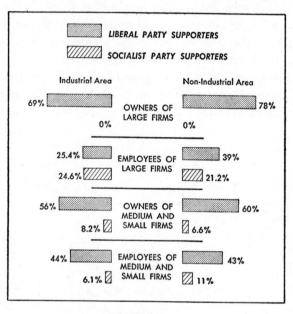

CHART 3

Relationship between party support and economic status.

Based on Royama, *Seiji ishiki no kaibo,* p. 31.

word would be passed around that a certain candidate ought to be supported for one reason or another. In some countries, voters of this kind would probably abstain from going to the polls, looking upon balloting as a chore. In Japan, however, the National Election Commission has conducted campaigns in recent years to reduce non-voting, and local communities have come to take pride in a high turnout. The campaign to get out the vote has been most effective in the rural areas where there is a general reluctance to go against the majority. The result is that the turnout is good, but this does not mean that those who go to the polls are necessarily well informed or have great interest in politics.[11]

The second type of citizen is one who votes as he is told out of fear. Theoretically, a secret ballot should enable everyone to vote as his conscience dictates; but in fact voters in rural areas are often coerced to vote for the office seeker who has made an alliance with some local boss. In the course of a lifetime, many an individual has had to seek assistance and favors from others, and such individuals become easy targets for political manipulators. Many people find that it does not pay to alienate bosses and influential people in the community. If, for example, one were in need of credit at a future date, he might find that no one would be willing to make him a loan.

But it might be asked: what is there to prevent a voter from promising to vote for one candidate but actually voting for another in the privacy of the polling booth? The answer is that there are ways in which political bosses can find out who "double crossed" them. First of all, if a person has been asked to vote for a particular candidate, he will, after he gets out of the polling booth, usually tell the political boss, "I voted for your man" (or words to that effect). But an individual who has voted contrary to instructions finds it difficult, if not impossible, to make such a remark with a straight face. A local leader has been quoted to the effect that when a voter has followed instructions he will usually drop in on the way home from the polls to report the fact, whereas someone who has not followed instructions will avoid him.[12]

Another way of guessing the identity of those voting contrary to instructions is to examine the marked ballots. Voters in

[11] Ariga Kizaemon, *"Senkyo no jittai"* (The reality behind elections), *Shakaigaku hyoron* (Japanese sociological review), I (May, 1951), pp. 71–2.

[12] See article entitled, *"Aru mura de kiku"* (We heard in a certain village), in *Asahi shimbun,* January 6, 1955.

Japan do not put "X" after a candidate's name, but instead they write in the name. Now there are several ways in which a man's name can be written; for instance, it can be written with phonetic symbols (*kana*) or in ideographs. Those who manipulate the vote sometimes instruct voters to write the candidate's name in a certain way—say in phonetic symbols—and later the ballots written that way are counted. Ballots from several hamlets and villages are supposed to be brought together before they are counted, but in practice ballots are often counted in each little locality, making it fairly easy for local bosses to find out how they were marked. If a boss had lined up, say fifty votes, and actually only forty-eight were cast, he can usually by a process of elimination find out who disobeyed him. Thus, in the Japanese social context, it is not easy for a voter to assert his will.

The "Floating Vote"

Politicians, as we have seen, often go to great lengths to line up votes for themselves; yet they will tell you that one cannot tell how an election will go until all the ballots are in and counted. One of the elements which can throw even the best of calculations out of kilter is the so-called "floating vote."

As the name implies, a "floating vote" is one that is not committed to one party or to an individual; and naturally this type of vote is found more frequently in urban areas where individuals can be more anonymous and free from community pressure. In terms of occupation, the "floating vote" is generally associated with white-collar workers, and with intellectuals. The "floating vote" is also more characteristic of youth than of the aged. Younger politicians who have not yet succeeded in building a *jiban*, and newcomers to politics find it to their advantage to run in electoral districts with a heavy "floating vote." Unlike the independent vote in American politics, the "floating vote" often is not motivated by a careful consideration of the issues based on informed thinking. Accordingly, the "floating vote" sometimes goes to a big name, for example, an ex-bureaucrat who decides to give up his career in the civil service and try his hand at politics.

To get the "floating vote" the candidate must make himself known to the electorate. A method used by all politicians is to rent sound trucks which stop at virtually every corner and blare out the candidate's name. The noise level rises appreciably during the weeks preceding an election; but no one knows exactly how effective such tactics are in corralling the vote for a candidate. Another technique used in the big cities is known as "*sakura senjutsu*" (literally cherry blossom tactics—cherry blossom being a euphemism for decoy). Campaign workers are planted in street cars and public baths to spread rumors of the virtues of the candidate in question and the asserted defects of rival candidates.

Voting and the Election System

Institutional arrangements invariably affect the way in which votes are cast, and the distribution of party strength in the legislature. Single member constituencies tend to favor the majority party, while proportional representation encourages the growth of minor parties. The present Japanese electoral system is neither single-member constituency nor proportional representation, but comes somewhere in between.

The country is divided into 118 electoral districts which send 467 representatives to the lower house. Every district, except one, chooses between three and five representatives, with an average of two-and-a-half to three times as many candidates running for office. In order to be elected, a candidate must place among the top three to five, depending upon the size of the district. Each voter, however, writes in the name of only one candidate.

It will be obvious that under this system, a successful candidate needs to have the support of only a minority of the voters in his district. Naturally the number of votes necessary to be included among the top three to five depends upon the number of candidates running and the spread of votes among them. In the 1955 elections, for example, the leading vote getter was Prime Minister Hatoyama Ichiro, who got 149,541 votes (or 27 per cent) in the first district in Tokyo, while Nikaido Susumu, a Liberal party member from the third district in Kagoshima got 24,748 votes (or 12 per cent) to win the dubious distinction of being elected with the least number of votes. There are always several contests in every election where the difference between success and failure is a few hundred votes.

For some reason Japanese voters do not like to "waste" their votes. They are therefore reluctant to vote for a candidate who clearly has no chance to win. By the same token, if they believe that a particular candidate will win by a wide margin, they might shift their vote to someone else. They feel that "he is going to win anyway, so why shouldn't I make my vote count by giving it to another candidate." There have been instances where a Diet member won the largest number of votes in one election, only to fail to make the grade in the next election. Under these circumstances, campaigning becomes a tricky art because the candidate must not give his supporters the impression that his cause is hopeless, and at the same time, he must not appear so confident that the people will think his victory was a foregone conclusion.

Because three to five candidates run in each district, it is essential from the party standpoint that the support it gets be distributed reasonably evenly among its candidates. For instance, if too many candidates are allowed to run, the vote will be spread too thin, with the result that some seats will be lost. A strong vote getter can sometimes be a handicap because he would get too many votes at the expense of his running mates. It is up to skillful campaign managers to try to manipulate the vote to avoid lopsided voting. In the pre-war days, Adachi Kenzo, who held the post of Home Minister in the Hamaguchi cabinet, had quite a reputation for being able to arrange the voting in such a way that it would be most beneficial to the party.

Chapter 11

The Mass Media and Public Opinion

All regimes, even those not dedicated to democratic principles, are sensitive to what the populace is discussing and thinking. An old Japanese saying runs to the effect that heaven has no mouth but it talks through the people. The element of public opinion, therefore, is everywhere present; nevertheless the attitude of the state toward political discussion provides one yardstick for judging whether or not the regime is democratic. Democracies allow relatively wide latitude to the discussion and dissemination of political opinions, even if such opinions are critical of the existing regime.

In the modern period, the mass media presumably play an important role in the moulding of political opinion. It is largely through the mass media that the average citizen learns what his government is doing, or is not doing, what the political opposition is saying, and what leading political organizations are advocating. What influence do the mass media in Japan exert on public opinion; and how does public opinion, in turn, affect the political process?

THE GROWTH OF MASS COMMUNICATIONS
The Press

Journalism in Japan is less than one hundred years old. The first newspaper is said to be the *Kampan Batavia Shimbun*, published by an agency of the Tokugawa government, and devoted largely to translations of material appearing in the foreign press. The first daily newspaper made its appearance in 1870, and in subsequent years many newspapers were founded.

With the establishment of political societies and parties in the 1870's, there appeared a number of papers which were either published by party leaders or by the parties or were closely identified with them. These papers naturally served more as vehicles for the dissemination of political opinions than for the reporting of news, and they contained a good deal of polemical material.

With the passage of years, newspaper enterprises became independent of political parties, and newspapers became "commodities," sold to the public for their news content. Very likely this development was accelerated by the Sino-Japanese War and the Russo-Japanese War, which whetted the appetite of the public for news. The big increase in newspaper circulation, however, came during the World War I period, and ever since then the sale of newspapers has increased steadily. For example, the circulation of *Osaka Mainichi* almost doubled between 1914 and 1919, and nearly tripled between 1919 and 1931 when it reached 2,400,000 copies.

At the present time, Japan ranks among the leading nations of the world in newspaper circulation. It is reported that in 1954, circulation hit the 34 million mark, or one copy per 2.43 individuals. The newspaper business is dominated by three large metropolitan dailies—*Asahi, Osaka Mainichi,* and *Yomiuri.* In 1951 the newsprint quota for the *Asahi* and *Mainichi* was set at just under three and a half million copies, and *Yomiuri* had one and three-fourth million. These three newspapers maintain large staffs, including correspondents in all of the major capitals of the world, and have a nationwide sales network. In addition each paper issues so-called "local editions," making it difficult for local papers to compete.

Compared to American newspapers, the Japanese dailies have fewer pages; for instance, the total number of pages of the morning and evening editions of *Asahi* for a whole month comes to about 375 at most. But the news content of the dailies is substantially similar to that of the American press. They contain international and domestic news, editorials, financial news, local news, news of radio and television programs, sports, feature articles, serialized fiction, and of course advertising.

Politically the large newspapers are "neutral" and do not openly support one political party or another. However, their political sympathies show up in the way they edit the news and in their editorials. By and large, *Yomiuri* and *Mainichi* are sympathetic to the conservatives, while *Asahi* leans towards the socialists.

The Radio

Like the press, the radio has seen remarkable growth since the first radio program was broadcast in 1925. In 1949, more than three fifths of urban families, and a little under one half of farm families had radio sets. Under the Allied Occupation, the broadcasting monopoly enjoyed by the Japan Broadcasting Corporation, a government corporation which, like the BBC, collects monthly fees from subscribers, was broken, and commercial broadcasting was also established. Today, two systems exist side by side; the stations operated by the Japan Broadcasting Corporation carry no advertising and are supported solely by fees collected from radio owners on a compulsory basis, while the commercial stations exist on advertising revenue.

The Japanese radio has felt, for better or worse, the effects of American broadcasting techniques, and there are a number of programs, for example, quiz programs, which were obviously copied from American models. Both the government stations and the commercial stations devote a certain amount of time to news broadcasts and to news commentary. They also schedule educational programs—round-table discussions of current topics, interviews of leading political personalities, as well as street-corner interviews of the "man in the street." When the Diet is in session, portions of the proceedings are broadcast and televised so that the legislators are in a sense performing before a large audience. As a medium for political education, the radio rivals the press.

THE EFFECTS OF MASS COMMUNICATIONS

Mass Communications and Their Audience

The development of the mass media suggests that they serve a useful function. Obviously these media survive because there is sufficient demand to justify their continued existence if not their gradual expansion. It is, however, not too meaningful to know merely that millions of people read the newspapers every day. What we would like to know, for instance, is what kinds of people read newspapers, and what effect this reading has on them.

Surveys of newspaper readers and radio audiences show that somewhere between 65 and 80 per cent of the population come into contact with the mass media every day. In general about one half of the population depend on newspapers for their news. The percentage of people who read newspapers is higher in the cities than in the countryside, where there is a tendency to depend more on radios. Older people and women, moreover, are inclined to depend on the radio as well as on word-of-mouth communication for their news. There is also some relationship between economic status and the purchase of newspapers and magazines in the rural areas. Those with higher incomes tend to be more interested in the mass media, and hence have more opportunities to become informed about political developments in the nation and in the world. It might be noted, in passing, that the mass media are a typically urban phenomena, and therefore are more suitable to urban rather than rural audiences.[1]

The next question is: what kind of news items and radio programs are people interested in? From the point of view of politics, the mass media are not important if it turns out that people read mostly news dealing with crime and listen only to soap operas, ignoring political news items and broadcasts. In a study made in one section of Tokyo, about one half of the men, and between one fourth and one third of the women, said they were interested in political and economic news appearing in the press. The figures were somewhat lower—ten per cent or a little more—in a rural area near Tokyo. There seems to be a positive correlation between the amount of formal education and interest —the more education the more interest in political and economic news. Age appears also to be a factor, with the greatest interest being shown by those in the 25 to 40 age bracket.

The percentage of people who say they are interested in news broadcasts and news commentaries runs somewhat higher than the percentage reportedly interested in political and economic news in the papers. About three fourths of the men and a little more than three fifths of the women questioned on this point in Tokyo replied that they were interested in news and news commentaries. Interest in the rural areas seems to be a little lower, and more so among women than among men; but in general it may be said that the difference between urban and rural audiences in the case of radio broadcasts is less sharp, suggesting that the radio plays a more important role, proportionately speaking, in the countryside. Some observers believe that

[1] *Asahi shimbun,* October 2, 1953; Royama Masamichi, et al., *Sosenkyo no jittai* (Survey of the general election) (Tokyo, 1955), pp. 85, 160.

radio is a more "personal" medium than newspapers and magazines, and hence appeals more to rural folk.[2]

The Effectiveness of Mass Communications

We have shown how the mass media have grown over the
decades and how substantial segments of the public are now exposed to the press, radio and other forms of mass communications. We have shown, moreover, that the political content of the
mass media managed to attract the attention of numerous people. The channels for the diffusion of political information, in
other words, are there for the public to use; and the evidence
suggests that they are indeed used.

It is tempting to proceed from these premises to the conclusion that the mass media therefore exert a powerful influence
on public opinion. As Bernard Berelson says, "by and large" the
mass media do affect public opinion; but "by and large questions
and answers" are not enough. What is needed is more detailed
information which isolates crucial factors and seeks to relate them
to other political phenomena. But when we come to specific
cases, we find ourselves on uncertain ground; and about all we
can do is to make some preliminary and highly tentative observations about the effectiveness of the mass media.

First of all, there is the matter of the actual transmission
of information and ideas. How well, for example, do the newspapers succeed in conveying news to their readers? Since this
is the kind of problem that affects the operations of newspapers,
publishers have given some thought to it. In the fall of 1953, for
instance, *Asahi* asked some of its readers to identify certain news
items then being prominently featured in the daily press. The
results are shown in the following table.

[2] Royama, *op. cit.*, pp. 88, 160; *Masu komunikashion koza* (Lectures
on mass communications), ed. by Shimizu Ikutaro (Tokyo, 1955), I, p. 200.

Readers' Knowledge of News Items

	PER CENT ABLE TO IDENTIFY	PER CENT UNABLE TO IDENTIFY
Crown Prince's trip abroad	93	7
The Rhee Line	64	36
MSA Aid to Japan	59	41

Source: *Asahi shimbun*, October 2, 1953.

Another test of reader information was undertaken by *Asahi* shortly after the outbreak of disorder in the Diet in the summer of 1954. Of those questioned, 75 per cent said they knew about the disorder (which, incidentally, was widely reported in the press, broadcast over the radio, and shown on newsreels); but when they were questioned in detail, 53 per cent revealed that they had no clear idea of what caused the riot to break out in the lower house.[3] These two surveys show that there is room for improvement; but before we criticize Japanese newspaper readers too sharply it is useful to remember that American readers might not fare much better if a similar survey were carried out in the United States.

There is one area of political activity where the mass media seem to make their weight felt, and that is in elections. Royama's study of the 1952 elections revealed, for example, that roughly one half of the voters got their information about the candidate and his program from the mass media. Even those who relied on rumors to get this information were, in many cases, ultimately dependent upon the mass media since these media were often the starting point of such rumors. Royama concludes that "the image of the political situation which the mass media psychologically implant in the minds of the electorate day in and day out exercises a very strong influence on the way in which they vote. We must say that on this point the effect of mass communications is indeed great."[4]

[3] *Asahi shimbun*, June 21, 1954 (Evening edition).
[4] Royama, *op. cit.*, p. 93.

Previously we pointed out that in general the radio seems to be a more effective medium in the rural areas; but when it comes to elections, the press probably exercises more influence. Royama and his associates asked voters in a rural area near Tokyo how they learned about candidates and their programs, and their responses showed that newspapers were the most important channel.

How Voters Learned About Candidates and Their Programs

	PRESS	SPEECHES	RADIO	GOV'T REPORTS	OTHER	NO REPLY	TOTAL
Men	49.4%	9.6%	10.8%	7.3%	19.5%	3.4%	100%
Women	33.1	8.8	16.1	8.3	30.8	2.9	100%
Total	40.8	9.2	15.7	9.0	25.0	0.3	100%

Source: *So-senkyo no jittai,* p. 161.

Thus the verdict is that the mass media do succeed—not fully to be sure, but to an important degree—in conveying news and information to the public. But what effect do the mass media have on basic political attitudes? This, of course, is crucial in assessing the long-run effects of the press, radio, and other forms of mass communications.

Specialists on public opinion have pointed out that the political content of the mass media is shaped by (1) the overt consideration of reader opinion by those who write and edit the mass media; and (2) unconscious similarity of ideology between those who produce the mass media and their consumers.[5] The result is that there is bound to be a large measure of correspondence between the basic political and social attitudes expressed in the mass media and those held by the masses who read them. One function of the mass media, therefore, must be to reinforce, by their reiteration, these basic attitudes. In this sense the mass

[5] Bernard Berelson, in *Mass Communications,* ed. by Wilbur Schramm (Urbana, 1949), p. 498.

media, whether intentionally or otherwise, stand on the side of conservatism.

One test of the "pull" exerted by the mass media would be to try to gauge their effectiveness among social groups, such as organized labor, which are frequently subjected to ideologies hostile to the existing order. Recently Professor Hidaka Rokuro and his associates undertook such a study of unionized workers employed in a steel mill in the Tokyo-Yokohama area.[6] The relevant data produced by this study, which adds significantly to our understanding of the role of mass communications in Japanese politics, will be summarized briefly here:

1. Workers in this steel mill were exposed to all kinds of media. The great majority of them read one or more of the metropolitan dailies, and many (71.5%) said they listened to the radio everyday. Both the Communist and the Socialist parties place special emphasis on organized workers who, according to Marxist theory, form the vanguard of the revolutionary movement. It is therefore interesting to note that seven out of ten workers said they didn't read either *Akahata* (Red Flag), the Communist newspaper, or *Shakai Taimusu* (Social Times), which was being published by the Socialists at the time this study was conducted. Employees who got low wages, such as temporary workers, had the highest percentage of readers of these left-wing papers, while workers in supervisory positions had the lowest. In addition to these media, workers in the steel mill were also given a paper put out by the company and another published by their union. These media seemed to be more popular than one might surmise; in each instance three out of five of those questioned stated that they read every issue. The most faithful readers of

[6] Hidaka Rokuro, et al., *"Rodosha to komunikeshon katei"* (Workers and the communications process), *Tokyo Daigaku Shimbun Kenkyujo kiyo* (Bulletin of the Institute of Journalism, University of Tokyo), IV (1955); also his *"Rodosha to masu komunikeshon to no musubitsuki"* (Workers and their relation to mass communications) *Shiso,* no. 370 (April, 1955).

the company paper as well as of the union paper were workers who earned higher pay.

2. Most interest in political news printed in the metropolitan dailies and broadcast over the radio was shown by those who held "staff" positions, that is technicians, office workers, and the like. The lowest interest in political news was shown by temporary employees. The difference between the two types of workers very likely stems from differences in the amount of formal education. By and large, those who have gone to school longer hold the better paying jobs; and there seems to be a correlation between interest shown in political affairs and the amount of schooling. The data turned up by the study suggests that those who are interested in politics tend to be receptive to all kinds of media, that is, they read the daily newspapers, listen to the radio, and read both the company and union publications. The fact that an individual is interested in political affairs does not, however, provide a clue to his political orientation. Both conservatives and radicals are found among those who pay close attention to political developments.

3. People may read newspapers with interest but this does not necessarily mean that they are influenced by what they read. (One possible exception is that those who read left-wing media tend to be left-wing in their political outlook.) The key factor is not exposure to the mass media, but credibility. Workers, according to the survey, are influenced only by those media in which they place some measure of confidence. In other words if a reader feels that the newspaper he is reading is biased, he will discount what he reads. It is significant, given these conditions, that many workers believe that the metropolitan dailies are "neutral" or are even "progressive" in their political orientation. There are some differences in the degree of confidence shown by workers in the large newspapers depending upon their position in the hierarchy within the plant. By and large, however, the higher the worker is in the hierarchy, the more faith he has in the mass circulation press.

4. Professor Hidaka and his associates started out to study the effect of mass communications on unionized workers, and in the course of their survey came to feel that personal communication, something that they had not intended to study, was very effective. Professor Hidaka's finding is one of several indications that the role of the mass media in Japanese politics cannot be fully understood without consideration being given to the element of personal communication.

Mass Communication vs. Personal Communication

One characteristic of mass communications is that it is a one-sided affair. The reporter who writes a news item and the man who reads it while riding to work on a subway train, the radio commentator speaking into a microphone and the listener sitting in his living room, have no personal contact. The one who receives the communication cannot say: "But I don't understand what you are driving at; please explain." For this and other reasons, there is a need for individuals who take what is contained in the mass media and informally interpret it and even relate it to other news and events. Such people, found in all social groups, are sometimes spoken of as "opinion leaders" or "opinion transmitters."

One student of Japanese public opinion maintains that there are certain "politically well-informed" people who make it a point to read the papers and keep up on political developments. He believes that such people are often found among barbers, priests, teachers, members of town and village councils, and the like. They are not professional commentators but are often instrumental in the transmission and formation of opinion among local groups.[7]

[7] Sato Tomoo, *"Masu komunikeshon to kojin teki iken dentatsu"* (Mass communication and the transmission of personal opinion), *Shakaigaku hyoron,* III (April, 1953), p. 35.

Professor Hidaka's study of the steel mill cited above has shown that leaders of the union organized within the plant appear to exercise considerable influence. The following table reveals differences in the degree of confidence shown by workers toward the mass media and toward their union leaders.

Confidence of Workers in Mass Communication vs. Personal Communication

WORKER'S STATUS	METROPOLITAN DAILIES	UNION LEADERS	CANNOT CHOOSE BETWEEN THE TWO	DO NOT KNOW; NO REPLY	TOTAL
Staff	46.4%	24.6%	23.2%	5.8%	100
Supervisory workers *	28.0	48.0	20.0	4.0	100
Ordinary workers	30.4	38.4	23.7	6.8	100
Temporary workers	31.9	34.0	29.8	4.3	100
Not clear	38.9	33.3	5.6	22.2	100
Total	32.8	36.4	23.6	6.7	100

Source: Hidaka, Rokuro, et al., *"Rodosha to masu komunikashion katei,"* p. 81.
* Japanese unions admit supervisory workers, on occasion even managerial employees such as department chiefs and section chiefs.

As the foregoing table shows, the mass media and union leaders seem to command about the same amount of confidence. This should serve as a caution to any temptation to ascribe excessive influence to the mass media. The table also shows that supervisory workers, that is, foremen and others who have men under them, place more confidence in their union leaders and less confidence in the mass media than do other workers. This may be explained in part by the identity which often exists between the foreman class and union leaders, that is, foremen can exercise a great deal of informal power in the plant, and they are able to use this power to work themselves into leadership positions in unions at the local level.

PUBLIC OPINION

Traditional Control of Public Opinion

"There has never been any lack of interest," writes Herbert Passin, "in the climate of public opinion on the part of government circles in Japan." [8] The state traditionally maintained a vigilant watch on what its subjects were saying and writing. Tokugawa history provides examples of thought control and political persecution, and not a few intellectuals and critics who dared to trespass the bounds of orthodoxy found themselves in prison. In 1875, a few years after its establishment, the Meiji government proclaimed its first press law; and the decades that followed saw censorship and thought control being exercised with varying intensity.

Before World War II, certain topics, notably matters relating to the Imperial House, were for practical purposes completely removed from the sphere of public discussion. Increasingly in the 1930's public discussion of the role of the military and of certain phases of foreign policy relating to Japan's adventure in China became enshrouded with taboo. As public discussion of many important issues diminished or ceased, those in policy-making positions necessarily became cut off from whatever guidance an informed public opinion could provide. They were working in the dark; and it became difficult for them to judge what the sentiments and feelings of the public were toward the policies they were formulating and putting into effect. Some attempts, to be sure, were made to sound out public sentiment. During the war, *Domei,* the official news agency, made occasional attempts to gauge the state of opinion and morale by collecting reports from its corps of correspondents, but its find-

[8] Herbert Passin, "The Development of Public Opinion Research in Japan," *International Journal of Opinion and Attitude Research,* V (Spring, 1951), p. 21.

ings were not distributed for fear of displeasing the military.[9] There is evidence that the secret police (*kempeitai*) gathered information during the war on rumors circulating among the populace, especially anti-government and anti-war rumors. Incidentally one study based on secret police documents shows that in about one fourth of the instances, people got rumors from strangers.[10]

The attempt of the state to control public opinion was not limited, of course, to censorship, which, after all, was more or less negative. As the masses became a weightier factor in politics, more positive steps to mould public opinion were also taken in the 1930's. The publication of documents like the *Kokutai no hongi*, discussed in Chapter 3 was one such step; another was the establishment of an information bureau within the cabinet, which issued a weekly bulletin (*Shuho*) giving the official interpretation of events and policies. Furthermore, the various mass communications media were put under pressure to shape their contents to conform to the officially inspired ideological line.

The purpose of the foregoing discussion on the traditional attitude of the state toward public opinion is to show the kind of legacy contemporary Japan has inherited from the past. Attitudes and habits inhibiting public discussion of issues which were nurtured over many decades cannot be quickly and easily altered. It is well to keep this in mind when we look at the state of public opinion in the contemporary period.

Public Opinion in Post-War Japan

As one of the many reform measures, the Occupation sought to free the mass communications media of the threat of censorship and control. The Occupation was not altogether con-

[9] Passin, *ibid.*, p. 22.
[10] Ikeuchi Hajime, "*Taiheiyo senso-chu no senji ryugen*" (Rumors during the Pacific War), *Shakaigaku hyoron*, II (August, 1951), p. 34.

sistent in this, since news and views derogatory to the Occupation were not permitted to be published; nevertheless, in all other realms, the mass media were able to operate in a relatively free atmosphere. Even such questions as whether or not the Emperor should be retained—something on which no one would have dared to express himself in print before the war—came to be openly discussed.

It was natural that as a part of the new era whose keynote was democracy, there should develop a new interest in the measurement of public opinion. The people, at least in theory, were now sovereign, and it was important to discover what they were thinking.

Public opinion polls were not altogether unknown in Japan. So far as is known, the first polls were undertaken in 1940 by *Mainichi*, which sought to ascertain public views on entrance examinations for middle school, and on proposals to revise the law on elections. It is noteworthy that in addition to people representing different occupations, *Mainichi* also polled 600 members of different associations, such as town and village agricultural associations, reservists' associations, town and *buraku* (hamlet) associations, and the like.[11] These are associations that include a number of locally prominent people, many of whom were no doubt in the category of "opinion makers."

The beginnings made in 1940 by *Mainichi*, however, were interrupted by the war, and it was not until after the surrender that the Japanese began to sample public opinion on a systematic and large-scale basis. All of the major newspapers set up departments for carrying on public opinion research; and a number of public opinion research institutes were established for the purpose of carrying on market research as well as for conducting polls on public issues. In 1949 the National Diet passed a law creating a National Public Opinion Research Institute, a government agency but controlled by a board of governors

[11] *Mainichi nenkan*, 1942 edition, p. 87.

elected by scholarly organizations. (The Institute was abolished in 1954.) As a result of the activities of these public opinion research organizations, there are now a large number of polls covering a wide range of topics from birth control and domestic relations to rearmament and international relations. Pre-election polls have also become an established feature of Japanese political life; prior to every election, the metropolitan dailies carry articles predicting the outcome based on a sampling of public opinion by their research departments.

At this point, the question of the validity of these polls may be raised. Quite naturally, the Japanese have relied heavily on American techniques which were imported into the country. Several American specialists were sent to provide guidance, and Japanese specialists came to the United States for training. Yet there is the problem of whether techniques evolved in America can be transplanted without making modifications to fit different conditions. For instance, it is reported that the Japanese are using in their sampling the same variables that are used in the United States, that is, age, geographical region, sex, and some economic measure. "Yet, is there any *a priori* reason to believe that the cultural determinants in America and Japan are so uniform that the same variables are the relevant determinants of attitudes in both cultures?"[12] A Japanese specialist believes that the occupational variable exerts a strong influence on opinions, but adds that this variable is difficult to work with, first, because occupations are difficult to classify in Japan, and second, because occupational change is relatively rapid.[13] The development of more accurate sampling methods will probably have to await further research in the theory of public opinion formation in Japan.

[12] Herbert H. Hyman, "World Surveys—The Japanese Angle," *International Journal of Opinion and Attitude Research*, I (June, 1947), p. 25.
[13] Yoneyama Keizo, "*Yoron*" in *Gendai shakai no kenkyu* (A study of contemporary society), ed. by Shakai Kagaku Kenkyujo (Tokyo, 1948), p. 251.

Another difficulty has to do with interviewing bias. Because of the tradition of thought control, many people are reluctant to reveal their real thoughts, particularly if they have some reason to believe that the interviewer might be a government official. Many people are also very much afraid of tax officials, since in these days of high taxes, tax evasion seems to take place on a fairly large scale.

On some questions, the percentage of "don't knows" runs high. Rural women in the older age brackets are likely to say "I don't know" to many questions other than those dealing with household matters, since they are either not interested in public issues or feel that it is inappropriate for them to express their views. For example, in 1948, the Nagasue Public Opinion Research Institute polled some men and women in Kyoto and got the following results:

Do you trust the present statesmen?

	TOTAL	MEN	WOMEN
Yes	6.2%	7.4%	5.0%
No	59.1	75.0	44.0
No opinion	34.7	17.6	51.0

Source: *International Journal of Opinion and Attitude Research*, II (Fall, 1948).

An American specialist who worked on public opinion problems in Japan, however, feels that in general the "don't know" response is not at all high compared with American results. In his view, moreover, surveys in Japan appear to be achieving valid results.[14]

One test of the validity of poll results is the accuracy achieved by pre-election polls. When they were first tried in the 1946 national elections, all of them proved to be inaccurate, leading to a loss of public confidence in polls, but since then pre-election polls have improved appreciably. For example, the fol-

[14] Hyman, *op. cit.*, pp. 20–1.

lowing table shows the pre-election forecast and the results of the gubernatorial election in Tokyo in 1947.

Pre-election Forecast and Election Result for Governor of Tokyo, 1947

CANDIDATE	FORECAST (per cent of votes)	ELECTION RESULT (per cent of votes)
Yasui, Seiichiro	54.1	48.1
Tagawa, Takichiro	42.3	42.0
Fukuda, Chotaro	2.5	2.9
Hibi, Chosaburo	0.5	1.1
Oyama, Zenryo	0.5	3.5
Hashimoto, Shonosuke		1.3
Tanno, Torakichi		0.7
Kitajima, Momotaka		0.3
Don't know; won't vote	50.5	43.8

Source: Makita Minoru, *"Seron chosa no keisei"* (The formation of public opinion), *Shiso*, 287 (May, 1948), p. 301.

In the 1955 national elections, *Asahi* undertook two pre-election polls, and on the basis of these forecast victory for the Democratic party. The *Asahi* forecast and the actual results can be compared in the following table:

Pre-election Forecast and Election Result in the National Elections, 1955

	1ST POLL	2ND POLL	ELECTION RESULT
Democrats	180 seats	188 seats	185 seats
Liberals	134	130	113
Left-wing Socialists	71	67	89
Right-wing Socialists	64	66	66
Others	18	16	14

Source: *Asahi shimbun*, March 28, 1955.

Asahi correctly forecast a Democratic victory, but underestimated the strength of the Left-Wing Socialists. This, however, can be explained in part by the fact that the Communist party withdrew a number of candidates on the eve of the election, thus throwing radical votes to the Left-Wing Socialists.

PUBLIC OPINION AND PUBLIC POLICY

The Appeal to Public Opinion

In addition to the question of the measurement of public opinion, there is a more fundamental one of the relation of public opinion to policy. There would not be much point in measuring public opinion if it should turn out that policy was formulated pretty much independently of it. It is perhaps a testimonial to the spread of democratic values that political leaders often seek to justify their actions (or failure to act) by appealing to "public opinion." Thus in the fall of 1951 when the dissolution of the Diet was a public issue, Hirokawa Kyozen, then a prominent member of the Liberal party, took a negative stand. He said: "It is evident from the results of the public opinion polls that the majority of the people clearly support the present cabinet and the Liberal party and do not look forward to the dissolution of the Diet." [15]

A more recent example of the appeal to public opinion is the successful maneuver on the part of left-wing parties and anti-Yoshida conservatives to drive Prime Minister Yoshida and his party from power late in 1954. In a speech in the House of Councillors, a member of the Left-Wing Socialist party demanded that Yoshida step down. "Ever since the peace treaty and the administrative agreements which bind Japan to a dependent status, maladministration and bad government on the part of the Yoshida cabinet have continued, until today public opinion is overwhelmingly in favor of the retirement of Prime

[15] *Asahi shimbun,* October 1, 1951.

Minister Yoshida." In defending himself against his critics, Prime Minister Yoshida also appealed to public opinion. In a speech on December 2, 1954 in the lower house he said: "Whether I will stay in office or retire will be decided by a party conference. There are voices among the people that urge me to carry on (laughter, applause). Not all of the people tell me to retire from office. There are some who tell me to carry on." [16]

Opinion and Policy

Are politicians really guided by public opinion or are they merely giving lip service to it? The answer to each question is probably yes and no. To the extent that politicians must rely on votes to get into office, they cannot afford to ignore the reactions of their constituents to public issues. On the other hand, the more a political leader depends on a political machine to deliver votes on election day, the less sensitive he needs to be to public opinion.

There is, however, another dimension to public opinion which must be considered in attempting to assess its influence on policy formation; and that is the element of intensity. Public opinion polls seldom measure this, and yet intensity is undoubtedly a factor. It makes a difference whether people feel strongly about an issue or are only mildly concerned. A Japanese student of public opinion maintains that the Japanese masses are quiet and have a sense of resignation toward great issues. This does not mean that they have no opinions, but that some believe it is a good policy to be quiet, and others lack the will power and emotional drive to make their views count in politics.[17] On-the-spot observation of Japanese behavior during crucial periods, such as elections and changes of cabinets, tends to confirm this

[16] Quoted in *Masu komunikashion koza,* II, pp. 176–7.

[17] Koyama Eizo, *Shimbun shakaigaku* (Sociology of newspapers) (Tokyo, 1951), p. 126.

view. Ordinarily, the Japanese are not an excitable and volatile people when it comes to politics. And perhaps this is the very reason that on occasion pent-up feeling seems to burst out in a spasm of violence, as it did, for example, during the rice riots which swept over the country in 1918.

Strictly speaking, public opinion exists only when there is an issue and when significant numbers of people take sides on that issue. Public opinion defined in this way can be said to exist in Japan in a much more rudimentary form than in the United States. Perhaps it would be more accurate to speak of mood rather than of opinion. Over a period of time the mood of the country seems to change, as it did, for instance, in the fall of 1954 when the Yoshida government which had been in power since 1949 became increasingly unpopular, partly as a result of disclosure of corruption within the government. To be sure, changes in mood are reflected in the mass media, and indeed they may find their origins, at least in part, in the press and other media; but in any case such changes in mood are usually not preceded by a "great debate" in which the issue or issues get a widespread and heated public hearing.

Opinion and Policy: A Case Study

One of the most persistent and far-reaching issues of recent politics concerns rearmament.[18] Although Article 9 of the post-war Constitution forbids Japan to have armaments, Japan has been in fact rearming since 1950 when a "Reserve police force" was established. However, because of the constitutional provision, Japan does not yet have an army but only "defense forces," and as yet there exists no full-fledged Ministry of Defense. Eventually the Constitution will in all likelihood be amended to per-

[18] Douglas H. Mendel, "Revisionist Opinion in Post-Treaty Japan," *American Political Science Review*, XLVIII (September, 1954), pp. 766–74.

mit rearmament on a larger scale; but the fact that this has not occurred to date is largely a result of hostile public opinion. A constitutional amendment must be approved by more than 50 per cent of the electorate; and so far most conservative political leaders who favor rearmament have been reluctant to put the issue up to the voters for fear that it would be turned down.

The following table shows the results of public opinion polls on the rearmament issue that were conducted by the newspaper *Yomiuri:*

Public Opinion on Rearmament

DATE	IN FAVOR	AGAINST	DON'T KNOW
Dec., 1950	43.8%	38.7%	17.5%
March, 1951	47.3	23.6	24.1
April, 1951	53.1	30.4	16.5
Aug., 1951	50.8	31.5	17.7
Oct., 1951	58.0	24.9	17.1
Feb., 1952	56.9	23.8	19.3
April, 1952	47.5	39.0	13.5
April, 1952	40.5	38.4	21.1
Jan., 1954	54.0	39.0	7.0

Source: Royama Masamichi, *Seron ni kansuru kangae-kata* (On public opinion) (Tokyo, 1955), p. 285.

Public sentiment, as measured by the polls, shows that roughly one-half of the population favors rearmament. The majority, however, is probably not yet large enough to give political leaders who favor rearmament sufficient assurance of success in case they attempt to push through a constitutional amendment. Here at least is one instance where there seems to be a close relationship between public opinion and public policy.

Chapter 12

The Intellectuals

One would judge, from the attention customarily given them, that Japanese intellectuals are regarded as playing an important, if not key, role in the political process. Prior to the war, Japanese government agencies, especially the old Home Ministry, went to great lengths and expense to keep intellectuals under surveillance, even resorting to stringent censorship and thought control when necessary. Presumably these steps were taken on the assumption that what the intellectuals wrote and did affected in a significant way the social and political order.

The various cultural and information programs sponsored at present by the United States government in Japan would also appear to rest fundamentally on similar premises. These programs, calling for the outlay of relatively large sums of money, operate at several levels. Through the exchange of persons program, the American government has made it possible for hundreds of Japanese educators, lecturers, research scholars, and specialists to travel and study in the United States, and for their American counterparts to journey to Japan. Another aspect of the program involves the maintenance of libraries stocked with American publications, the translation and publication of American books in Japan, the sponsorship of lectures, exhibitions, concerts, and the like. This effort falls in the broad field of cultural exchange; and it goes without saying that it is directed, in the main, at that strata of the population which has had the benefit of considerable formal education. In short, it is proper to think of these activities as seeking to influence the attitudes and behavior of intellectuals, broadly speaking.

Cultural exchange is a worthwhile endeavor, deserving to be encouraged whenever and wherever possible.[1] But it would be less than honest to shut one's eyes to the practical political considerations that often accompany the desire for cultural exchange. Stated bluntly, one objective of work in this area is to create attitudes, and, if possible, behavior friendly to the United States; and the theory, either explicitly or implicitly held, is that an effective way to achieve such an objective is to work through intellectuals. It would be pertinent, given these considerations, to raise the question of the role of intellectuals in Japanese politics.

A SOCIOLOGICAL VIEW OF INTELLECTUALS

In the beginning we may ask: who are the intellectuals? Intellectuals are a heterogenous lot, and hence difficult to define. Perhaps more so than others, those who deal with ideas tend to be individualistic and nonconformist. One must, accordingly, avoid the impression that they form a cohesive group, bound together by a common set of assumptions, sentiments, and values. Nevertheless, intellectuals sometimes develop group attitudes and group interests, making it possible to think of them as a social group.

As a rule, higher education is required for an individual to become an intellectual; but not all those with higher education are necessarily intellectuals. According to the 1950 census, there

---

[1] Those interested in the history of cultural relations between the United States and Japan will find some interesting comments in Robert Schwantes, *Japanese and Americans* (New York, 1955).

were a little more than two million individuals 25 years of age or over who had completed 13 years or more of schooling. These individuals represent 5.7 per cent of the population in this age bracket. A further breakdown by sex reveals a disproportionate ratio, since 10 per cent of the males and only 1.8 per cent of the females in this age group have completed 13 years or more of schooling. These two million men and women then may be thought of as *potential* intellectuals.

The active (as opposed to potential) intellectuals are, of course, substantially fewer in number. According to Schumpeter, intellectuals are people "who wield the power of the spoken and the written word, and one of the touches that distinguish them from other people who do the same is the absence of direct responsibility for practical affairs." [2] If we follow this definition, the following types of people would be included among intellectuals: first and foremost are the "professors" who teach and do research in the institutions of higher learning. Others are political commentators, who write in magazines and speak over the radio on current political affairs; journalists who report and comment on politics; novelists, especially those who deal with political and social themes; translators, and artists. In terms of the entire population, active intellectuals form a tiny minority. In 1953 there were just under 33 thousand teachers in all the universities in Japan.[3] A 1951 directory of people who hold copyright on published works contains a little more than 10,000 names.[4] Obviously there is duplication since some university teachers are included in the directory. On the other hand, the directory would not include all intellectuals as we have defined them. Nevertheless, we can get a rough idea of the order of magnitude

[2] Joseph A. Schumpeter, *Capitalism, Socialism, and Democracy* (New York, 1950), p. 147.

[3] *Nihon gensei* (Japan's present situation), 1954 edition, ed. by Kyodo Tsushin-sha (Tokyo, 1953), p. 149.

[4] *Bunka jimmeiroku* (Who's who in the cultural field), ed. by Nihon Chosakuken Kyogikai (Tokyo, 1951).

involved from these two figures just cited. One would suppose that a generous estimate of the number of those "who wield the power of the spoken and written word" would be in the neighborhood of 50,000 men and women.

We see then that active intellectuals, as defined above, form a small group. But numbers alone do not tell the whole story. In traditional Japanese culture, the teacher commanded prestige, and intellectual activity was highly valued. In recent decades, the prestige once enjoyed by intellectuals has been seriously eroded; money is to an increasing degree replacing family background, official position, and education as the standard of valuation. Professors, before the war, were able to lead an upper-middle class life; but today inflation has played havoc with professorial salaries, until it is well nigh impossible for a university teacher to subsist without outside income. Moneywise the professor has a low rating; but there still is a carry-over from the past so that intellectual endeavor continues to command some measure of respect. It is worth noting in this connection that the survey cited in Chapter 2, which tried to assess the relative importance of 30 occupations, placed professors in the second position from the top, while journalists came about one third of the way down the list.

The Social Role of Intellectuals

Arnold Toynbee notes in his famous work, *A Study of History*, that when one civilization is forced to adapt itself to another there emerges a special social class which performs the functions of a "transformer." Just as a transformer converts electrical current from one voltage to another, so this special class—which he calls the intelligentsia—learns the tricks of an intrusive civilization and teaches them to the rest of the community.[5] In Toynbee's view, the first recruits to this class are the military

[5] (London, 1954) V, p. 154.

and naval officers, followed by diplomats, merchants, and eventually schoolteachers. In the Japanese instance, intellectuals can lay claim to having served as "transformers." They were deeply involved in the transformation of Japan into a modern nation.

There are at least two major ways in which intellectuals have helped to introduce Western ideas, techniques, and institutions to Japan. One is travel and study abroad. Precise data on the number of teachers and students who have journeyed to foreign lands in the modern period is not available; but it is safe to say that over the years, thousands have gone to the great intellectual centers of the world to study every conceivable subject—higher mathematics, physics, biology, Greek philosophy, German metaphysics, French literature, and American science. The importance attached to Western training may be attested to by the custom which prevailed in government universities prior to World War II. Before a teacher became a full professor, he was usually awarded a government scholarship which enabled him to spend a year or two in a European or an American university, and upon his return he was given a professorial chair.

Another approach to Western civilization has been through the study of European languages. Even a cursory examination of footnotes in Japanese scholarly works will show the extent to which Japanese scholars use source materials in German, French, and English. One result of this interest in foreign works is the incorporation of a large number of foreign words into the Japanese language. Terms like "humanism," "communication," "proletariat," and many others can be found even in the daily newspapers. A related phenomenon is the extensive body of translations of foreign works which indefatigable translators have made available to the Japanese public. Statistics compiled by the Japanese government show that between 1881 and 1920 some 6,800 translations were issued.[6] The *Index Translationum*

---

[6] Compiled from statistics in *Shuppan nenkan,* ed. by Tokyodo, 1931 edition, pp. 72–3.

(no. 6, 1954) published by UNESCO lists 1,298 translations of Western works into Japanese, issued mostly in one year, 1953. Most of the major Western works ranging from Shakespeare to Steinbeck, from Plato to Gide, can be read in translation. It is clear that many Japanese intellectuals are preoccupied with things foreign.

So far we have been speaking in general terms about the long-term orientation toward the Western world; but a more detailed examination would show the existence of cyclical trends. There are periods when the national mood is one of receptivity to foreign influences; and these are always followed by periods of relative hostility to foreign ideas and institutions. (One is hard put to explain how and why these cycles operate; but their existence is clear.) There have been in the history of modern Japan three periods when the nation seemed to look outward, ready to accept new and foreign influences. The first period began with the Restoration in 1868 and lasted until about 1888. There then followed a period of reaction, during which a critical eye was cast on things foreign, and emphasis was placed on traditional values and methods of doing things. The end of the Russo-Japanese war in 1905 opened another era of rapid Westernization, and it continued until about 1930. From 1930 until the end of World War II in 1945 the Japanese nation looked inward and to its past for inspiration. Everything foreign fell under a cloud of suspicion and hostility. The surrender in 1945 and the subsequent Allied Occupation again opened the flood-gates to foreign, particularly American, influences. Present-day Japan is still in this cycle, although there are signs that the downward phase has already begun.

It is almost axiomatic that the influence exercised by intellectuals is related to these cycles. Since one of the important functions of intellectuals is to introduce Western ideas and techniques into the country, their services are actively sought and their advice is taken more seriously in those periods when the national mood is one of receptivity to foreign influences. Conversely, in periods of reaction, they are likely to feel the heavy hand of censorship and suppression.

Intellectuals and Their Outlook

The existence of cycles, and the alternate periods of hostility to Western influences and by extension to intellectuals, may help explain one feature of Japanese intellectual life which stands out. That is, in studying the Western world, Japanese intellectuals have been propelled by a sense of urgency. In the early years of the Meiji era, intellectuals found that they had much to learn because the West had managed to get a head start. Ever since then they have been obsessed by the feeling that they are lagging behind the West, and that they therefore must exert great effort to close the gap. And even if they reach a point where they have almost caught up with the West, they again are left behind in periods when the national mood is unfriendly to Western influences. The sense of urgency may be one reason Japanese intellectuals have had a tendency to seize upon one thing, only to cast it off in favor of something new. As yet, no intellectual history of modern Japan has been written; but when such a history is set down by a competent historian, it will tell a fascinating story for in the course of the past century Japan has seen waves of foreign ideas sweep over the intellectual world: utilitarianism, social democracy, anarchism, Wilsonian democracy, communism, liberalism, fascism, and most recently existentialism, have come and gone. Decades ago, Natsume Soseki, a brilliant novelist with a penchant for social criticism, likened this process to a man who starts to eat a dish placed before him at a dinner table only to find it taken away before he has had a chance to finish it, and replaced by another.[7]

[7] *"Gendai Nihon no kaika"* (Enlightenment in contemporary Japan), in *Soseki zenshu* (Collected works of Natsume Soseki) (Tokyo, 1936), XIII, p. 375.

A useful guide to current trends of thought among intellectuals are the "journals of opinion," which are monthly magazines written in the main by intellectuals. These journals carry articles, quite often of a scholarly nature, on current political, economic and international questions, literary essays and short stories. Almost every issue carries several articles by leading academic people. One would be hard put to find exact counterparts of such journals in the United States; perhaps they may be best characterized as representing a combination of *Harpers* or *Atlantic*, the *Yale Review*, plus the *New Republic*. At the present time there are four journals which are worthy of mention. Proceeding from right to left in terms of their general political orientation, we find that *Bungei shunju* (Annals of literature and arts) is the most conservative and literary of the group; *Chuo koron* (Central review), the oldest, having been in existence for 70 years (as of 1955), occupies a more or less centrist position by Japanese standards; *Kaizo* (Reconstruction) founded during World War I, has always been leftist; and *Sekai* (World) which began publishing in 1946, is even more radical than *Kaizo*. All of the four journals have behind them the resources of large publishing houses, a factor which helps explain why they are able to survive in a field where the mortality rate is rather high.

It is said that *Chuo koron* has a circulation of a hundred thousand copies or so a month. Obviously, *Chuo koron* cannot be thought of as a mass circulation magazine, but neither can it be dismissed as a highbrow journal with a small coterie of admirers. So far as is known, no scientific reader survey has been made to to find out just who buys and reads journals of this type. One thing is fairly certain, however, and that is that young white-collar workers and university and college students form an important group of readers. A recent survey of student reading habits has brought out that these four journals rate rather high in student popularity:

Percentage of Students Reading Certain
Journals (*October, 1953*)

JOURNAL	TOKYO UNIVERSITY	WASEDA UNIVERSITY
Sekai	35.4	14.7
Bungei shunju	26.5	28.1
Shukan Asahi	22.1	29.1
Chuo koron	15.2	14.0
Shizen	8.2	1.4
Sunday Mainichi	7.0	12.6
Kaizo	6.2	6.5
Shosetsu shincho	5.4	8.6
Shincho	5.4	5.5
Reader's Digest	3.9	5.8
Asahi camera	0.8	6.5

Source: *Nihon dokusho shimbun,* December 8, 1953.

It might be said in passing that we have here a situation in which embryonic intellectuals (i.e., students) and potential intellectuals (white-collar workers) provide the audience for intellectuals.

One would surmise that the reason these journals are read widely enough to enable them to survive is that they perform a useful function. First of all, these journals help intellectuals (and their audience) keep abreast of latest developments both in the domestic and foreign scene. They serve, in other words, as convenient sources of information. Second, these journals provide a handy forum for the exchange of views and ideas among intellectuals. By reading these magazines, intellectuals can ascertain what other intellectuals are thinking and what stand they are taking on controversial issues. Here we come to a rather interesting characteristic of Japanese intellectual life. Every year there are two or three important intellectual free-for-alls which bring forth much discussion and debate. These free-for-alls remind one of boxing or wrestling matches in that there is the promoter in the form of a magazine editor who persuades some prominent intellectual to take a position on some topic of current interest. In the succeeding months other intellectuals join in the fray, writing rebuttals and counter-rebuttals in other journals. Almost always there is in the exchange a liberal use of innuendo and insinuation. Any person who wishes to be regarded as an intellectual must follow the verbal battle with care; and when a group of intellectuals assemble, there is heated discussion as to whether intellectual A got the better of B or vice versa. A third function of these journals is to serve as an outlet for protest. Schumpeter has remarked that intellectuals take a critical attitude toward affairs partly because they lack first-hand knowledge, and partly because the main chance they have of asserting themselves lies in their actual or potential nuisance value.[8] One of the functions of Japanese intellectuals is to serve as critics; and it is therefore fashionable to be critical.

It would appear that Marxism has had some relation to social criticism and protest. Since the World War I period, Marxism has apparently made a deep and lasting impression on many intellectuals. This is not to say that all intellectuals subscribe to Marxian tenets; there are many who do not. It is also important to note that there are a variety of Marxists, ranging all the way from those who are members of the Japanese Communist party to those who are quite apolitical, and merely use certain Marxian ideas as conceptual tools in their research. In any case, many of the most articulate intellectuals have accepted Marxian principles in varying degrees, and the influence wielded by Marxists and crypto-Marxists is such that it cannot be ignored.

Historically, the first mention of Marx in Japan is to be found in an essay published in 1881; but for at least two decades thereafter, Marxism remained a rather obscure subject. Then in 1904, on the eve of the Russo-Japanese war, two well-known so-

[8] *Op. cit.*, p. 147.

cialists, Kotoku Shusui and Sakai Toshihiko, published a translation of the "Communist Manifesto" in their weekly newspaper, *Heimin Shimbun*. But this incurred the wrath of the authorities and the issues containing the translation were banned. In the following year, Kawakami Hajime, who later became a leading Marxist scholar, wrote a book based on Edwin Seligman's *The economic interpretation of history*. Other works followed; but it was not until after World War I, when interest in the subject was aroused in part by the success of the Russian Revolution, that Marxism became the subject of serious study. In 1919 Kawakami started a magazine which he wrote and edited called, *Shakai mondai kenkyu* (Study of social problems), and in it he published his studies on Marxian economics and on historical materialism. The following list pinpoints some of the highlights in the development of Marxian thought.

1919—Sakai Toshihiko published "From the point of view of historical materialism"; and "From the point of view of socialism."

1919—Takabatake Motoyuki published a translation of Kautsky's work on *Das Kapital*.

1920–1924—Japanese translation of *Das Kapital* issued.

1924—"Marukusu-shugi" (Marxism), an intellectual journal devoted to Marxism, founded.

1926—Collected works of Lenin issued in translation.

1927—A number of publishers competed to bring out translations of the collected works of Marx and Engels.

1927—"Intanashunaru" (International), a journal devoted to the international developments in Marxism, founded.

It has been said that in the 1920's, Japan ranked next to Soviet Russia and Germany in the number of books and articles published on Marxian questions.

The popularity of Marxism reached its peak toward the end of the 1920's, and then began to decline, partly as a result of strong government action. At that time, thousands of suspected communists were arrested, leading Marxist professors were driven from their academic posts, and most of the leaders of the Communist party were imprisoned or forced to flee the country. The decline of Marxism became even more pronounced after the invasion of Manchuria in 1931 when a wave of nationalistic sentiment swept over the country.

During the 1930's and the war years—the period which Japanese intellectuals, especially those belonging to the left, describe as the "dark ages"—Marxism was kept under wraps but by no means discarded. Marxism apparently managed to survive censorship, political persecution, and thought control and to remain rooted in Japanese intellectual life, because with the end of the war it witnessed a quick and vigorous revival. The post-war period is very much reminiscent of the 1920's when Marxian literature enjoyed such a vogue. In recent years, publishers' lists have contained many translations of Marx, Lenin, Stalin, and Mao Tse-tung, as well as works which give a Marxian interpretation of Japanese history and social development.

Until a systematic and careful study of the role of Marxism in Japanese culture is undertaken, we cannot begin to understand with any feeling of certainty the reasons so many Japanese intellectuals find it a congenial doctrine. Pending such a study we can only speculate. It may be that Marxian analysis provides a reasonably plausible explanation for some of Japan's persistent problems: the trend toward economic concentration, the coming and going of economic depressions, and the presence of poverty on a large scale. It may also be that some people take up Marxism as a kind of protest against their social system. Roberto Michels once said of intellectuals that "since their intellectual pursuits bring them into contact with theories and information not available to others they often come to regard the social order in which they find themselves as anachronistic with reference to ideas and institutions developed elsewhere or at other periods." [9] Michels

[9] "Intellectuals" in *Encyclopedia of the Social Sciences.*

believed that the intellectuals therefore "acquire an intellectual motive for urging change." And one may surmise that Marxism would be especially appealing because it not only purports to explain the causes of social change, but also provides a specific program which would presumably facilitate and direct social change.

An important social phenomenon which would encourage intellectuals to throw their weight on the side of social change is the matter of their own chronic unemployment. Toynbee makes the point that it is more difficult to stop than to start the process of creating intelligentsia to act as transformers and that there soon develops an oversupply, leading to the building up of an intellectual proletariat. The problem of unemployed intellectuals has been serious in Japan since about the 1920's.

Traditionally, Japanese culture has placed a premium on non-manual work; and that this attitude still exists can be seen from the survey already cited. High status, prestige, and economic security accrue (or perhaps more accurately used to accrue) to those who are in government service or in the professions. Hence every school boy, particularly from middle class families, is encouraged to set his sights on these occupations.

There is an additional factor which has contributed to the problem of the creation of an intellectual proletariat. The modern period has been one of rapid change; and it has led to an intensification of the feeling of insecurity. Families which were once well off have met with misfortune, while upstart families have risen to take their places. Ownership of land, business enterprises, or bonds and stocks no longer afforded a full measure of security. In the 1920's many middle class families came to consider higher education for their sons as the most stable form of investment.[10] At the same time, educational facilities were rapidly expanded in the post-World War I period, with the result

[10] Oya Shoichi, *"Shushokunan to chishiki kaikyu no kosokudo-teki botsuraku"* (The difficulties of finding employment and the rapid rate of decline of the intellectual class), *Chuo koron*, March, 1929, p. 73.

that the output of college students was greatly accelerated. In 1920 there were 21,914 students enrolled in government and private universities, or a little less than 1 per cent of the male population between the ages of 20 and 24. By 1930 the figure had risen to 69,605, or 2.5 per cent of the male population between these ages. In 1950, 557,000 or 5.9 per cent of those between 19 and 24 were attending school.[11]

Even then, as these figures show, Japan was not (and is not at present) producing in terms of absolute numbers a vast army of intellectuals. We cannot help but suspect that the problem here is one of underconsumption as much as it is of overproduction. But in any case, too many talented young men were being channeled into "white-collar" occupations, upsetting the balance of supply and demand. Some insight into the situation may be gained from the fact that in the 1930's thousands of young men competed for a few hundred government positions. The following table shows the situation in 1934.

Number of Candidates for Examinations for the Higher Civil Service, 1934

TYPE OF EXAMINATION	NO. OF CANDIDATES	NO. PASSING WRITTEN TESTS	NO. PASSING ORAL TESTS
Administration	3,072	303	302
Judicial	3,779	315	331
Diplomatic	321	74	14
Total	7,172	692	647

Source: *Teikoku Daigaku nenkan,* 1935–36, p. 635.

The situation in the post-war period appears to be no better. In 1950 the Tokyo newspaper, *Asahi,* had ten openings in its editorial department, and found itself in the fortunate position of being

[11] Based on statistics in Naikaku Tokei Kyoku, *Nihon teikoku tokei nenkan* (Statistical yearbook of the Japanese empire) 1933 edition, and Bureau of Statistics, Office of the Prime Minister, Population census of 1950, III, pt. 1.

able to choose from among 1,083 applicants. Under the circumstances, thousands of young men who belong to the intellectual proletariat can only look forward to a state of chronic unemployment. One would scarcely expect such young men to be the most ardent supporters of the social system.

THE POLITICAL ROLE OF INTELLECTUALS

It is one thing to be dissatisfied with the way things are, and quite another to "do something about it." It would seem, at first glance, that in a country like Japan where they are held in esteem, intellectuals would be able to wield considerable influence in public affairs. It is true that some intellectuals have identified themselves with the existing regime, and have tried to formulate political doctrines whose ultimate aim is to rationalize the existing political and social order. It is true, also, that some academic people, especially those in government universities, have served from time to time as consultants to one government agency or another, and have also participated in advisory committees. Since most of the bureaucrats are trained in government universities, teachers in these institutions are involved indirectly, if not directly, in public affairs. Robert Merton has called intellectuals of this type "bureaucratic" intellectuals.[12]

But aside from these instances, the main body of intellectuals has remained aloof from government, their main function being, as we have already noted, to act as critics. These are the "unattached" intellectuals whose clientele is the public. In Japan there has been little interchange of government and academic personnel. The intellectual world has remained pretty much to itself.

A rather illuminating illustration of the isolation of intellec-

[12] *Social Theory and Social Structure* (Glencoe, Illinois, 1949), p. 165.

tuals is afforded by the behavior of the literary elite. An outstanding peculiarity of Japanese fiction is the preponderant position held by the so-called "I novel." The essential feature of this literary form is that the novel is strictly autobiographical. The novelist writes about himself and his experiences, and about those around him. Since the novelist writes about himself, he must, if he is to have something interesting to say, have unusual experiences; and this, as a rule, takes the form of leading an unconventional life. The novelist, therefore, thinks of himself as a different breed, and lives in a detached literary world, and from his detached position he looks out at the world like a monk in a monastery. One might say that Japanese novelists show few signs of social consciousness. Instead of writing about social themes, they turn their attention to the contemplation of nature and natural beauty, for their main concern is to escape from the cares of the world.[13] The novelists probably represent an extreme case of withdrawal from the practical world; but the example is useful in that it points up a state of affairs which is common in varying degrees to all intellectuals.

There is another aspect of isolation which is probably inherent in the intellectual's function as "transformers." One may distinguish two facets of the problem. First, the very fact that they are "transformers" implies that they are living in two worlds. As intellectuals they are oriented toward the West, and their problem is to study and to understand the Western world, its techniques of social analysis, its philosophical systems, and its values. Much of the West is understood intellectually, but its applicability to the Japanese scene always remains a stumbling block. The ideas derived from the Western world cannot easily

---

[13] Ito Sei, *"Kindai Nihonjin no hasso no sho-keishiki"* (The various forms of expression among modern Japanese), *Shiso*, no. 344 (February, 1953) and no. 345 (March, 1953); also his *Shosetsu no hoho* (The method of the novel) (Kawade bunko series) (Tokyo, 1955). Howard S. Hibbett, "The Portrait of the Artist in Japanese Fiction," *Far Eastern Quarterly*, XIV (May, 1955), pp. 347–54.

be made an integral part of life situations. Karl Löwith, a German philosopher who taught in a Japanese university before the war, summed it up rather neatly when he said that Japanese intellectuals reminded him of a two-story house. The first floor was in Japanese style where its inhabitants felt and thought in traditional Japanese ways. The second floor was a large library filled with the great works of the Western world, ranging from Plato to Russell. And Löwith commented that there appeared to be no stairway linking the two floors.[14] Since, as Löwith implies, it is not at all easy to reconcile or "synthesize" the two civilizations, Japanese intellectuals often find themselves in a dilemma. As they become more Westernized they are likely to become more deviant in their own society, and hence to become alienated from other social groups.

The second facet of the problem has to do with intellectual communication. The literary output of intellectuals represents a form of discourse intelligible only to a rather small and select portion of the population. If we borrow Löwith's analogy, the people on the first floor have only a faint understanding of what goes on above them, partly because they live in a different world, and partly because, literally and figuratively, "it is over their heads." The journals of opinion, which are the favorite outlets for the literary endeavors of intellectuals, contain for the "man in the street" difficult ideas written in a formidable language. Much has been said about compulsory education and the high literacy rate; yet there is some doubt about the effectiveness of the present educational system to teach people to read much beyond the elementary level. A large scale study of literacy undertaken several years ago by a group of linguists and anthropologists produced the conclusion that only 6.2 per cent of a sample of the Japanese population could achieve a perfect score (allow-

[14] Karaki Junzo, *"Kindai Nihon no shiso bunka"* (Intellectual life in modern Japan), in *Sekai shi to Nihon* (World history and Japan) (Tokyo, 1953), p. 106.

ance being made for "careless mistakes") in a literacy test made up of words taken from the mass media and regarded as essential for one to know if he is to "lead a normal social life." [15]

Isolation, then, may help account for the paradoxical situation in which intellectuals find themselves. They enjoy social prestige, and yet, as they so often lament, they are unable to become influential politically. The answer to this paradox may lie in the inability of intellectuals to mobilize the masses and win their support. And without this support they cannot hope to become a potent political force.

A crucial question here is the relation of the intellectuals to the "middle strata" who provide a focal point of power in thousands of communities throughout the land. Maruyama has suggested that the middle strata serve as a kind of transmission belt for the spread of ideas to the masses. Through word-of-mouth communication, those who form the "middle strata" exert influence on the formation of public opinion.[16] They therefore stand between the intellectuals and the masses; and since the "middle strata" are conservatively inclined, the radicalism of the intellectuals is "filtered out" in the transmission process which carries ideas from one strata to another. If this analysis is correct, it is clear that until such time as the intellectuals can find the means of carrying their message directly to the masses and of influencing the political behavior of the masses, they will continue to be relatively ineffectual in Japanese politics.

---

[15] Tokyo Daigaku Shuppanbu, *Nihonjin no yomi-kaki noryoku* (The ability of Japanese to read and write) (Tokyo, 1951), p. 335.

[16] *Nihon fasshizumu no shiso to undo,* pp. 149 ff.

Chapter **13**

Violence in Politics

Physical coercion, or the threat of it, is part and parcel of political rule. When the great majority of the governed accept the political myths on which the regime rests; and when the political system is so organized that conflicting interests between various social groups can be reconciled and resolved by discussion and debate, the impulse to use force and violence recedes to the background. But even under these circumstances, there is, as V. O. Key says, the tacit assumption that one faction or another seeking ascendancy will resort to violence.[1]

Some political analysts make a distinction between force and violence. The criterion is that of legitimacy: force being looked upon as the legitimate use of coercion, and violence the illegitimate use of coercion. "In the social context," says Sidney Hook, "violence may be defined roughly as the illegal employment of methods of physical coercion for personal or group ends."[2]

[1] *Politics, Parties, and Pressure groups,* 2nd edition, p. 620–1.
[2] "Violence," in *Encyclopedia of the Social Sciences.*

THE TRADITION OF VIOLENCE

The Japanese feudal code of ethics which prevailed until the beginning of the modern state in the middle of the 19th century sanctioned the use of force and violence by the samurai or warrior class. A famous injunction stated that "The samurai is not to be interfered with in cutting down a fellow who has behaved to him in a rude manner." [3] According to Japanese feudal ethics, samurai were to be prepared at all times to serve their feudal lords with unswerving devotion and to face death with equanimity.

The samurai class as such was abolished early in the Meiji era; but some of the social attitudes and ideals associated with the samurai class were carried over into the modern period. Since many leaders in the political, economic, and cultural fields were drawn from the old samurai class, it was natural that samurai attitudes should be valued by the elite, and sometimes consciously inculcated among the masses through education and propaganda. The Japanese army in particular was strongly influenced by samurai traditions and certain types of behavior, such as resorting to mass suicide to avoid surrender, no doubt could be traced to these traditions.

Survivals of samurai attitudes can be found in several sectors of contemporary culture. Probably the most celebrated play in the repertoire of the Kabuki theater is *Chushingura*, a bloody tale of 47 samurai whose thoughts and actions are dominated by one idea—avenging the death of their feudal master. Japanese movies make frequent use of samurai themes which call for sword fighting and violent death. The number of pictures using such themes has increased in recent years. Finally, one might note that the most successful novelist in terms of income received from writing is Yoshikawa Eiji, whose specialty

[3] Quoted in E. H. Norman, *Ando Shoeki and the Anatomy of Japanese Feudalism,* published as a volume in the series, The Transactions of the Asiatic Society of Japan. Third series, II (December, 1949), p. 113.

is melodramatic novels featuring the adventures of swashbuck-ling samurai.

When the samurai class was abolished, some individual samurai who were unable to make the adjustment to new condi-tions became *soshi* or professional bullies, who attached them-selves to underworld gangs, ultra-nationalistic societies, such as the so-called "Black Dragon Society" (more appropriately the Amur River society), and even to political parties.

Soshi were sometimes responsible for political assassina-tions, which until recent times were a characteristic feature of Japanese political life. A number of prominent political figures have fallen victim to assassins in the modern period, and many more have barely escaped injury or death. In fact even a cursory examination of the memoirs of statesmen who held office in the 1930's shows that those who occupied the higher echelons of gov-ernment in that era lived in the shadow of fear—fear of assassina-tion. The veteran correspondent, Hugh Byas, who wrote about political developments in the 1930's appropriately called his book, "Government by Assassination."

The way in which a culture looks at and evaluates acts of violence like political assassinations is important. In Japanese culture, assassination generally does not arouse strong feelings of revulsion. It is tolerated, condoned, even approved, depend-ing on individuals and circumstances. Assassins, when brought to trial, have rationalized their actions by arguing that they per-petrated the deed to bring about political reform, to get rid of evil advisers around the Throne, to gain eternal fame for them-selves, and so on. Assassination has often had the tacit approval of the public; and this undoubtedly helps to account for its rel-atively high incidence in Japan. When the young army officers who assassinated Prime Minister Inukai Tsuyoshi in 1932 were brought to trial, counsel for defense "presented 111,000 letters ap-pealing for clemency, many of them written in blood." [4]

[4] Hugh Byas, *Government by Assassination* (New York, 1942), pp. 41–2.

Political assassination, which aims to remove a few people who are close to the center of power, is perpetrated by an individual or a small group of individuals. Uprisings and riots, in contrast, involve a larger number of participants, and their potentialities both for changing the power structure and for dramatizing demands and issues may be even greater. Japan has a long tradition of peasant uprisings. There were in the Tokugawa period alone several hundred peasant uprisings, some involving as many as a hundred thousand angry peasants who burned houses of officials and money lenders, and demanded a reduction in taxes. Peasant uprisings continued into the early years of the Meiji era but their frequency tapered off, the last uprisings of any significance taking place in the 1880's. In recent decades peasant uprisings have given way to tenancy disputes and to organized political action through peasant unions and left-wing parties.

Two notable urban riots have occurred in the modern period. The first was a riot in Tokyo in 1906 brought on when the police authorities banned a political rally protesting the provisions of the Portsmouth Treaty which followed the Russo-Japanese war. Angry mobs swarmed through the center of the city, attacking a pro-government newspaper and the Foreign Office, setting fire to the official residence of the Home Minister, demolishing police boxes, and overturning street cars. When the disturbance became of such a magnitude that the police were unable to cope with it, troops were called out to put down the rioting.

The second was the famous rice riots (1918), which started in a fishing village when housewives took action against the exorbitant price of rice. Rioting soon spread to other areas, including the major cities, where rice shops were attacked and warehouses set on fire. Troops were called out to restore order, and the government took measures to bring down the price of rice which had risen precipitously during the World War I period.

The military uprisings of the 1930's differed somewhat from the peasant uprisings and urban riots in that they involved, by and large, one section of the government using violence against another, in this case the younger officers putting pressure on the senior officers and the civilian government. Compared to assassinations, peasant uprisings, and urban riots, this type of uprising had, of course, much greater potentialities for upsetting the political status quo. In the beginning the senior officers used the army revolts as a lever to get a greater voice in the government for the military branch; but eventually they saw the dangers, and after the big uprising of young officers in February, 1936, they took stern measures, thus bringing revolts to an end.

In the post-war period, violence has often accompanied labor disputes. When picket lines are drawn and tempers become frayed, fists are likely to fly in Japan as elsewhere. Strong-arm squads have been used by both employers and unions; and violence has also flared up in intra-union controversies. "The tradition of the *ronin* or adventurer and the *soshi* or professional bully," notes Miriam Farley, "is strong in Japan and it was not surprising that it manifested itself on both sides in labor controversies." [5]

All revolutionary movements will resort to force at one point or another in order to gain power. In the early years of the Occupation, the Japanese Communist party played down the element of force and sought to gain popular support by becoming a "lovable Communist party." The emphasis on a "peaceful revolution," however, was abandoned after the Cominform criticism of Japanese Communist strategy in 1950, and thereafter the Japanese Communist movement became more militant. The highpoint was reached on May Day, 1952, when Communist-led demonstrators clashed with the police in the Imperial plaza, and some American service men were thrown into the Imperial moat and American cars were overturned by the mob. By resorting

[5] *Aspects of Japan's Labor Problems*, p. 86.

to violence, the Japanese Communists became more unpopular with the Japanese public, and the police were forced to take more stringent measures against them.

Before bringing this discussion of the tradition of violence to a close, it is appropriate to mention briefly the occurrence of violence within the Diet. Parliamentary government is the epitome of government by discussion and debate; yet the Japanese Diet has been the scene of violent outbreaks from time to time. In the pre-war period, parties used to assign seats nearest the aisle to nimble members who could get to the speaker's chair in a hurry when an argument broke out. Name plates on members' desks were sometimes used to strike opponents, and so eventually they came to be fastened down.[6] At times political parties resorted to bringing in *soshi* to intimidate political opponents.

Occasional violence and unbecoming behavior have marred post-war sessions and has served to reduce the prestige of the legislative body. In 1947, for example, some Diet members appeared on the floor in an intoxicated state, leading to a resolution to prevent intoxicants from being sold in the dining room:

> At the Socialist party Diet members meeting on 22 November, Sato, Kanjiro (Aichi Ken), Nogami, Kenji (Oita Ken) and Nishimura, Eiichi (Osaka Fu) presented the following motion: "Liberal Party Chief Secretary Ono and others were in a slightly intoxicated state when they attended the plenary session held on the evening of 21 November, and they created considerable disturbance. In order to protect the prestige of the Diet and the sacredness of the House, wine must not be served in the dining-room of the Diet Building." The motion was unanimously approved and presented to the Diet steering committee.[7]

[6] Arima Yoriyasu, *Seikai dochuki* (Travels in the political world) (Tokyo, 1951), pp. 39–41.

[7] *Tokyo Mimpo,* November 24, 1947, and translated in ATIS *Press Translations,* December 2, 1947.

Later the motion was withdrawn on the understanding that the Speaker would send a warning to the members involved.

In the summer of 1953 a Liberal party member of the Diet got into an argument with the Socialist chairman of the labor committee and kicked him, causing an injury which required medical treatment. Later in the same summer, violence again broke out in the plenary session of the House of Representatives when Arita Jiro, deputy-secretary general of the Liberal party turned to the socialists and shouted: "Shut up, street walker!" to Mrs. Tsutsumi Tsuruyo, a Right-Wing Socialist who was heckling a Liberal party member speaking against a non-confidence resolution. At this point, "Irate Opposition members rushed at Arita, who was sitting at the rear of the hall, leaping over desks in the process. Government party members tried to check the onrush causing a deafening roar and confusion." [8]

A more recent disturbance in the Diet occurred in June, 1954, when the Liberal party, then in power, introduced a resolution to extend the session an additional two days in order to permit consideration of a bill creating a centralized police system. The Socialists, who were opposed to the police bill, tried to prevent extension of the session, arguing that such extension was illegal. At 10:35 p.m., June 3, 1954, the bell signaling the beginning of another Diet session rang, but by this time Socialist members had occupied the speaker's chair and seats reserved for the Prime Minister and other cabinet members. The Socialists, moreover, had blocked the entrances to the chamber. The Liberals formed a flying wedge and tried to break through the blockade in order to get the speaker into his chair. Fighting broke out around the speaker's chair, which was surrounded by the Socialists. After a struggle the speaker was hoisted into his chair, only to be quickly ejected and eventually forced out of the chamber.

At this point, the Speaker of the House of Representatives summoned 200 policemen, and with their help and that of the Liberal party members, he tried to reenter the House of Repre-

[8] *Nippon Times*, August 2, 1953.

sentatives. There was another clash between the Liberals and the Socialists, who were still intent on preventing the speaker from getting to his chair. At midnight, the Socialists withdrew, asserting that the move to extend the session had been defeated, but the Speaker maintained, with the support of the conservative parties, that a resolution to extend the session had been passed at 11:57 p.m. This was the first time in the history of the Diet that police were brought to the floor of the Diet to quell a disorder.

The pattern of disturbance in the Diet suggests that violence is most likely to occur when there is disagreement over what one might call the "rules of the game." There is a good deal of criticism in the Japanese press and elsewhere about the abuse of power by the majority. Democracy rests on the principle of government by majority, but the power of the majority is always restrained by rules, both explicit (e.g., requiring two-thirds majority in certain instances) and implicit (e.g., the majority will not vote to get rid of the democratic system). When the "rules of the game" become clarified and firmly anchored through long practice, the impulse to resort to violence loses its force. The fact that parliamentary proceedings in Japan have been marred by the outbreak of violence from time to time attests to the immaturity of parliamentary government.

VIOLENCE AND POLITICS

Max Lerner once wrote that assassination was "an index of the gap between the driving political impulses of men and the limits of their attainment set up by the existing political forms." [9] A Japanese government study of "The causes of violent crimes" published in 1935 came to the conclusion that a smoothly operating parliamentary system which reflected the political conscious-

[9] "Assassination," in *Encyclopedia of the Social Sciences*.

ness of the people provided a safety valve, and that defects in the parliamentary system were a basic cause of the rise of right-wing and left-wing movements in Japan.[10]

Several days after Prime Minister Hara Kei fell victim of an assassin, Inukai Tsuyoshi, who himself was to die at the hands of another assassin a little more than a decade later, said:

> The act of assassination occurs when the people get into a melancholy mood. When a dark shadow falls across the political situation, assassinations come with regularity. If we create a period when dishonest acts of officials are done away with, and politics are discussed by means of true words, assassinations will disappear.[11]

The consensus of views cited above is that assassinations (and by extension other acts of violence) occur because of defects and rigidities in the political system. Acts of violence, in other words, may be regarded as belonging in the realm of social and political pathology.

A phenomenon often associated with violence, and which also pertains to social pathology, is the activities of so-called "anti-social" groups. The modernization of Japan has not yet succeeded in eliminating certain social groupings organized on the *oyabun-kobun* basis and resting fundamentally on the use of physical coercion and force. These "anti-social" organizations engage in activities like gambling, blackmail, levying tribute on street stalls and booths where cheap merchandise is sold, selling protection to dance halls and prostitutes, etc. They are essentially groups of racketeers who prey on the weak and on those who belong in the fringes of society. Harry Emerson Wildes has characterized them as follows:

[10] Shigetomi Yoshio, *"Shudan-teki boryoku hanzai no genin," Shiho kenkyu* (Studies in the administration of justice), no. 19 (1935).

[11] Quoted in Shimizu Ikutaro, *"Ansatsu"* (Assassination), *Chuo koron*, September, 1949, p. 25.

All such groups are conservative, all have a certain degree of cohesiveness based upon their family-like exclusiveness, their nostalgic feeling of reliance upon orders from above, their hunger for sonorous instructions, and their complete devotion to the Emperor as the soul and symbol of Japan. Professing a passionate devotion to justice, charity, love, and mutual obligation, they regard themselves as the embodiment of the true Japanese spirit.[12]

Curiously, although such "anti-social" groups are feared by those in the lower reaches of society, they are not necessarily disliked. For instance when an *oyabun* was arrested in Tokyo some people said that he was a generous and good man. One comment was that "he is the type of person who would even take the shirt off his back for people who are weak or are in trouble. He gave fifty to eighty per cent of the contributions in the community. He is greater than those who always talk [but do not act]; and he should be respected."[13] Apparently *oyabun* and their followers have succeeded in convincing others that they are devoted to justice, charity, and love.

One reason these "anti-social" organizations are able to generate tacit support among the lower classes is that they perform certain functions. As the foregoing quotation shows, they sometimes help the weak and the poor, although the ultimate source of their funds may be tribute levied on those who often can ill afford to pay such tribute. Occasionally, in a very flashy kind of way, they donate to community enterprises. Moreover, some of their activities have a quasi-political coloring. They may mediate in disputes and personal quarrels. They may, by resorting to strong-arm methods, or the threat of them, force debtors to pay long over-due bills. In other words, these groups sometimes take over some of the functions performed by the legal profession and the courts in American so-

[12] "Underground Politics in Post-War Japan," *The American Political Science Review,* XLII (December, 1948), p. 1159.

[13] Iwai Koyu, *"Han-shakai-teki shudan to shakai kincho"* (Social tensions and anti-social groups), *Shakai-teki kincho no kenkyu,* p. 110.

ciety. They are a part of the system of "informal government" which was discussed in Chapter 4.

These considerations suggest that there are deficiencies in the existing apparatus of state. The average citizen tends to feel that a great gap separates him from his government. In one of Yoshikawa Eiji's novels, a person asks where he can find the local government office, whereupon people tell him that it is no use going there to seek help because officials are not interested in helping the people, and they direct him to the local *oyabun*.[14]

The gap between the citizen and the government can be bridged, when needed, by the use of an intermediary or intermediaries with prestige and "face." Those who belong to the lower classes and have no influential friends and supporters are often impelled to turn to "anti-social" groups for assistance and protection. In other words, "anti-social" groups help fill the vacuum between the average individual and the government.

The political role of "anti-social" groups is often enhanced by the fact that politicians and political parties, especially the conservative variety, are not loath to make connections with such groups. Moreover, *oyabun* sometimes manage to get themselves elected to ward assemblies and city councils, and one well-known *oyabun*, Ozu Kinnosuke, ran unsuccessfully for the lower house in 1947 on the Liberal party ticket. It is easy to see that since these organizations can often control blocs of votes, they would be sought after by politicians bent on building a political machine.

Concluding Remarks

We have tried to show in the foregoing pages that violence and organizations whose stock in trade is the use of violence

[14] Takeda Kiyoko, "*Yoshikawa Eiji no shiso to sakuhin*" (Yoshikawa Eiji's thought and works), in *Yume to omokage* (Dreams and shadows), ed. by Shiso no kagaku kenkyukai (Tokyo, 1950), p. 92.

are an integral part of Japanese political life. Students of politics will recognize, of course, that violence, or the threat of it, is always present in political situations and hence this is not something that is unique to Japan. A more important question is the relative weight violence exerts in the political process. And here we are handicapped by the fact that as yet we have no method of accurately measuring the "violence level," so to speak, of a political system. We must, therefore, rely on impressions and observations when we try to make comparisons between one political system and another. On the basis of available information, it is hard to escape the conclusion that violence plays a more important role in Japanese politics than in American politics.

Chapter 14

The Decision-making Process

After the end of World War II, the victorious powers, breaking precedent, established international tribunals for bringing to trial German and Japanese leaders deemed responsible for starting the war. Twenty-eight of Japan's highest officials were indicted and brought before the International Military Tribunal for the Far East, which had been created to try and punish those who had committed crimes against peace, conventional war crimes, and crimes against humanity. In the course of lengthy proceedings which began in 1946 and lasted two years, hundreds of witnesses were called to testify and thousands of documents were introduced as exhibits in order to establish who had been responsible for the decisions which led to war, for the mistreatment of prisoners of war, and for atrocities committed by Japanese troops.

A striking feature of the trial was the denial of responsibility by the defendants. Except for ex-Prime Minister Tojo Hideki, who in a forthright fashion assumed full responsibility for his acts, all of the defendants tried either to prove that they had not been responsible for important decisions made by the government, or to minimize the part they had played. The civilian officials tried to shift the blame to the generals and admirals, arguing that they had been coerced by the military. On the problem of the mistreatment of prisoners of war, members of the war ministry and general staff asserted that armies in the field were responsible, while the field commanders claimed that they were merely following orders issued by the government.

It is understandable that men should be reluctant to assume responsibility for their actions when at a later date such actions are judged illegal or immoral, and especially when the penalty is long imprisonment or execution. Nevertheless, it would seem incorrect to attribute the evasion of responsibility entirely to the frailties of human nature. A part of it undoubtedly resulted from the structure of Japanese government and the process by which important state decisions were reached.

Decision-making as it occurs in the Japanese social context has not yet been adequately studied; but certain general characteristics are discernable, and on the basis of these a preliminary analysis can be made.

SOME FEATURES OF DECISION-MAKING

Political Fragmentation

We have alluded on several occasions to the matter of political fragmentation. Outwardly the Japanese state—particularly in the pre-war era—looked like a tightly-knit monolithic state in which decision-making was highly centralized. Appearances to the contrary, the Japanese state was in fact one without an effective head, and many important decisions were often taken by one division or another of the government, with little attempt being made to secure coordination or integration of the various units.

An illuminating example is provided by the decision to launch a surprise attack on Pearl Harbor. The idea of a carrier-based surprise air attack originated with the late Admiral

Yamamoto Isoroku, commander-in-chief of the combined fleet, early in 1941. Yamamoto's idea ran counter to the plan worked out by the naval general staff, and hence he was not able to "sell it" to the navy for a number of months. It was not formally accepted by the Japanese navy until October, 1941, some two months before the Pearl Harbor attack. The planning and preparation for the attack was carried out in strict secrecy and few outside of the navy were aware of it. "The prewar system of Japanese government," writes Robert Ward, "was such that no outside sanction was necessary for the adoption of the Pearl Harbor plan. Technically this was a command decision, a matter of purely naval strategy, despite its world-shaking implications. . . . There appears to be a fairly good possibility that even Tojo, then serving as both Premier and Minister of the Army, learned of the existence of the Pearl Harbor plan for the first time at a liaison conference held on November 30, 1941." [1]

Although it is difficult to get concrete data to substantiate it, very likely there is less fragmentation in the post-war political system. One gets the impression that the power of the political parties and of the Prime Minister has been increased substantially, thereby providing more centralized control of the government.

Decision by Consensus

Whenever possible, Japanese organizations, private and official, avoid arriving at a group decision by majority vote. The preferred way is by consensus. "The code calls for the group to reach decisions together—almost by a sort of empathy. The function of a chairman is, therefore, not to help people express themselves freely, but to divine the will of the

---

[1] Robert E. Ward, "The Inside Story of the Pearl Harbor Plan," *United States Naval Institute Proceedings,* LXXVII (December, 1951), p. 1279.

group, to express this will, and to state the decision reached, presumably on the basis of the divined will." [2]

The fact that a group will reach a decision by consensus does not mean that every member of the group is in agreement with the decision and is prepared to support it. Decision by consensus does prevent friction and conflict from coming out into the open, thereby preserving outward unanimity; but it does not necessarily lead to real compromise and accommodation. It would appear that this type of decision-making would be effective only if the meeting (or meetings) at which the group decision is arrived at is preceeded by long informal discussions among those in positions of influence. The real decisions are probably made in these informal discussions, and the meeting or conference is more for the purpose of putting the formal stamp of approval on a decision made previously.[3]

Consensus and Inter-Personal Communication

"When the nature of the task," says Alex Bavelas, "is such that it must be performed by a group rather than by a single individual, the problem of working relationships arises. One of the more important of these relationships is that of communication. Quite aside from a consideration of the effects of communication on what is generally called 'morale,' it is easily

[2] Fred N. Kerlinger, "Decision-Making in Japan," *Social Forces,* XXX (October, 1951), p. 38.

[3] See Robert E. Ward, "The Socio-political Role of the *Buraku* (hamlet) in Japan," *The American Political Science Review,* XLV (December, 1951), pp. 1030–1.

The following account of Hatoyama's election as president of the Liberal-Democratic party on April 5, 1956 is interesting: "His election, however, did not come about as many of his supporters might have wished. Contrary to traditional unanimous installation of a new president in keeping with a prearranged understanding, the choice this time took the form of balloting, which also publicly exposed intra-party strife." *The Japan News Letter,* No. 14 (April 6, 1956).

demonstrated that for entire classes of tasks any hope of success depends upon an effective flow of information." [4]

An outsider looking into the Japanese political process is struck by the relative lack of effective communication. A part of the difficulty appears to rest on the lack of precision in the Japanese language together with the rather slipshod manner in which the language is sometimes used. Anyone who has ever tried to translate Japanese into English, both in its oral and written forms, soon becomes keenly aware of the difficulties involved in communicating through the medium of the Japanese language. A more fundamental problem, however, has to do with the psychological barriers which seem to lie in the way of inter-personal communication. Many people are prevented by training and social custom from saying what they think and of revealing their real and innermost feelings and thoughts. The pressure for social harmony and for outward unanimity is too strong. Individuals who grow to maturity in such an environment must learn to fathom another's thoughts, feelings, and intentions by reading between the lines, by observing indirect signs, and by resorting to a kind of intuitive process. Some idea of the difficulties encountered in interpersonal communication among the political elite during the war may be gained from Robert Butow's study of the behind-the-scenes maneuvering to bring the war to a close.[5] Indeed, one is tempted to suggest that the chief reason political "deals" and decisions were often made (and continue to a lesser extent to be made) in geisha houses was that these houses provided a more suitable atmosphere for letting down the psychological bars and facilitated heart-to-heart talks.

In the following pages two case studies of important decisions will be given in order to provide more concrete data in support of the general propositions made above.

[4] "Communication Patterns in Task-Oriented Groups," in *The Policy Sciences,* ed. by Daniel Lerner (Stanford, 1951), p. 193.
[5] *Japan's Decision to Surrender,* especially Chapter 3.

DECISION-MAKING AND WORLD WAR II

The decision to declare war on the United States and the Allied nations was undoubtedly the most momentous decision made in the history of modern Japan. On that decision rested the future of Japan as a world power.

It is useful, therefore, to retrace as best we can, on the basis of available documentary evidence, the important steps which led Japan's leaders to choose war as a course of action. It appears in retrospect that the issue of war or peace was not settled in any one top-level conference; but rather the decision to declare war was the culmination of a long evolutionary process. A whole series of decisions of limited scope were taken, each one building on the other and pushing the nation that much closer to war. An important milestone was the Imperial conference of September 6, 1941, which put a time limit on attempts to reach settlement by peaceful means, and which permitted the armed forces to ready the machinery of war for action.

Since no decision is ever made in a vacuum, it is helpful to summarize briefly the setting in which the Imperial conference took place. By this time Japanese armies had bogged down in China and there was little prospect that the Chungking government under Chiang Kai-shek would capitulate, bringing the war in China to a victorious end. Nazi Germany had overrun Europe, and was advancing eastward into the Soviet Union. Japan was committed to the Axis pact and to the establishment of a "New Order in East Asia." As a result of Japanese policies in Asia, Japanese-American relations had approached a breaking point, and hence negotiations were being carried on in Washington to seek a settlement of some of the outstanding issues. In June, 1941, the Japanese army had pushed into French Indo-China, obtaining air bases and the right to station troops in that area. This action provoked the American government into freezing Japanese funds in the

United States, and into declaring an embargo which stopped the shipment of oil to Japan. The oil embargo forced the Japanese navy, dependant upon foreign supplies of oil, to move in favor of an early war before its stockpile of petroleum was exhausted. In general the course of events in the summer of 1941 strengthened the hand of those groups in Japan which argued that drastic action was called for since Japan was getting weaker in relation to the United States with the passage of time.

Of those in the armed forces, the men at the top levels of the Japanese navy were the least bellicose, since they were not at all confident that Japan could win a protracted war against the United States. However, many officers at the lower levels, that is, men who headed the various bureaus and other departments in the navy, were more militant; and it was these officers who drafted in August, 1941, a document called "An outline plan for carrying out the national policy of the Empire." [6] The gist of this document was that preparations for war would be completed toward the end of October, and that if Japan's demands could not be gained through diplomatic negotiation by that time, Japan should go to war. This policy document was first discussed at a conference of bureau chiefs of both the army and navy on August 16, and other conferences were held every few days throughout the remainder of the month. Many army leaders were in favor of a firm commitment to go to war, since the army could not mobilize a large number of men and prepare for war without such a commitment. The navy, on the other hand, was not under the same pressure, because it could prepare for war without losing its ability to return to the status quo ante fairly easily in case diplomatic negotiations were successful. Hence in the conferences held on August 27 and 28, Admiral Oka Takasumi,

[6] A convenient source for following the developments of this period is Hattori Takushiro, *Dai To-A senso zenshi* (History of the war in Eastern Asia) (Tokyo, 1953), I, pp. 177 ff.

chief of the naval affairs bureau of the navy ministry, argued against a firm policy to go to war and in favor of waiting to see how things would turn out in Europe. Despite objection of this kind, the original policy statement was accepted without major changes by the various bureaus in the Ministries of War and Navy, and also by the two chiefs of staff. It was therefore put on the agenda of a liaison conference on September 3, which lasted from 11 a.m. to 6 p.m.

The liaison conference, composed of the principal cabinet members and their chief assistants, the president of the Privy Council, the two chiefs of staff and their principal assistants, was the top body for deciding grave issues involving diplomacy and war. As in the case of other deliberative bodies, decisions were by unanimous agreement rather than by majority vote. After opening remarks by Admiral Nagano, chief of the navy general staff, Admiral Oikawa Koshiro, the navy minister, offered an amendment to one clause of the document which stated: "We are determined to commence war with the United States (Britain and the Netherlands) immediately in the event that by the early part of October our demands are not accepted." Oikawa proposed that it be changed to read: "We will take the last step for self-defense and self-preservation in the event that there is no prospect of our demands being accepted by the early part of October." After some debate Oikawa's proposed amendment was discarded and agreement was reached on the final version which stated: "We are determined to commence war with the United States (Britain and the Netherlands) immediately in the event that there is no prospect of our demands being accepted by the early part of October." Neither Konoye Fumimaro, the Prime Minister, nor Admiral Toyoda, the foreign minister, raised objections to the policy statement. Apparently neither realized that by this decision Japan had become committed to war and that hostilities could be averted only if the United States reversed its previous position and acceded to Japanese demands.

Having successfully cleared the liaison conference hurdle, the policy statement was next put before the Imperial conference, held in the presence of the Emperor. In practice the Imperial conference merely put the stamp of formal approval on decisions arrived at previously in the liaison conference. Prior to the Imperial conference, scheduled for September 6, 1941, the Emperor was briefed by the Prime Minister on the agenda of the meeting. The Emperor was disturbed. "This," he said, "would seem to give precedence to war." The Prime Minister declared that this was not the intention, that war would be declared only if diplomatic efforts failed. At the Emperor's insistence, the two chiefs of staff were summoned to the Imperial presence and questioned, whereupon they also said they gave precedence to diplomacy.

The Emperor was advised by the Lord Keeper of the Privy Seal not to ask further questions in the Imperial conference to be held the following day in order to avoid stirring up trouble, and it was arranged tha Hara, president of the Privy Council, should put the questions in his stead. At the Imperial conference Hara got up and asked: "In reading the statement it appears that war takes precedence over diplomacy. But is it proper to interpret it to mean that getting ready for war is to be prepared in case diplomacy fails, and that at the present time we will do our utmost to seek a diplomatic solution, and will go to war in the event that diplomatic negotiation is not possible?" The chief of staff was about to stand to reply when Navy Minister Oikawa spoke up and affirmed that Hara's interpretation was correct. Following this the Emperor read a poem composed by his grandfather, the Emperor Meiji, asking why it is that there are turbulent waves when universal fraternity prevails over the four seas. There was silence throughout the hall, and then the two chiefs of staff replied that they concurred in what Hara had said. The Imperial conference of September 6 cleared the way for the army and navy to prepare for action. Japan stood committed to war under the circumstances.

Several conclusions may be drawn from this brief account of the September conference and the background of events leading to it:

(1) The policy statement which was finally adopted originated somewhere below the top levels of the navy ministry. It shows that in Japan, as elsewhere, the ultimate contributor to a decision need not necessarily be high in the hierarchy.

(2) Quite clearly the intent of those who drew up the document was to commit Japan firmly to a policy of war with the United States. Those who favored such a policy were able to get it adopted despite opposition from a number of people who occupied top positions in the formal structure of authority.

(3) Although the purpose of the policy was to commit Japan to war, some of those who participated in the decision to adopt this policy were under a somewhat different impression. Those who hoped to stave off war were probably not fully aware of the implications of the decision they had helped make. If by group decision is meant a situation in which there is a flow of information and communication among those involved, leading to a common understanding of what was being agreed upon, the September 6 conference may be said to represent only a partial decision.

DECISION-MAKING AND THE RESIGNATION OF PREMIER YOSHIDA

A more recent case study of decision-making is afforded by the resignation of Premier Yoshida Shigeru in December, 1954. During the six years he had held office, Yoshida's popularity had waned considerably, partly because of his dictatorial methods, and partly because he was singularly inept in public relations, causing him to antagonize the press which seemed to go out of its way to portray him in a bad light. During the fall of 1954, the Premier took a trip abroad, and on his way home he stopped at Washington for a round of conferences with State Department and other officials. He was, in his negotiations with American officials, unable to get anything in the way of major concessions; and so he was unable to make a dramatic return and capture the public imagination.

Meanwhile, during his absence factional strife within his Liberal party, which experienced considerable difficulty in absorbing depurged political leaders, had reached a critical stage, leading to a walkout of 33 members of the House of Representatives under the leadership of Hatoyama Ichiro. These ex-Liberals then joined with the Progressive party to form a new Democratic party with Hatoyama as its president. The new conservative party, moreover, temporarily joined forces with the Socialists to prepare a non-confidence resolution, which, if introduced, was certain to pass, now that Liberal party strength had been depleted in the lower house.

Prior to this, Yoshida made public toward the end of November, 1954, a letter he had written to the leaders of his party, putting in their hands the question of his continuing to head the party or resigning. This gesture strengthened the position of those who opposed him within his own party and who were gravitating around Ogata Taketora, then being mentioned as Yoshida's successor.

The political situation reached a crisis stage early in December when the opposition made ready to present the non-confidence resolution. The Liberal party was now confronted with the choice of dissolving the Diet and calling for new elections, or resigning and permitting the opposition to form a new government. The Prime Minister made it very clear that he favored the former course, and documents were even being prepared toward that end. The rank and file, however, strongly opposed dissolution for two reasons. The big business firms whose financial contributions made election campaigns possible came out openly against dissolution at this time. An early December dissolution meant, also, that the campaign would have to extend through the holiday season when it would be extremely difficult to get the attention of the public. It is perhaps characteristic of Japanese organizations that communication between leaders and followers which is essential for group decision and action often breaks down. This certainly seems to have been the case in this instance.

The story is told that Ikeda Hayato, secretary-general of the Liberal party and a trusted follower of Yoshida, wanted to convey to the Premier what the rank and file of the party were thinking on this issue, but he was reluctant to tell Yoshida directly. Accordingly, Ikeda had a close friend write him a letter, and he took this letter to Yoshida with the remark that he had received this letter and others like it which show that the Prime Minister's intentions were misunderstood. Yoshida is said to have retorted that these letters no doubt contained nothing but criticism and refused to look at the one Ikeda brought.[7]

In any case, the rank and file soon showed its disaffection by circulating a petition urging resignation of the Cabinet; and before long some 120, or about two thirds, of the Diet members in the Liberal party affixed their signatures to it. Even when confronted by this concrete indication of rank and file revolt, Yoshida persisted in his determination to dissolve the lower house.

On December 6, the top leaders of the Liberal party met at the Prime Minister's residence to discuss the issues at hand.[8]

[7] Shimada Goro, *"Geki-teki naru saigo kakugi no jikkyo"* (An account of the dramatic last cabinet session), *Bungei shunju* (Annals of art and literature), special issue, *Sengo saidai no seihen*, January, 1955, p. 74.

[8] This account is based on material in Shimada, *op. cit.*, and *Yomiuri shimbun*, *Asahi shimbun*, and *Mainichi shimbun*, all for December 8, 1954.

Secretary-general Ikeda supported Yoshida's position, while Ono Bamboku, an old-time politician and chairman of the executive committee, opposed Yoshida and urged resignation. Some other party leaders maintained a neutral stand and remained silent. While the meeting was going on, some Diet members who had signed the petition went to the Prime Minister's residence, and, according to one account, called the leaders out of the meeting one by one and put pressure on them to vote for resignation. Another account differs somewhat and states that these representatives sent in a memorandum urging resignation. In any case, it is clear that there was a strong rank-and-file movement in favor of resignation.

Late the same day, Ogata met with Yoshida and tried to persuade the Prime Minister to agree to the resignation of the Cabinet, but the latter was adamant. Yoshida next conferred with Ikeda to prepare a program for the following day—a meeting of party leaders, followed by a cabinet meeting, an executive committee meeting, a meeting of the Diet members, and dissolution to be voted in the plenary session starting at one o'clock.

The next morning, December 7, Ogata met again with Yoshida, this time threatening to resign from the party and taking his followers with him if Yoshida insisted on pursuing his policy. Apparently Yoshida failed to realize until this juncture that Ogata was so firmly opposed to dissolution. It is an interesting commentary on the state of inter-personal communications that the Prime Minister was apparently unable to fathom correctly the feelings and intentions of the man he was grooming to be his successor. Despite Ogata's threat, the Prime Minister went into the meeting of party leaders still intent on carrying out his policy. In the meeting Ono and others opposed Yoshida and it ended with no decision being reached. A cabinet meeting followed in which there was the expected division: some supported Yoshida, others opposed him, and the remainder were non-committal. Angered by the opposition, Yoshida shouted that only those in favor of it need sign the order dissolving the lower house and asked the secretary of the Cabinet to bring in the documents for signature. A cabinet officer muttered that all those refusing to sign the document would first have to be relieved of their posts and that this would take time. The secretary of the Cabinet, seeing that the Cabinet was split, suggested that a recess be called in order to allow time for informal discussions. During the recess Yoshida was called to his study; and he never returned to another cabinet meeting. In his study Yoshida conferred individually with various party leaders and advisers and cabinet members; and several hours later bowed to party pressure. The cabinet meeting was resumed under the leadership of Ogata, who announced that he would like to have the Cabinet vote for resignation and who circulated among his colleagues for signature a document announcing the resignation of the Yoshida cabinet.

Chapter 15

Conclusion
and
Summary

Political power is found whenever and wherever men live in groups. In this sense it is universal. Nevertheless, the study of power is always fascinating because there are wide variations in the manner in which power is gained, retained, and exercised. Not only does the nature of power vary from one historical epoch to another, but it also varies from culture to culture. In the foregoing pages we have tried to analyze the way in which power is exercised in Japan in terms of the historical, social, ideological, and institutional setting, and the dominant political forces—business, labor, and agriculture.

In the course of our discussion, we have also referred to several major themes which relate to Japanese politics. It will be our task in this concluding chapter to try to bring these themes together and to see how they are interrelated.

The Persistence of Traditional Values

Japan is in many respects a modern nation. A Westerner feels pretty much at home in a big city like Tokyo with its office buildings, hotels, department stores, and subways. An American scientist will have much in common with his Japanese counterparts; and a European concert pianist will find an appreciative audience in Japan.

Yet for all its modernity, the culture still pays its homage to the past; and tradition and custom make their influence felt in a myriad of ways. The weight of the past seems particularly heavy in that facet of the culture which has to do with social behavior.

We have seen how traditional values emphasized the subordination of the individual to the group. The family, hierarchically organized, was looked upon as the model for social organization; and the family and the nation were considered fundamentally similar in character. The Meiji elite used old values to justify, sustain, and channelize social change, and later these values were inculcated through the educational system and through propaganda. Many of the traditional values were explicitly enunciated in formal documents like the Imperial Rescript on Education and *Kokutai no hongi* which were intended to serve as guideposts for moral education. Propaganda and indoctrination no doubt helped to perpetuate old values, but it is hard to believe that the perpetuation of old values was achieved through propaganda alone.

We should also look for other forces which were at work to preserve traditional values. Japanese statesmen have often considered agriculture as the fountain-head of conservatism, and in this they were correct for undoubtedly the agricultural way of life made (and continues to make) family and group solidarity a condition of survival. The way of life which prevails in Japanese rural communities fosters group solidarity and discourages the development of an individualistic spirit.

Another element which has probably contributed to the persistence of values calling for group solidarity is the problem of personal insecurity. In a stratified and slowly changing society every individual has his niche, and social rewards—material and immaterial—are distributed more or less in accordance with the position one enjoys in the society. In periods of rapid economic change, the situation becomes more fluid, and an individual's chances of improving his social and economic position are enhanced, but so are his chances of falling in status. One may rise from rags to riches; but by the same token one may fall from riches to rags. Presumably in those countries which have experienced large-scale geographical and economic expansion in modern times, the possibilities of an individual rising in social status have increased. Fragmentary evidence suggests that there has been a substantial measure of social mobility in Japan during the last century, and that some families which were once prominent have fallen by the wayside, while other families have managed to push ahead socially. Nevertheless, the range of opportunities for achieving a high social status through one's own efforts appear to be more limited than in the United States.

Because Japan was relatively heavily populated when she began her modernization program, because the large reservoir of surplus labor in the countryside tended to depress wage scales, and because colonial expansion on the scale that Western Europe experienced following the opening up of the New World was not possible, the average individual in Japan did not have many opportunities to accumulate sufficient savings to provide a substantial measure of economic (and with it) psychological security. An individual was often exposed to many uncertainties such as illness, unemployment, and business failure. Very likely because of the rapidity of change in the past century, the level of uncertainty has remained fairly high. One suspects that a common method of alleviating some of these uncertainties was through mutual aid, first within the family, and second, within the small group, which we called the "human group" in an earlier chapter. The individual, therefore, remained rather firmly anchored in his group, and through group ties and group action found security—both economic and psychological.

One consequence of the preoccupation of individuals with

their families and the small group has been the underdevelopment of more impersonal and formalized relationships. To be sure, Japanese society has large associations—indeed it cannot get along without them—but the fact remains that often individuals feel uncomfortable when put in impersonal situations, and many large organizations as a result become in actuality a conglomeration of numerous small groups.

The Role of the "Middle Strata"

The small group mentioned above may be thought of as forming the "cellular units" of Japanese society, and those who exercise influence within such units often belong to the "middle strata." Such individuals are found in tens of thousands of communities scattered over the land. Some are office holders, others are not; but all play a part in the political process. Viewed in terms of their functions, they are, first of all, leaders in informal government. They act, for instance, as mediators in local disputes, and in this way contribute to the maintenance of social harmony. They participate, moreover, in the transmission of political views and the formation of public opinion. Because their views are usually considered authoritative, they are in a position to "interpret" the news and opinions carried by the mass media and in this way they can often help create a climate of opinion which is at variance with the opinions expressed in the media.

Furthermore, they often serve as officials and informal leaders of local organizations, such as farm organizations, neighborhood associations and the like, and thus they are able to build up an organized following. Working through organizations of this kind, local leaders are in a position to manipulate the vote in favor of one candidate or another, and because of their ability to "deliver the vote" they become cogs in political machines. Another function of leaders belonging to the "middle strata" is to serve as intermediaries between the citizenry on the one hand and the formal institutions of government on the other. Thus, for example, a farmer or a retail merchant who finds that he must have dealings with one government agency or another is likely to first contact a local leader, who in turn will probably approach some member of a political party, requesting intercession on behalf of the individual in question.

Traditionally, local leaders were drawn from long established landed families. This is still the case in many rural communities; but changes have also occurred as a result of the decline of traditionally prominent families, especially as a result of the land reform program. There are indications that in some instances, professional people like school teachers are playing a more important role. Moreover, with industrialization and urbanization, new types of leaders have come to the fore. Building contractors, foremen in factories, officials of merchant associations, to mention a few representative types, now exercise leadership at the local level in towns and cities.

Local leaders are by their very nature dispersed geographically, and in terms of occupational status they are a heterogeneous lot. Yet they are a potent political force partly because they share an important characteristic, namely a common ideological orientation toward traditional values. It is in traditional values that these leaders find a rationale for their power position; and as a result they are understandably staunch defenders of such values.

The Challenge to Old Values

If, as we have mentioned, old values have persisted, they have also been challenged. Those in power in the Meiji era put high priority on the attainment of military power and economic development toward the end that Japan might achieve a prominent position in the international community. To promote economic development the government supported business enterprise by various direct means. In addition, it indirectly assisted business by providing compulsory education as well as technical education and by removing legal and other restraints on business activity which had been in effect during the Tokugawa period. The development of capitalistic enterprise and the spread of capitalistic ethos which followed could not help but affect the relation of the individual to the social order. Individual ownership of private property was given legal recognition. A competitive spirit came to permeate the society; and increasingly wealth became a measure of individual success. In the economic sphere at least there was a basis for the rise of individualism. At the same time, the disparity in the amount of wealth held by different families and individuals became more marked and gradually consciousness of class divisions became increasingly acute.

The growth of industry attracted an increasing number of people to the cities. To a certain extent urban life detached individuals from their old social moorings and subjected them to new influences, social as well as intellectual. New types of associations such as labor unions gradually developed to claim the allegiance of those belonging to the working class. Moreover, mass education and the development of mass communications paved the way for the spread of new ideas—including alien social and political doctrines like individualism, democracy, socialism, and communism—which were not consistent with the dominant political doctrines and myths. These new doctrines had appeal, especially among the intellectuals, probably because the harsh realities of economic life—competition and conflict among classes, exploitation, the creation of a property less proletariat—could not be easily reconciled with traditional values which taught that the nation was a family living in harmony.

What occasions surprise is not the fact that such new and heady political doctrines found an audience, but that they made, relatively speaking, so shallow an impact in terms of changing the modes of social behavior. Japanese intellectuals have produced an extensive literature arguing the pros and cons of every conceivable kind of social theory. Yet these discussions appear to have remained pretty much confined to the intellectual class, and social theory does not seem to have directly affected the masses in a significant way.

A part of the answer to this puzzling situation would appear to lie in the isolation of the intellectuals and the strong position held by the "middle strata." Another important factor was the way in which new techniques and institutions were often incorporated into the existing system. For example, even though Japan became industrialized, personnel management in many factories and companies rested on the ideal of paternalism in which management was likened to a benevolent father.

It would seem, nevertheless, that in the long run traditional values are destined to be changed fundamentally, and that such changes will come less from the intellectual appreciation of new political doctrines than from slowly accumulating changes in social needs and habits. Among those changes, the ones relating to the family are of basic importance. There are signs that sharp differences of opinion now exist between the older generation and the youth of Japan on such vital issues as whether arranged marriages are more desirable than romantic marriages, and whether a son's first loyalty should be to his parents rather than to his wife. There is a trend, particularly in the cities, toward a nuclear family more akin to the American family than to the traditional Japanese family.

Changes are also occurring in other sectors. For instance, Mischa Titiev noted in his study of neighborhood associations in the Okayama area that there was a trend "away from reliance on and cooperation with relatives and toward greater ties with nonkin," and he expressed the belief that it probably represented a "Japanese manifestation of a basic trend that is going on in all contemporary nations and that may be seen, for example, in conjunction with the universal shift from rural to urban centers of population as a country becomes increasingly industrialized."[1]

Profound modifications will most certainly appear in the Japanese political system as further urbanization and industrialization take place, leading to the growth of a more formalized and impersonal pattern of social relationships. It is difficult, of course, to predict with any feeling of certainty the course of future events, but it seems reasonable to assume that, among other things, the position and role of the "middle strata" will be altered significantly, that the structure and role of political parties will change and that decision-making will be less by consensus and more by majority vote. But in the meantime, the fact remains that at present highly personalized relationships still predominate; and we may now turn to a consideration of some of the implications of this state of affairs.

Schism in the Body Politic

Before the war the problem of conflict between the traditional system of values and changing social conditions was not solved through accommodation and compromise; but rather was hidden from public view through the suppression of ideas which ran counter to the dominant political doctrines and myths. The political and social tensions resulting from the conflict between old values and new conditions were not released but were suppressed. It would appear reasonable to suppose that outbreaks of violence in the pre-war period were related to the suppression of these social and political tensions, and that the use of violence had a certain amount of cathartic effect.

There is a significant difference between the pre-war and

---

[1] "Changing patterns of *kumiai* structure in rural Okayama," *Occasional Papers*, University of Michigan, Center for Japanese Studies, No. 4 (1953), p. 11.

the post-war political situations with regard to the use of authoritarian measures to overcome tensions. The freedom of political expression which has come to prevail in the post-war period has done much to relieve some of the tensions. Moreover, the emergence of a relatively strong Socialist party now provides those who find the traditional order to their disliking with a vehicle for registering political protest.

But in politics, as in other aspects of social life, long-established habits are slow to change. The preference which still persists for highly personalized and enduring social relationships results in the fragmentation of Japanese society into numerous small groups. The existence of small groups, in turn, encourages its individual members to seek solutions to their problems, if possible, within the framework of the small group. Quarrels are mediated, economic aid is provided, moral support is given in crisis situations by the members of the group. But such a society must also pay a price—and the price is political apathy. For many people government remains something remote, something not intimately connected with their lives. Many an individual finds that "informal government" is more immediate and more important than formal political institutions.

On the other hand, political and economic groups which want to further their interests through political action make it a practice to establish contacts with the political parties and the bureaucracy either through organized effort or through personal connections. This means that those who have economic interests to defend, and hence are likely to feel strongly about politics are in a position to secure access to government agencies to present their case.

Thus, the Japanese political structure may be thought of as a bifurcated one. On the one hand, the great mass of citizens are governed by "informal government" while, on the other hand, powerful interest groups are closely tied to the formal institutions of the central government. Links between the two parts of the political structure are provided by local leaders, who overtly or covertly exercise influence, and by the political parties.

It will be readily seen that one weakness of this kind of political structure is that the "public interest" is likely to come out second best. There seems to be no agency within the Japanese government which serves as the defender of the public interest; and thus unless it should so happen that competing interests cancel themselves out, the special interests will most certainly gain their ends at the expense of the public interest.

Another weakness is the difficulty of carrying through political action which requires mass participation for its success. Because of the political structure, it is no easy task to launch and generate enthusiasm for a national campaign aimed to achieve some public good which involves voluntary action on the part of many people. This kind of political system can be highly resistant to change initiated and directed by the central government authorities. For this reason the task of political leadership in Japan is a formidable one. A country like Japan must make the best use of her meager resources and plan intelligently for the future if she is to survive in the modern world. Hence much will depend on whether capable and far-sighted political leaders will appear and whether they will be able to develop effective programs and "sell" such programs to the people.

Having called attention to the more obvious disadvantages of political fragmentation, we should also note some of the advantages. As historical experience has shown, a society organized on the basis of small groups has a remarkable capacity for survival in times of severe dislocation and distress. Unlike a highly integrated political system whose proper functioning is dependent upon direction from the center, a loosely organized system can continue to operate even if the center becomes disorganized or even paralyzed. By the same token, the Japanese political system contains within it elements of stability; and hence the possibilities of the social order breaking down as a prelude to revolution seem rather remote.

Political analysts will be able to find many seeming defects and weaknesses in the Japanese political system; yet the fact remains that many people are apparently reasonably content with the way in which the system works. And in the last analysis, this is of cardinal importance in politics.

❋ *Works Consulted*

1. NEWSPAPERS

Asahi Evening News
Asahi Shimbun
Dokusho Shimbun
Nippon Times
Press Translations and Summaries by Allied Translator and Interpreter Section

2. BOOKS IN ENGLISH

Allen, G. C.: *A Short Economic History of Modern Japan.* London: G. Allen & Unwin [1946].

Benedict, Ruth: *The Chrysanthemum and the Sword.* Boston: Houghton Mifflin Company, 1946.

Bisson, T. A.: *Zaibatsu Dissolution in Japan.* Berkeley: University of California Press, 1954.

Borton, Hugh (ed.): *Japan.* Ithaca: Cornell University Press, 1950.

Butow, Robert J. C.: *Japan's Decision to Surrender.* Stanford: Stanford University Press, 1954.

Byas, Hugh: *Government by Assassination.* New York: Alfred A. Knopf, 1942.

Colbert, Evelyn S.: *The Left Wing in Japanese Politics.* New York: Institute of Pacific Relations, 1952.

Cooper, John L.: *Development of Agricultural Cooperatives in Japan.* Tokyo: Supreme Commander for the Allied Powers, Natural Resources Section, 1949.

Embree, John Fee: *Suye Mura, a Japanese Village.* Chicago: The University of Chicago Press [1939].

Farley, Miriam S.: *Aspects of Japan's Labor Problems.* New York: The John Day Company, 1950.

Friedrich, Carl J.: *Constitutional Government and Democracy.* Boston: Little, Brown and Company, 1941.

Gerth, Hans, and Mills, C. Wright: *Character and Social Structure.* New York: Harcourt, Brace, 1953.

Hall, Robert King: *Shushin: The Ethics of a Defeated Nation.* New York: Bureau of Publications, Teachers College, Columbia University; 1949.

Hunter, Floyd: *Community Power Structure.* Chapel Hill: University of North Carolina Press [1953].

Ike, Nobutaka: *The Beginnings of Political Democracy in Japan.* Baltimore: The Johns Hopkins Press, 1950.

Ishino, Iwao, and Bennett, John W.: *The Japanese Labor Boss System.* Columbus: The Ohio University Research Foundation, 1952.

Japan. Ministry of Education. *Kokutai no hongi.* Trans. by John Owen Gauntlett. Cambridge: Harvard University Press, 1949.

Japan. Office of the Prime Minister. Bureau of Statistics: *Japan Statistical Yearbook.* Tokyo, 1949–

Key, V. O., Jr.: *Politics, Parties, and Pressure Groups.* Second Edition. New York: Thomas Y. Crowell Company, 1947.

———: *Southern Politics in State and Nation.* New York: Alfred A. Knopf, 1949.

Lamott, Willis: *Nippon; the Crime and Punishment of Japan.* New York: The John Day Company, 1944.

Lerner, Daniel (ed.): *The Policy Sciences.* Stanford: Stanford University Press [1951].

Lockwood, William W.: *The Economic Development of Japan.* Princeton: Princeton University Press, 1954.

MacIver, R. M.: *The Web of Government.* New York: The Macmillan Company, 1947.

Merriam, Charles Edward: *Systematic Politics.* Chicago: The University of Chicago Press [1945].

Merton, Robert K.: *Social Theory and Social Structure.* Glencoe: Free Press, 1949.

Nagai, Michio: *Dozoku: a Preliminary Study of the Japanese "Extended Family" Group and Its Social and Economic Functions.* Columbus: The Ohio State University Research Foundation, 1953.

Norbeck, Edward: *Takashima: a Japanese Fishing Village.* Salt Lake City: University of Utah Press, 1954.

Norman, E. Herbert: *Ando Shoeki and the Anatomy of Japanese Feudalism.* The Transactions of the Asiatic Society of Japan. Third Series, Vol. 2 (December 1949).

————: *Japan's Emergence as a Modern State.* New York: Institute of Pacific Relations, 1940.

Obata, Kyugoro: *An Interpretation of the Life of Viscount Shibusawa.* Tokyo, 1937.

Reischauer, Edwin O.: *Japan, Past and Present.* Second Edition. New York: Alfred A. Knopf, 1953.

————: *The United States and Japan.* Cambridge: Harvard University Press, 1950.

Sabine, George H.: *A History of Political Theory.* New York: Henry Holt and Company, 1937.

Sansom, G. B.: *Japan in World History.* New York: Institute of Pacific Relations, 1951.

————: *The Western World and Japan.* New York: Alfred A. Knopf, 1950.

Scalapino, Robert A.: *Democracy and the Party Movement in Prewar Japan.* Berkeley: University of California Press, 1953.

Schumpeter, E. B. (ed.): *The Industrialization of Japan and Manchukuo, 1930–1940.* New York: The Macmillan Company, 1940.

Schumpeter, Joseph A.: *Capitalism, Socialism, and Democracy.* Third Edition. New York: Harper and Brothers, 1950.

Schramm, Wilbur (ed.): *Mass Communications.* Urbana: University of Illinois Press, 1949.

Schwantes, Robert S.: *Japanese and Americans.* New York: Harper and Brothers, 1955.

Smith, Thomas C.: *Political Change and Industrial Development in Japan; Government Enterprise, 1868–1880.* Stanford: Stanford University Press, 1955.

Stoetzel, Jean: *Without the Chrysanthemum and the Sword*. New York: Columbia University Press, 1955.

Supreme Commander for the Allied Powers: *Political Reorientation of Japan*. Two volumes. Washington: U.S. Government Printing Office [1949].

Swearingen, Rodger, and Langer, Paul: *Red Flag in Japan*. Cambridge: Harvard University Press, 1952.

Toynbee, Arnold J.: *A Study of History*. Vol. 5. London: Oxford University Press, 1954.

Truman, David B.: *The Governmental Process*. New York: Alfred A. Knopf, 1951.

U.S. Mission on Japanese Combines: *Report of the Mission on Japanese Combines*. Part I. Washington: U.S. Government Printing Office, 1946.

White, Leonard D. (ed.): *The Civil Service in the Modern State*. Chicago: The University of Chicago Press, 1930.

Wildes, Harry Emerson: *Typhoon in Tokyo*. New York: The Macmillan Company, 1954.

3. ARTICLES IN ENGLISH

Beardsley, Richard K.: "The Household in the Status System of Japanese Villages." *Occasional Papers*. University of Michigan, Center for Japanese Studies, No. 2 (1951).

Colton, Hattie Kawahara: "The Workings of the Japanese Diet." *Pacific Affairs*, Vol. 28 (December, 1955).

Colton, Kenneth: "Conservative Leadership in Japan." *Far Eastern Survey*, Vol. 24 (June, 1955).

Dore, R. P.: "The Ethics of the New Japan." *Pacific Affairs*, Vol. 25 (June, 1952).

Dull, Paul S.: "Mano Tokuichi; a Case Study of a Political Boss in a Japanese Town." Mimeographed. [1954].

————: "The Senkyoya System in Rural Japanese Communities." *Occasional Papers*. University of Michigan, Center for Japanese Studies, No. 4 (1953).

Esman, Milton J.: "Japanese Administration—a Comparative View." *Public Administration Review*, Vol. 7 (Spring, 1947).

Hibbett, Howard S.: "The Portrait of the Artist in Japanese Fiction." *Far Eastern Quarterly*, Vol. 14 (May, 1955).

Hyman, Herbert H.: "World Surveys—The Japanese Angle." *International Journal of Opinion and Attitude Research,* Vol. 1 (June, 1947).

Japan. The House of Peers, 90th Session of the Imperial Diet: *The Official Gazette.* English Edition. Extra No. 40 (October 7, 1946).

Karasawa, Tomitaro: "Changes in Japanese Education as Revealed in Textbooks." *Japan Quarterly,* Vol. 2 (July–September, 1955).

Kerling, Fred N.: "Decision-making in Japan." *Social Forces,* Vol. 30 (October, 1951).

Levine, Soloman B.: "Prospects of Japanese Labor." *Far Eastern Survey,* Vol. 23 (May, 1954).

McCamy, James L.: "Analysis of the Procegss of Decision-making." *Public Administration Review,* Vol. 7 (Winter, 1947).

MacDonald, Hugh H., and Esman, Milton J.: "The Japanese Civil Service." *Public Personnel Review,* October, 1946.

Maki, John M.: "The Prime Minister's Office and Executive Power." *Far Eastern Survey,* Vol. 24 (May, 1955).

Mendel, Douglas H.: "Revisionist Opinion in Post-Treaty Japan," *American Political Science Review,* Vol. 48 (September, 1954).

Okawa, Kazushi, and Noda, Tsutomu: "Measurements of the Standard of Living in Japan." *Keizai Kenkyu* (Study of Economics), Vol. 2 (January, 1951).

Passin, Herbert: "The Development of Public Opinion Research in Japan." *International Journal of Opinion and Attitude Research,* Vol. 5 (Spring, 1951).

Roser, Foster: "Establishing a Modern Merit System in Japan." *Public Personnel Review,* Vol. 11 (October, 1950).

Shirvens, Maynard, and Speicher, Joseph L.: "Examination of Japan's Upper Bureaucracy." *Personnel Administration,* July, 1951.

Smith, Thomas C.: "Old Values and New Techniques in the Modernization of Japan." *Far Eastern Quarterly,* Vol. 14 (May, 1955).

Smythe, Hugh H., and Watanabe, Masaharu: "Japanese Popular Attitudes Toward the Emperor." *Pacific Affairs,* Vol. 26 (December, 1953).

Steiner, Kurt: "The Revision of the Civil Code: Provisions Affecting the Family." *Far Eastern Quarterly,* Vol. 9 (February, 1950).

Titiev, Mischa: "Changing Patterns of *Kumiai* Structure in Rural Okayama." *Occasional Papers.* University of Michigan, Center for Japanese Studies, No. 4 (1953).

Totten, George: "Problems of Japanese Socialist Leadership." *Pacific Affairs*, Vol. 28 (June, 1955).

Ward, Robert E.: "The Inside Story of the Pearl Harbor Plan." *United States Naval Institute Proceedings*, Vol. 77 (December, 1951).

————: "The Socio-political Role of the *Buraku* (hamlet) in Japan." *American Political Science Review*, Vol. 45 (December, 1951).

Wildes, Harry Emerson: "Underground Politics in Post-War Japan." *American Political Science Review*, Vol. 42 (December, 1948).

Williams, Justin: "Party Politics in the New Japanese Diet." *American Political Science Review*, Vol. 42 (December, 1948).

Yamanaka, Tokutaro: "Japanese Small Industries during the Industrial Revolution." *The Annals of the Hitotsubashi Academy*, Vol. 2 (October, 1951).

————: "The Nature of Small Industries." *The Annals of the Hitotsubashi Academy*, Vol. 4 (October, 1953).

4. BOOKS IN JAPANESE

Adachi, Tadao: *Kindai kanryo-sei to shokkai-sei* (Modern bureaucracy and job classification). Tokyo, 1952.

Arima, Yoriyasu: *Seikai dochuki* (Travels in the political world). Tokyo, 1951.

Fukutake, Tadashi: *Nihon noson no shakai-teki seikaku* (The social character of Japanese farm villages). Tokyo, 1949.

Furushima, Toshio: *Kaikaku tojo no Nihon nogyo* (Japanese agriculture in the process of reform). Tokyo, 1949.

Harada, Kumao: *Saionji Ko to seikyoku* (Prince Saionji and the political situation). Eight volumes. Tokyo, 1950.

Hattori, Takushiro: *Dai To-A Senso Zenshi* (History of the war in eastern Asia). Four Volumes. Tokyo, 1953.

Hijikata, Seibi: *Zaisei shi* (History of Finance). (*Gendai Nihon Bummei Shi*, Vol. 4). Tokyo, 1942.

Hirose, Ken'ichi: *Saha Shakaito no jittai* (On the left-wing Socialist party). Tokyo, 1955.

Ifukube, Takahiko: *Un, don, kon* (Fate, dullness, perseverance). Tokyo, 1952.

Iizuka, Koji: *Nihon no guntai* (Japan's army). Tokyo, 1950.

Imai, Kazuo: *Kanryo, sono seitai to uchimaku* (Bureaucrats, their mode of life and behind-the-scenes activities). Tokyo, 1953.

Inagaki, Tatsuo: *Gendai seito ron* (Contemporary parties). Tokyo, 1949.

Ishida, Takeshi: *Meiji seiji shiso shi kenkyu* (A study of Meiji political theory). Tokyo, 1954.

Ito, Sei: *Shosetsu no hoho* (The method of the novel). Tokyo, 1955.

Japan. Keizai Shingicho: *Nihon keizai to kokumin shotoku* (Japanese economy and national income). Tokyo, 1954.

Japan. Kokkai: *Futo Zaisan Torihiki Chosa Tokubetsu Iin Kaigi Roku* (Proceedings of the Special Investigating Committee on Illegal Property Transactions). Second Session, 1948.

————: *Shugiin Mombu Iinkai Kaigiroku* (Proceedings of the Education Committee of the House of Representatives). Twelfth Session. No. 4 (November 26, 1951).

Japan. Sorifu. Kokuritsu Seron Chosajo: *Shakai kyoiku ni tsuite no seron chosa.* (Public Opinion Survey on Social Education). Report No. 51 (March, 1953).

Kakehi, Katsuhiko: *Kokka no kenkyu* (A Study of the state). Tokyo, 1930.

Kanzaki, Hiroyoshi: *Noson jinko ijiron* (On Maintaining the agricultural population). Tokyo, 1944.

Kawai, Etsuzo: *Noson no seikatsu* (Life in the farm villages). Tokyo, 1952.

Kawashima, Takeyoshi: *Kekkon* (Marriage). Tokyo, 1954.

Koyama, Eizo: *Shimbun shakaigaku* (Sociology of newspapers). Tokyo, 1951.

Kyochokai: *Kosaku sogichi ni okeru noson jijo* (Conditions in areas which were the scene of tenancy disputes). Tokyo, 1934.

Kyokuto Kokusai Gunji Saiban Kenkyukai: *Kido nikki* (Kido diary). Tokyo, 1947.

Maki, Kenji: *Nihon kokutai no riron* (The theory of Japan's *kokutai*). Revised Edition. Tokyo, 1940.

Maruyama, Masao: "Meiji kokka no shiso" (The ideology of the Meiji state) in *Nihon shakai no shi-teki kyumei* (A historical study of Japanese society), ed. by Rekishigaku Kenkyukai. Tokyo, 1949.

————: *"Nihon fasshizumu no shiso to undo"* (The ideology and structure of Japanese fascism) in *Sonjo shiso to zettaishugi* (The pro-emperor ideology and absolutism), ed. by Toyama Shigeki. Tokyo; 1948.

Masu komunikashion koza (Lectures on mass communications). Six Volumes. Published by Kawada Shobo. Tokyo, 1955–56.

Minami, Hiroshi: *Nihonjin no shinri* (The psychology of the Japanese people). Tokyo, 1953.

Morita, Yoshio: *Waga kuni no shihonka dantai* (Organizations of capitalists in our country). Tokyo, 1926.

Nakamura, Akira (ed.): *Gendai seiji no kiso chishiki* (Basic knowledge about contemporary politics). Tokyo, 1952.

Nakaoka, Hiroo: *Nihon-teki sekaikan josetsu* (An introduction to the Japanese world-view). Tokyo, 1944.

Natori, Giichi: *Sei-zaikaijin no meiun* (The fortunes of leaders in the political and financial world). Tokyo, 1952.

Natsume, Soseki: "Gendai Nihon no kaika" (Enlightenment in contemporary Japan), in *Soseki zenshu* (Collected Works of Soseki), Vol. 13. Tokyo, 1936.

Nihon gensei (Japan's present situation), ed. by Kyodo Tsushin Sha. 1954 Edition. Tokyo, 1953.

Nihon Jimbun Kagakukai: *Shakai-teki kincho no kenkyu* (A Study of social tensions). Tokyo, 1953.

Nihon Seiji Gakkai: *Nihon seijigaku nempo* (Annuals of the Japanese political science association), Vol. 1 (1950).

Nochi Kaikaku Kiroku Iinkai: *Nochi kaikaku temmatsu gaiyo* (A report on the land reform). Tokyo, 1951.

Ohara Shakai Mondai Kenkyujo: *Nihon rodo nenkan* (Japan labor yearbook).

Okochi, Kazuo: *Nihon rodo kumiai ron* (On Japanese labor unions). Tokyo, 1953.

Osatake, Takeshi: *Nihon kensei shi taiko* (An outline of Japanese constitutional history). Two Volumes. Tokyo, 1939.

Royama, Masamichi (ed.): *Nihon no seiji* (Japanese politics). Tokyo, 1955.

Royama, Masamichi: *Noson jichi no henbo* (Changes in local government in rural areas). Tokyo, 1948.

—— (ed.): *Seiji ishiki no kaibo* (An analysis of voting consciousness). Tokyo, 1949.

————: *Seron ni kansuru kangae-kata* (On public opinion). Tokyo, 1955.

Royama, Masamichi, et al.: *Sosenkyo no jittai* (A survey of the general election). Tokyo, 1955.

Sakurai, Takeo: *Nihon nohonshugi* (Agriculture as the basis of the state in Japan). Tokyo, 1935.

Sawamura, Yasui: *Nogyo dantai ron* (On agricultural organizations). Tokyo, 1936.

Sengoku, Kotaro, and Shimada, Hideo: *Nihon noson sangyo kumiai no tembo* (The outlook for Japanese agricultural cooperatives). Tokyo, 1936.

Sengo Nihon no seiji katei (Post-war Japanese politics), 1953 issue of *Nihon Seiji Gakkai Nempo.*

Shakai Kagaku Kenkyujo: *Gendai shakai no kenkyu* (A study of contemporary society). Tokyo, 1948.

Shimmin no Michi (The way of the subjects), published by the Ministry of Education. Tokyo, 1941.

Shiso no Kagaku Kenkyukai: *Watakushi no tetsugaku* (My philosophy) and *Watakushi no tetsugaku, zoku.* Tokyo, 1950–51.

————: *Yume to omokage* (Dreams and phantoms). Tokyo, 1950.

Shuppan nenkan (Publishing yearbook), ed. by Tokyodo, 1931 Edition. Tokyo, 1931.

Sobunsha: *Sekaishi to Nihon* (World history and Japan). Tokyo, 1953.

Suehiro, Gentaro: *Nihon rodo kumiai undo shi* (A history of the Japanese labor movement). Tokyo, 1950.

Suzuki, Eitaro: *Nihon noson shakaigaku yoron* (The essentials of rural sociology). Tokyo, 1949.

Suzuki, Yasuzo: *Nihon seiji no kijun* (The basis of Japanese politics). Tokyo, 1941.

Tohata, Seiichi: *Nihon nogyo no tenkai katei* (The development of Japanese agriculture). Tokyo, 1939.

Tokyo Daigaku Shuppanbu: *Nihonjin no yomi-kaki noryoku* (The ability of Japanese to read and write). Tokyo, 1951.

Tsuchiya, Takao: *Nihon shihonshugi no keieishi-teki kenkyu* (A historical study of entrepreneurs in Japanese capitalism). Tokyo, 1954.

Tsuji, Kan'ichi: *Jingasa* (Rank and file). Tokyo, 1953.

Tsuji, Kiyoaki: *Nihon kanryosei no kenkyu* (A study of the Japanese bureaucracy). Tokyo, 1953.

Washio, Yoshinao (ed.): *Seikai gojunen: Kojima Kazuo kaikoroku* (Fifty years in the political world: the Memoirs of Kojima Kazuo). Tokyo, 1951.

Yagi, Yoshinosuke: *Beikoku toseiron* (On rice controls). Tokyo, 1934.

Zenkoku Noson Sangyo Kumiai Kyokai: *Dai rokujushichi gikai ni okeru beikoku san-ken ryo-hoan o meguru sangyo kumiai to sho-undo* (The activities of the rural cooperatives with reference to two bills on rice and raw silk in the 67th session of the Diet). Tokyo, 1935.

5. ARTICLES IN JAPANESE

Ariga, Kizaemon: *"Senkyo no jittai"* (The reality behind elections). *Shakaigaku hyoron* (Japanese sociological review). Vol. 1 (May, 1951).

"Aru keisu-jo no ketsuron" (A certain statistical conclusion). *Shakai undo tsushin* (Report on social movements), No. 448 (February 23, 1955).

Hayashi, Shunzo: *"Rippo no doki oyobi kore ni kansuru jakkan no mondai ni tsuite"* (Motivation for legislation and several problems related to it). *Jiyurisuto* (Jurist), No. 35 (June, 1953).

Hidaka, Rokuro, et al.: *"Rodosha no komunikashion katei"* (Workers and the communications process). *Tokyo Daigaku shimbun kenkyujo kiyo* (Bulletin of the Institute of Journalism, University of Tokyo), Vol. 4 (1955).

Hidaka, Rokuro: *"Rodosha to masu komunikeshion to no musubi-tsuke"* (Workers and their relation to the mass communications). *Shiso* (Thought), No. 370 (April, 1955).

Hisha, Kimpachi: *"Keizai dantai no uchimaku"* (Behind-the-Scenes of economic organizations). *Toyo keizai shimpo* (Oriental economic review), Bessatsu, No. 7 (March, 1952).

Ikeuchi, Hajime: *"Taiheiyo senso-chu no senji ryugen"* (Rumors during the Pacific War). *Shakaigaku hyoron* (Japanese sociological review), Vol. 2 (August, 1951).

"Ima no mama de wa sa-ha shinshutsu ni genkai ga aru" (If present conditions continue there are limits to the rise of the left-wing

Socialists). *Shakai undo tsushin* (Report on social movements), No. 379 (May 6, 1953).

Ishikawa, Ichiro: *"Shin keidanren no shimei"* (The task of the new Federation of Economic Organizations). *Jitsugyo no Nihon* (Industrial Japan), Vol. 56 (January 1, 1953).

Ito, Sei: *"Kindai Nihonjin no hasso no sho-keishiki"* (The various forms of expression among modern Japanese). *Shiso* (Thought), Nos. 344, 345 (February, March, 1953).

Kawashima, Takeyoshi: *"Giri"* (Obligation). *Shiso* (Thought), No. 327 (September, 1951).

————: *" 'On' no ishiki no jittai"* (On the consciousness of "on"). *Chuo koron* (Central review), March, 1951.

————: *"Risshin shusse"* (Success in life). Tembo (Outlook), No. 69 (September, 1951).

Kyogoku, Jun'ichi: *"Gendai Nihon ni okeru seiji-teki kodo-yoshiki"* (Political behavior in modern Japan). *Shiso* (Thought), Nos. 339, 340, 342 (September, October, December, 1952).

Makita, Minoru: *"Seron chosa no keisei* (The formation of public opinion polls). *Shiso* (Thought), No. 287 (May, 1948).

Maruyama, Masao: *"Nihon ni okeru nashionarizumu"* (Nationalism in Japan). *Chuo koron* (Central review), January, 1951.

Matsuoka, Saichi: *"Nihon nomin shiso no hensen ni tsuite"* (On changes in the ideology of peasants in Japan). *Shiho kenkyu* (Study of the administration of justice), Vol. 17 (March, 1933).

Nakagawa, Zennosuke: *"Oyagoroshi"* (Patricide). *Tembo* (Outlook), No. 68 (August, 1951).

Ota, Kaoru: *"Rodo sensen toitsu no shin hoko"* (A new departure in the unified labor front). *Chuo koron* (Central review), March, 1954.

Oya, Shoichi: *"Shushokunan to chishiki kaikyu no kosokudo-teki botsuraku"* (The difficulties of finding employment and the rapid rate of decline of the intellectual class). *Chuo koron* (Central review), March, 1929.

Sato, Tatsuo: *"Horitsu ga dekiru made"* (Until laws are made). *Horitsu jiho* (Law review), Vol. 25 (January, 1953).

Sato, Tomoo: *"Masu komunikeshion to kojin-teki iken dentatsu"* (Mass communications and the transmission of personal opinion). *Shakaigaku hyoron* (Japanese sociological review), Vol. 3 (April, 1953).

Shigetomi, Yoshio: *"Shudan-teki boryoku hanzai no genin"* (Causes of violent crime). *Shiho kenkyu* (Studies in the administration of justice), No. 19 (1935).

Shimada, Goro: *"Geki-teki naru saigo kakugi no jikkyo"* (An account of the dramatic last cabinet session). *Bungei Shunju* special issue: *"Sengo saidai no seihen,"* January, 1955.

Shimizu, Ikutaro: *"Ansatsu"* (Assassination). *Chuo koron* (Central review), September, 1949.

Shiso no Kagaku Kenkyukai: *"Nomin no uso to makoto"* (Falsehood and truth among peasants). *Chuo koron* (Central review), August, 1951.

"Sohyo taikai sokkiroku kara (From the transcript of the proceedings of the Sohyo convention). *Shakai undo tsushin* (Report on social movements), Nos. 388, 389 (August 5, 12, 1953).

"Sonzoku shogai chishi hiroku jiken" (Case of fatal injury of an ascendant). *Saiko Saibansho hanreishu* (Supreme Court reports), Vol. 4 (December, 1950).

Tsurumi, Shunsuke: *"Nichijo no ronri"* (Everyday logic). *Shiso* (Thought), No. 325 (July, 1951).

————: *"Nihon shiso no tokushoku to tenno-sei"* (Special characteristics of Japanese thought and the emperor system). *Shiso* (Thought), No. 336 (June, 1952).

Ukai, Nobushige: *"Koba rodosha no tohyo kodo"* (Voting behavior of factory workers). *Sekai* (World), No. 84 (December, 1952).

Yakabe, Katsumi: *"Sohyo no tatteiru chiten"* (Where Sohyo stands). *Chuo koron* (Central review), September, 1953.

Yoshimura, Tadashi: *"Giin rippo no kompon mondai"* (The basic problem of member-sponsored legislation). *Senkyo* (Elections), Vol. 5 (October, 1952).

% *Index*

Achievement: as social goal, 110
Adachi, Kenzo, 210
Adachi, Tadao, 154 *n*
Advisory committees, 183
Agriculture: and cost of industrialization, 116–17; and industrialization, 117–22; and traditional values, 115; as family enterprise, 118; basis of state, 114–16, 278; cleavages in, 122–5
Akahata, 219
Akebono, quoted, 186
All Hope is not Lost, 52–3
All-Japan Agricultural Affairs Association, *see Zenkoku Nojikai*
All-Japan Association of Rural Cooperatives, *see Zenkoku Noson Sangyo Kumiai Kyokai*
Allen, George C., quoted, 88–9
Amano, Teiyu, 53–4
Amaterasu-o-mikami, 39
Anti-social groups, 259–61; and political parties, 261
Ariga, Kizaemon, 207 *n*
Arima, Yoriyasu, 256 *n*
Arita, Jiro, 257
Asahi Evening News, 157 *n*, 164 *n*
Asahi Shimbun, 149, 157, 161, 162, 178, 179, 184 *n*, 187 *n*, 207 *n*, 212–13, 215 *n*, 216–17, 228 *n*, 229, 246, 274 *n*
Assassination, 253–4, 259
ATIS Press Translations, 98 *n*, 99 *n*, 167 *n*, 172 *n*, 256 *n*

Bavelas, Alex, quoted, 266
Beardsley, Richard, 32 *n*

Benedict, Ruth, quoted, 30–2
Bennett, John W., quoted, 25, 26 *n*, 27
Berelson, Bernard, 216; quoted, 218 *n*
Black Dragon Society, 253
Borton, Hugh, 102 *n*
Budget, 70, 155–56
Bungei Shunju, 240
Bureaucracy: and interest groups, 160–4, 285; as source of political leaders, 174–5; core of government, 143; *see also* Civil service
Bureaucrats: social origins of, 144
Business organizations: as pressure groups, 92–5; history of, 92–3; in post-war period, 93–5
Businessmen: as political leaders, 175; change in social position, 81
Buraku, 14, 75
Butow, Robert J. C., 44 *n*, 267
Byas, Hugh, 253

Cabinet, 70–1; under Yoshida, 272-6
Campaign funds, 200–2
Campaign techniques, 193–4, 209–10
Capitalistic enterprise, 282
Censorship, 223–4, 233
Chamber of Commerce and Industry, 93
Chamberlain, Basil Hall, 39 *n*
Chiang Kai-shek, 268
Chinese influences, 4
Chu, 42
Chukanso, 15, 250, 280–1, 284
Chuo Koron, 240

A NOTE ON THE TYPE

The text of this book is set in Caledonia, a Linotype face designed by W. A. Dwiggins. This type belongs to the family of printing types called "modern face" by printers—a term used to mark the change in style of type-letters that occurred about 1800. Caledonia borders on the general design of Scotch Modern, but is more freely drawn than that letter.

Composed, printed, and bound by KINGSPORT PRESS, INC., *Kingsport, Tenn. Paper made by* P. H. GLATFELTER CO., *Spring Grove, Pa. Typography by* GUY FLEMING.